The law changes, but Nolo
ways to make sure you an

Nolo's Legal Upd

We'll send you an em
is published! Sign up

Updates @ Nolo

Check **www.nolo.**
in the law that affec

3 **Nolo Customer**

To make sure that t
recent one, call us a
our friendly custom
Or find out at **ww**

Work Less, Live More

The New Way to Retire Early

by Bob Clyatt

FIRST EDITION	OCTOBER 2005
Editor	BARBARA KATE REPA
Cover & Book Design	SUSAN PUTNEY
Index	SONGBIRD INDEXING SERVICES
Proofreading	ROBERT WELLS
Printing	DELTA PRINTING SOLUTIONS, INC.

Clyatt, Bob.

    Work less, live more : the new way to retire early / by Bob Clyatt ; edited by Barbara Kate Repa -- 1st ed.

      p. cm.

    ISBN 1-4133-0200-9 (alk. paper)

     1. Finance, Personal. 2. Retirement income. 3. Retirees--Finance, Personal . I. Repa, Barbara Kate. II. Title.

    HG179.C6518 2005

    332.024'014--dc22

                             2005047250

Quantity sales: For information on bulk purchases or corporate premium sales, please contact the Special Sales Department. For academic sales or textbook adoptions, ask for Academic Sales. Call 800-955-4775 or write to Nolo, 950 Parker Street, Berkeley, CA 94710.

Dedication

To our Teachers

Acknowledgments

My thanks to the many early retirees who shared their stories and their insights so that others might follow a little more confidently. Particular thanks to the gang at www.early-retirement.org who are always ready to help, 24/7.

Keith Marbach of Zunna.com generously ran study after study to help refine, test, and update the Safe Withdrawal Method and programmed the needed enhancements to model The 95% Rule in Chapter 4. Keith also wrote the code for the WATS Simulator, which has been used for his own published research as well as for academic researchers, foundations, and retirees.

Paul Fendler, my longtime accountant and friend, graciously provided instant feedback on all manner of tax questions and strategies throughout the writing of this book. Paul's guidance, clarifications, and the many hypothetical tax returns he produced for illustrations can be seen wherever tax matters arise in the book, notably in Chapter 5.

Tom Orecchio, of Greenbaum & Orecchio in Old Tappan, New Jersey, an advisor with Dimensional Fund Advisors (DFA), helped refine and test my early ideas about the Rational Investing Portfolio and turn it into something worth sharing. Tom graciously and regularly ran scenarios and portfolios through his software getting me updated and historical statistics that provided the meat of Chapter 3's data.

We are all indebted to a small number of independent thinkers who pioneered the research, created the products, and stood up against the ridicule of Wall Street to make the Rational Investing Method viable for the little guy. First among them is John Bogle, the founder of Vanguard and developer of the first low-cost index funds. William Bernstein's research and pragmatic explanations provided me and many others with the "Aha" moments. And Eugene Fama and the folks at DFA have given all serious asset allocators the building blocks we need to understand and implement Rational Investing.

My finance professors at MIT's Sloan School lectured us on the fine points of Modern Portfolio Theory, efficient markets, and asset allocation in the 1980s. Twenty years later—my thick-headedness, not their teaching—I have finally begun to understand and apply their powerful ideas, the foundation of Rational Investing.

My editor Barbara Kate Repa and the Nolo team instantly understood the value of this book to help guide people toward safer, more rewarding early retirements. I will always be grateful to Barbara Kate for her painstaking dedication to this book and for providing much needed structure to my ideas.

And last, to my family, who understood and supported me—and left me alone to write.

Table of Contents

CHAPTER 2

Live Below Your Means

CHAPTER 3

Put Your Investing on Autopilot

CHAPTER 4

Take 4% Forever

CHAPTER 5

Stop Worrying About Taxes

CHAPTER 6

Do Anything You Want, But Do Something

CHAPTER 7

Don't Blow It

CHAPTER 8

Make Your Life Matter

APPENDIX 1

The Asset Classes in the Rational Investing Portfolio

APPENDIX 2

Resources

INDEX

Introduction

There are a number of reasons why you might want to stop working full-time well before you reach traditional retirement age. You may be reasonably happy at work, saving money, but wondering how long you can hold out against the gnawing sense that you're trading your life away. Or you may be a little further along, with ample savings, agonizing about whether you need to keep pounding away at a full-time career that no longer fires you up the way it once did. You may have tired of the long hours, the bills, the pressure, and the feeling there is never enough time to do the things that are important. Or you may just be ready to move on from what has come to feel like a constant diet of compromises, working for the man. You ask yourself: Do I really have to do this until I'm 65? Can I turn all this hard work into a ticket outta here?

> *There must be some kinda way outta here...*
>
> —FROM "ALL ALONG THE WATCHTOWER," BOB DYLAN

By husbanding your financial resources, managing your expenses, and making a commitment to graduate from the traditional workplace, you can safely cut back your time on the job by years, even decades. Lots of people are doing this now, leaving full-time work in their 40s and 50s, even some precocious ones in their 30s. They have plenty of time to relax and focus on living a life of clarity and purpose. And you can, too.

A. Something Wrong in Paradise

Working life was never supposed to be as stressful as it has become. A vibrant modern economy full of opportunity and well-paying jobs was supposed to mean we would all be happily challenged, with enough money to buy the things we needed. Then we would enjoy this bounty during the leisure time freed up by our sparkling efficiency.

At least that was the theory.

But something happened to derail that vision. Instead of enjoying more leisure as our earning power went up, we decided we'd have to work even more to pay for all the goodies we couldn't live without. In fact, we really needed two incomes just to afford a place in a decent neighborhood. Now, rather than feeling energized and challenged by work, we feel stressed and trapped. The problem has less to do with the nature of the work and more with the amount of time we spend there: The hours that American workers put in today should really be called Overwork. Most career-track professional employment requires 55 or more hours a week of sustained in-the-workplace effort, along with more labor at home or on the road checking email and catching up on relevant business news. The average American worker logs nearly 48 hours a week on the job.

Some people can put in fewer hours, but the pace in their workplaces often makes it feel like more. And for many, leaving work early is like pasting a big target on their backs marked Fire Me First. With a mortgage, credit card debt, and an endless parade of bills, missing a few paychecks could even spell ruin. Life for many full-time workers has become an adrenaline rush of long hours, big spending, unrelenting stress, and poor health.

RETIRING RETIREMENT?

Plenty of people are uncomfortable using the term "retirement" to describe their lives after leaving full-time work. For them, that word conjures up images of frail elderly people who have hung up their spurs. If someone asks them what they do they simply say, "I take French lessons." Or "I am an investor." Or for the historically inclined, "I am a gentleman of leisure." They think of themselves as just living life—not withdrawing from it in any sense. Even people who retire in their 60s often feel the term simply doesn't connote their active new lifestyles, with the phrase "phased retirement" now being used to refer to a raft of semi-retirement alternatives.

Until a better term is coined, this book uses the terms "early retirement" and "early semi-retirement" to describe using all available financial resources to leave full-time career work before age 65.

You decide what words best describe that state of grace, freedom, and adventure that you'll be living. And perhaps your new moniker will help retire the term "retirement" once and for all.

B. The Solution: Early Semi-Retirement

Early semi-retirement—reclaiming a proper balance between life and work by leaving a full-time job—offers a way out of this madness. By reducing spending and switching to a pared back but more satisfying lifestyle, less money goes out the door. Tapping into accumulated savings in a sensible way provides a steady annual income. Any shortfall can be filled with a modest amount of work, done in an entirely new state of mind: With less need to work for the largest paycheck possible, you can find low-stress work that you truly enjoy, on a schedule that gives you time to breathe.

Doing some amount of engaging work offers a comfortable transition between full work mode and full retirement mode, making early semi-retirement a good fit for middle-aged people and their families. With a modest income from part-time work, early semi-retirees may not have to face the dramatic downshifting in spending and lifestyle that so often confronts those who simply retire early, with a plan to never work another day in their lives. Early semi-retirees learn that a bit of work, even unpaid work, keeps them energized, contributing, and sharp. (See Chapter 6 for specific ideas on types of activities you might seek.) For those who are mentally ready and who align their spending and financial means, early semi-retirement can be the ideal course for navigating a long, healthy, and happy life.

If the entire early semi-retirement movement were simply about working less and relaxing more, critics might feel that it was somehow depleting the dynamism of our economy or creating a new parasitic aristocracy. But personal experience and the passionate convictions of many other early retirees have shown otherwise.

Early semi-retirees are reclaiming their health and zest for life, re-energizing their communities with talented volunteer work, staying fit, becoming more accessible parents, and mentoring young people who increasingly grow up without much meaningful interaction with adults. By being calm and composed during the time they do spend working, early semi-retirees can bring co-workers perspective and balance too often in short supply in the workplace. By being hands-on investors, they provide angel investment funds

and expertise to growing firms, invest in franchises, or improve neighborhoods through rehabbing homes and rental properties. With time to tinker,
think, and develop ideas about which they are passionate, early semi-retirees
are inventing new products and technologies, writing articles—and contributing in other ways that may show no immediate profit but have a longer-
term benefit to the economy or society.

LUCKY FOR SOME?

Though you might find it hard to believe, early retirement is not restricted
to just the people who ride in private jets and ski in the Alps with minor
European royalty. Recent data indicate that large numbers of people can
pursue early retirement and early semi-retirement. In 2004, some four million still-working households in the United States had net financial assets
—not including homes and personal property—of over $1 million dollars.

Even more people, about a quarter of all American households, could
today choose to dump the car, sell the house, pocket the home equity,
and move abroad to one of the many early-retirement meccas—living
quite comfortably on just $500,000 in assets.

Hard as it may be for coastal high-earners to believe, early retirement
chat groups are full of folks living singly or as a couple on $20,000 or
$25,000 a year in rural parts of the U.S., shopping at discount stores,
buying used cars, and relishing lives of financial independence.

*Sources: TNS Affluent Market Research Program; UBS Paine Webber/AB Financial,
Spectrem Group, Chicago, www.early-retirement.org surveys*

C. Escaping the World of Work: One Story

Early on in my work life, I discovered a book about early retirement and set
about making plans to get there. Seeing my own life slipping away in stress
and overwork sent me searching for a sane alternative that would bring work,
family, and personal time into balance—a way to slow down, have time to
breathe, think, and just live.

No Pollyanna, I knew I'd need to provide for longer term financial needs. I thought in terms of becoming my own rich uncle, giving myself a sort of lifetime endowed professor's chair or trust fund, an annual lottery payout, and buying back my freedom. In preparation, I built the family savings to the point that they provided a safe annual income for life so I would never have to work again.

And so in 2001, after 20 years of sustained high-pressure work, the last seven spent battling in the Internet wars, my wife Wonda and I chucked it in, mothballed our suits, rented a small summer house in Italy, and began our new lives as early retirees. The biggest change that first year, and my biggest luxury, was time: time to plan, time to think, time to take care of all of life's niggling chores, time to be with the family, work on the boat, exercise, read, and relax. We loved every minute of it. I assured myself that I never wanted to work another day in my life, and never would.

Friends began confiding their anxiety and curiosity: Have you really managed to slip out of the rat race? How does it work financially? What do you do all day? Can you tell me how to do it, too? To better answer their questions, I continued to dig deeper into investing research and retirement finance theory and got hit with a shock: It appeared that by the most conservative measures, we came up a bit short—especially given the abysmal financial market performance of the day. My days turned into long stressful sessions doing Internet-based stock research and plugging new assumptions into the retirement savings calculators. I began to fret about our daily investment performance and struggled with uncertainty about the future. At the same time, I was getting restless and uncomfortable having no work or income whatsoever, and began to wonder whether retiring early was such a good idea after all.

The solution that arose from this experience, and what our family has been living for the past several years, is early semi-retirement. It captures the best of both worlds: plenty of free time and the opportunity for good healthy living that early retirement offers, combined with the psychological benefits and long-term financial security of a modest amount of part-time work—a hybrid that works for large numbers of people.

D. How This Book Can Help

This book can help you, too, find that different road outside the fast lane. Some who contemplate early retirement long to spend their days teaching disabled people how to program computers, organizing art classes at the neighborhood senior care center, or leading environmental trips at a nearby estuary. Others want to do a lot of fishing, motorcycle maintenance, and golf. Your idea of a perfect life after early retiring will be uniquely yours.

In these pages you'll find lots of encouragement and ideas of what other early retirees are doing. And this book will help you understand that early retirement may be possible for you, that it opens a doorway to a new place where you leave the madness behind and have the time and energy to do the things you are inspired to do.

You'll not only get a roadmap for the psychological and emotional sides of living in early retirement, but also for the crucial hard-nosed financial planning needed to shape the investing and tapping of your savings to support you through the years ahead. If you've been fortunate enough to have saved diligently or to have vested in a solid pension, this book will show you how to manage those savings and live from them throughout the rest of your life. If you are still getting started, the ideas in these chapters will arm you with the vision and tactics to reach your goals.

As you free yourself from the pressures of a traditional fast-lane career, you can start to experience the life you've always wanted: a life that can change the world for the better, that makes you excited to get up every morning, that has a chance to be an inspiration to young people and friends. You will find your way to the type of work, paid or unpaid, that you can feel passionate about, that uses your unique gifts, and makes a difference in others' lives—work in just the right doses that leaves you energized, not spent. You'll have the time to get healthy and stay that way. Your relationships will deepen and strengthen. You'll be living life the way it was meant to be.

> **WARNING**
>
> (!) **A WORK IN PROGRESS.** This book should serve as the beginning of a conversation. Feel free to ask questions, bring up early retirement concerns, and suggest new ideas for future editions. Contact me at bob@workless-livemore.com.

E. A Look at Some Typical Early Retirees

It may help you to know that certain models of early semi-retirement have emerged that work for different types of people. They are described here not to limit your thinking, but to give you an idea of the diversity of people and paths available.

1. MBA Moms Pulling Back

Vast numbers of women have been practicing early semi-retirement for years, dialing up and down their involvement in the workplace to accommodate career development, kids, a need for extra income, eldercare obligations, or more time for personal growth. Those with more family income have, as a group, opted for less work.

EXAMPLE: An Artist Freed From the Law

Wendy was one of those kids who always wanted to be a lawyer. Ever since she came to the United States from Asia as a girl, she pushed herself to succeed in school even harder than her anxious parents pushed her. Graduating from law school and clerking for a judge set the stage for building a private practice helping scientists and other professionals immigrate to America. But after 15 years, the constant drains of dealing with government bureaucracy and stressed-out clients were taking a toll.

Wendy and her husband Ron had been planning early retirement for years, and they decided that it made sense for Wendy to start first. She helped her staff find new jobs and gradually shut down her practice, finishing off old cases and refusing new ones.

The transition out of full-time work was a breeze for Wendy. With two sons in elementary school, she began at once to improve her network of nonworking friends and moms and discovered a whole new world of activities were now available: book clubs, lunches, play groups, events, as well as the informal information network of what was really going on around town. And she finally had time to commit to caring for her aging parents.

During that first year, Wendy also rediscovered her love of costume jewelry, and began designing and creating pieces for sale. She hosted trunk shows in her home and set up displays at art fairs and charity benefits, taking great pleasure in seeing her creations worn and appreciated by other women.

Wendy is now active in a number of community organizations, including having been appointed to the local Human Rights Commission, joining a yacht club, becoming a member of the Garden Club, and actively volunteering at church and a local nature center.

"None of this ever had a chance to come out when I was working fulltime," muses Wendy, describing this creative side that has flowered since she left law. Lifelong stomach problems have disappeared, sleep is complete and restful, and she looks vibrant. "The boys have really benefited, too," she adds. "The extra time we've been able to spend with them has turned around a few potentially messy developmental issues."

2. Geeks on Permanent Vacation

Early semi-retirees fitting this profile tend to be highly intelligent and independent engineering or scientist types who love nothing more than working absorbedly in their shops or labs. These innovators long ago decided that most bosses cramped their styles and so they used their skills to earn enough money to leave more traditional workplaces.

With plenty of free time to follow their passions, they continue to invent or innovate, do consulting or project work for money, and keep their skills fresh while crafting lives with plenty of time for families and hobbies alongside their work.

EXAMPLE: Working Hard—and Hardly Working

As a young graduate facing the job market about 25 years ago with a fresh mechanical engineering degree, Chet had a few early career positions designing nuclear submarine and HVAC systems. But the coat and tie chafed at him, and he longed to get back out into the field and get his hands on some tools.

At night and on weekends, he and his wife Valerie worked on a handful of apartments or homes they bought, and slowly transformed those dilapidated San Francisco properties back into things of beauty. They had started in the mid 1980s, while still in their 20s, and rode a wave of appreciation in California real estate.

But a decade later, feeling the city wasn't the best place to raise their kids, Chet and Valerie did the math and realized they could almost live off the rents from their homes. They piled their two young daughters in a station wagon and began driving around the Western states, seeking a new rural home with a good quality of life. Settling on a small town in Northern California, they began building a house, home schooled their daughters, and got actively involved in the community.

Chet built a big workshop and began fabricating electromechanical pumping and filtration systems for a small company in the California wine industry. He works when he feels like it, only taking jobs that he knows will be interesting and lucrative. His schedule runs the gamut from an occasional intense workweek to time off for an extensive camping trip around the Western states. The income from the real estate covers the family's main living expenses, while any outside income goes toward travel or other hobbies. If outside income is curtailed for any reason, they know they can cut back on the luxuries without any worries.

Recently, Chet converted a VW Bug to run on battery power— and now tools around town in an odd vehicle that looks like some kind of pickup truck, with the batteries lined up under the truck bed. In his spare time around home, he tinkers with alternative energy inventions or helps coach his daughters' baseball and soccer teams. He has finagled life to give him exactly what he wants: plenty of free time to work on all his projects and enough money so he never has to worry about finances.

3. Perpetual Travelers

Living out of a backpack and exploring the world may not be everybody's idea of a perfect life, but it has a strong pedigree in early retirement circles. Settling down for a month or a year in places such as Argentina or Thailand, house sitting in a luxury home in Hawaii, working as a resort manager or bartender during the season in Costa Rica, then moving back to a no-maintenance home base in the U.S. to reconnect with family and culture—this is the Perpetual Traveler's life.

Not only do such folks see the world and meet incredible people while they are young and energized, they are able to do it on a budget that makes even rural American early retirees look profligate.

EXAMPLE: Wildflowers Don't Care Where They Grow

For 14 years, Billy and Akaisha have moved between home bases in Arizona, Chiang Mai, Thailand, and Mexico to points throughout South America, Southeast Asia, and beyond.

They are passionate about their travels and about volunteering or helping people along the way—teaching English, visiting western prisoners, or cleaning gravesites of locals and Americans buried overseas. The local American Legion keeps them apprised of volunteer opportunities and needs. During the '90s, they lived for a number of years in Chapala, Mexico, where they helped local photographers develop a postcard business, and got a basketball scoreboard donated, from the U.S., for the local high school gym. (Billy was coaching the basketball team and despaired at the way scores and times were mangled under the antiquated flip charts and stopwatch methods in use when he arrived.) His pride and joy was volunteering to raise funds to build five municipal tennis courts for the town, then overseeing their construction.

By renting homes and moving slowly, Billy and Akaisha make lots of new friends as they get to know locals and other travelers, becoming part of the community. When a situation feels right, they'll take on jobs along the way—usually resort restaurant or bar management for free room and board types of roles, but sometimes they house sit. Akaisha had a thriving cards business in Mexico which gave jobs to local women artisans and brought in several thousand dollars a year at its peak. These work gigs help cover their already-low expenses and fit into their philosophy that they are living a lifestyle, not a vacation.

As a practical matter, they keep U.S. catastrophic health insurance, but pay locally for health care; it is cheap and high quality. They return home roughly once a year, to a low-maintenance co-op style house in which they store Akaisha's art supplies, the cooking equipment needed for their foodie habit, and other personal effects. Email lets them keep up with family and friends, and receive reports from neighbors about anything needing attention at their home in the states. On their Web page at www.geocities.com/ba264, they report about their travels and opine about the early retirement lifestyle.

Early semi-retirement has been perfect for Billy and Akaisha, affording them flexibility, for example, to provide end-of-life care for parents and to be with family for extended periods. Convinced that more people could early retire as perpetual travelers and enjoy life a lot more, Billy quips, "Half of California could sell the house and do what we do."

4. The Millionaires Down the Road

These early retirees take advantage of the low cost of living and lack of pre-tension in rural areas to retire comfortably, on their own terms, without a huge financial strain. Sometimes referred to as The Millionaires Next Door, a term coined by author Thomas Stanley who catalogued their behavior, these unassuming people often invest in real estate, start and sell businesses, or just save diligently. Although they typically have at least a million and a half dollars in combined savings and real estate, they live frugally, and make that money last.

Living for them means not working for someone else and having lots of time for family and toys and fun—fishing, motorcycles, or wind-generating power plants. Their 14-year-old pickup truck not only helps hold down expenses, but allows them to keep a low profile despite their business and financial sophistication. And to compensate for geographic remoteness, they use the Web and national media to stay abreast of trends and information that interest them. Typically, their kids are grown and have moved away from home.

EXAMPLE: The Good Life in the Heartland

Bob epitomizes the values and behavior of The Millionaire Next Door—living frugally but comfortably in a small Iowa town, driving used cars, and feeding a family of four on just $400 a month. He and his wife Julia actually got a relatively late start financially; it wasn't until Bob was 38 that they really started saving. In just 14 years, though, he and Julia amassed enough for him to leave his job and retire. For them, saving became almost a family hobby, as they socked away more than 50% of their gross pay.

Not only do Bob and Julia live below their means, but they live in a place in which means are themselves well below the national average: plenty of nice homes in the area are priced in the $50,000 to $80,000 range. Bob has been working on creative ways to save for years, even speaking to his daughter's college president to appeal for a better financial aid package. In the end, the president wouldn't overturn his financial aid officer's decision, but did offer Bob's daughter a job in his office—an opportunity that opened many career doors for her, and incidentally, kept the contribution toward their daughter's state college education to just $7,000 for the full four years.

All told, Bob, Julia, and their family live very comfortably on about $42,000 a year, including health insurance, taxes, car amortization, and fund management fees.

Now in early retirement, Bob and Julia are contemplating a move to a college town in northwest Iowa where Bob's parents live, as he expects to be providing more care for them in the coming years. Julia expects to continue to work ten or 12 hours a week, something she very much enjoys, and the new locale will provide opportunities for concerts, lectures, ethnic restaurants, and a whiff of excitement. Bob may pick up a writing project in the future, but for now he is just enjoying having plenty of free time.

Bob believes that a low tolerance for BS at work is often the trigger that gets the early retiree to start planning an exit, but the ones who actually make it tend to be creative, self-sufficient, intelligent—and completely committed to financial independence.

5. The Half-Millionaires in the Next Apartment

These early retirees have taken frugality to the farthest comfortable limits. They live, perhaps singly or as a couple, on about $25,000 a year, usually with no kids. Renting an apartment can help keep more money free to invest.

Their budget secrets: Drive an old car, eat simply, keep the heat turned down. But never compromise on high-speed Internet connectivity. That's the lifeline to their world, including consulting or freelance work that helps pay the bills. They camp or stay with friends when they travel; hotels are for somebody else.

EXAMPLE: Walden on the Bay

Phil lives simply in the San Francisco studio apartment he owns, spending just $1,000 a month. He never liked having a job, so the financial sacrifices he makes to be early semi-retired seem well worth it, and are, in any event, consistent with his deeply green, conservation-oriented beliefs.

Even though he is able to eat organic food and eat often at Thai restaurants, he makes sacrifices in other areas, using electricity for little more than his small refrigerator, a computer, and a reading light. Candles look better anyway, and he saves money by using the Internet at the library.

Phil carries a high-deductible health insurance policy, but walks or bikes everywhere as he chooses not to own a car. Expenses are further curtailed by the fact that he has not had to pay income taxes for years.

Phil spends his days volunteering in environmental projects and activities, including some that have taken him to the Amazon or Europe; a major environmental organization provides him free travel, willingly paying to get his specialized skills. On Saturdays, you can often find him at a nearby national park giving free tours to visitors. Volunteering as an usher at a local movie theater gets him plenty of free tickets to art house movies.

He loves his life, feeling liberated by its simplicity, and feels no sense of deprivation. In fact, Phil considers himself a bit of a spendthrift compared to other folks following the simple-living lifestyle.

6. Bankers With Off Switches

These overachievers got stock options or bonuses for enough years so that accumulating savings was never a problem. But with corporate mergers and the inexorable narrowing of the pyramid, they found themselves in their 40s increasingly turned off by the high stress and competitiveness of their careers. Realizing they don't need to overwork, they do the math on their municipal bond portfolio alone and take the exit package.

Once their noncompetes expire, some start a little hedge fund, some join a few boards and make some angel investments, and others start actively trading a large personal stock portfolio a few hours a day. Women on this track may switch to full-time motherhood, perhaps as a spouse or partner continues to work.

These early retirees tend to stay in the same homes and communities they lived in while they were working, and if they have children, they keep them in the same schools, perhaps planning to move when the kids are off to college.

EXAMPLE: Type A From the Bottom Up

Following a rapid and stellar career in finance, Duncan, at the age of 44, was weary of the unrelenting pressure on Wall Street. His financial needs had long since been met, so he resigned as the CEO of a major investment firm to take some time off and regroup.

It was a difficult adjustment. Duncan's career focus had left him with few outside interests and it was taking time to grow them again. His consulting and unpaid work on nonprofit boards and in local government was fulfilling, but as someone who had once managed 750 people and a billion dollars of revenue, he kept hearing about friends getting big jobs with big salaries and began to fear that early semi-retirement had been a huge mistake.

After a year, he agreed to a friend's request to interview for a senior position at one of Wall Street's most prestigious investment banks. But if he had any doubts about early retirement before, he put them to rest that day. Not one of the managing directors at the firm seemed to want to talk about his experience solving a major financial crisis or hear how he had worked to unravel the fraud at a major bank. Instead, they wanted to talk about early retirement. Every single managing director looked wistfully at Duncan, and in a lowered voice, asked what his days were like, whether he was able to live off his savings, how much time he got to spend with his kids. Duncan realized then that these titans of Wall Street envied him; they felt trapped and they wanted out. That was enough to convince him that early semi-retirement was his path, and he has never looked back.

In the last several years, Duncan has blended involvement in financial startups and investments in local real estate partnerships with an active community life, helping the local YMCA raise several million dollars for a new building and being elected to the local city council. Duncan is involved with several nonprofit boards and keeps healthy with regular yoga and running. His interest in health and wellness has led him to take classes in homeopathy, which may someday even lead to a new avocation.

Duncan's recap after four years of early semi-retirement: "Type A people need to feel they are changing the world, and in business you are used to doing that from the top down. Now my activities have impact from the bottom up, one person at a time, but the impact is just as meaningful and even more satisfying for me."

7. Exotic Transplants

These early semi-retirees do the math on how much it costs to live in the United States and take off for distant parts. They tend to congregate in a handful of expat-friendly countries such as Mexico, Costa Rica, and Thailand—though a new generation is finding that Panama, the Dominican Republic, Vietnam, and Ecuador are less discovered and offer better value. Typically they do not have children or their children are grown, and they find the lower cost of living outside the United States helps make early retirement possible years before it would be at home.

They may start a small hotel or business, catering to foreign tourists or importing and exporting products. Quality of life can be quite high. Costs of living can range between $1,000 per month on the low end to $3,000 per month for multiple full-time domestic staff and all they can eat or spend. They pay locally for medical care, and as American citizens, must pay U.S. taxes on investment income, but avoid U.S. property and state income taxes. And when the time comes, they know that Social Security checks will follow them overseas.

EXAMPLE: Where the Grass Truly Is Greener

Beginning in the 1970s, Willem and Ruth worked hard, extensively remodeling their penthouse apartment a few blocks from New York's World Trade Center, and traveling the world with their two kids. As layoffs and mergers went on around him, Wil continued to defy the odds, staying employed for more than 20 years through much tumult at his large global information firm.

In the late '90s though, with the writing on the wall, Wil and Ruth began looking for a place to early retire. They had always loved Central America, and began scouting properties and locations there for the next chapter in their lives. Antigua, Guatemala, offered a perfect setting—its Spanish colonial architecture beautifully preserved since the early 1800s when a rumbling nearby volcano convinced the town fathers to move the nation's capital from Antigua to Guatemala City. They bought a property in the center of town and began making plans.

A few years ago, Wil and Ruth sold their penthouse apartment—creating the bulk of their early retirement portfolio—loaded up a tractor trailer with all their personal goods and another truck full of plumbing fixtures, which they sold quite profitably, and drove to their new home. They spent the next three years doing what they do best—renovating a charming old property—and now own a home, several spacious apartments, and a few shops on the main street in Antigua. They rent shops and the apartments to Americans; many international aid organizations have staff locally, and American families regularly need to stay for a few months while adopting Guatemalan children.

As they have always done, Ruth and Wil jumped into civic life in Antigua, creating a beautification committee that raises funds and has now built over 100 minigardens in public spaces all over the city. Wil raves about the great Internet connectivity, dirt cheap cell phone service, and their four full-time staff—a housekeeper, cook, handyman, and gardener—who together cost just $700 per month. Wil built and maintains a website for Antigua, whose advertising revenues support a local hospital for severely handicapped children. With annual expenses of less than $30,000, and income from their new guesthouses, Ruth and Wil are living comfortably on their portfolio, donating generously to local causes, and living the life of their dreams in a beautiful location.

8. Government Employees

These early retirees, from among the one in seven U.S. employees in the public sector, find the challenge and security of government jobs, along with the attractions of a government retirement package, are ample compensation for forgoing the higher salary they might have earned in the private sector. Then they find the right spot—not all government pensions are created equal—max out their 403(b) and other savings plans and count the years until early retirement becomes available, typically after 20 to 30 years of service.

Their generous health care benefits, full inflation-adjusted pensions, and the power of governments to tax to ensure the benefits remain intact signal the gold standard for secure retirement packages. Still, because of their low salaries while on the job, the only assets these retirees may have are their pensions, so it is crucial for them to save along the way to provide for extras.

EXAMPLE: The Slow Lane to Success

"Fifty and out!" chuckles Marty as he describes the plan he and Carlos, his partner of 32 years, had been working on for more than 20 years. Marty credits this vision to seeing his father retire early and thinks that role model was crucial to his retirement planning. From the start, in the 1970s, Marty chose to work for the State of California, vesting in a safe pension, and laying the groundwork for his early exit from the workforce.

Since Marty retired at age 50 in 1997, he and Carlos have been living comfortably but modestly on the gains they realized from their real estate holdings and pensions, including Carlos's long-term disability from his job as a building inspector in San Francisco. Although Marty only receives about 30% of his former salary, the proceeds from the couple's real estate sales are easily keeping them solvent until they can begin tapping their IRAs or Marty's savings plan.

Once financial matters were in place, the two quickly moved on to the things that inspired them in life. "I really like to restore things, create things," says Carlos. He and Marty had profitably bought and remodeled two houses in San Francisco during their years there, and on moving to Portland, Oregon, soon after retiring, they plunged into their third real estate project: restoring a three-story 1910

Craftsman-style home. Marty volunteered in his neighborhood association and was soon elected its president. He admits that it "turned out to be more than a full-time job," but learned a lot from the experience.

Feeling the need to step back from their overly ambitious commitments, and relishing their freedom to change course, they sold their Portland home and moved to New York City. For the past several years, they have been exploring all that New York has to offer. Carlos continues to find "treasures" in thrift shops that he lovingly restores, and Marty is able to sit on the board of the YMCA Camp he attended as a youth. Marty's French lessons give a clue to their next goal: regularly spending a few months at a time in Europe.

In the meantime, they have plenty of time to visit Carlos's family in Ecuador and Marty's family and friends. They have developed a laundry list of strategies for living modestly in the Big Apple, including buying into a beautiful, though far uptown, neighborhood, and cashing in on Carlos's uncanny ability to land inexpensive last-minute tickets to Broadway shows. "You've got to be flexible," he advises, then waxes philosophical: "Figure out what's important in life. Too many Americans are driving themselves crazy buying things." Marty adds: "Once you leave full-time work, you've got to develop pillars to give your life some sense of structure." ●

How to Use This Book

Creating your early retirement can be the best thing you ever do for yourself. Start by envisioning what you'd like your life to be like, if you only had more time. Then lay the plans that will take you to the point at which you can stop working full time and devote your time and energy to uncovering and developing those more meaningful pursuits. Once you are in early retirement, you'll need regular tune-ups to stay on track—ways to remind yourself of your initial goals and keep moving toward them—and this book offers plenty of practical advice for that.

Each chapter explains a rule, eight in all—your guideposts to a successful early retirement distilled from the combined experience of hundreds of early retirees. You'll meet some of them throughout these pages and learn their stories and their tips and get their encouragement for you at each stage of the early retirement process.

A. Stages of Early Retirement

This book is written for four main types of people who will either be planning or already living in early semi-retirement. You may find that you fall into one of these categories. If so, the suggestions below describe how you might use this book to your best advantage.

1. Young Dreamers

You are in your 20s or 30s, starting to get serious about saving—and just beginning to think you might not want to work forever. You need some help and encouragement to Just Say No to the constant parade of pressures that beckon you to blow your savings or go into debt to buy more things. And you may be looking for a way to plan your finances for the long run.

FAST FORWARD

HOW TO USE THIS BOOK BEST. If you fit this mold, just knowing there is a path up and out of the salt mines can be an inspiration. For you, the beginning of this book should give a clear vision of what life off the treadmill can be like, keep you focused on your goals, and help you plan for the day when you can leave bosses and commuting behind. Concentrate on these possibilities when reading Chapter 1. Begin adopting some of the long-term budgeting and investing techniques outlined in Chapters 2 and 3. Think about alternative work options from Chapter 6. And read Chapter 8 for inspiration.

EXAMPLE: Keeping Their Eyes on the Prize

Paul, a 31-year-old bank credit analyst, and his wife, Paige, have been sharing their dream of early retirement for several years, making big sacrifices and developing a Spend Less, Save More lifestyle. Throughout their 20s, they maxed out 401(k) and Roth IRA plans and saving after tax money in a brokerage account; they now find their net worth puts them in the top 10% of households for their age group. A few years back, both Paul and Paige were working full time and pursuing advanced degrees at night to move to higher-paying jobs in their fields. Now with a one-year-old daughter and one or two more kids in their future, Paige runs a small business from home while Paul pursues a professional degree.

Now on their second home, the couple has done well in real estate. They were able to sell their first home, a condo, for more than twice what they paid for it in just a few years, giving them a profit of about $100,000. They have decided they will probably sell their current home, too, when the time comes to early retire. They like the neighborhood and the job opportunities, but believe the high cost of living will force them to move once Paul stops working. Paul handles the family's investments and was pleasantly surprised this year to update their Total Savings Worksheet (See Chapter 2, Section D5) and discover that instead of being 15 years from their goal as he had thought, they were closer to 12 years away.

Working for large companies has benefits for Paul, but he smacks up against frustrations frequently. "Our management treats us like kindergarteners despite our advanced degrees, requiring frustrating remedial courses for everyone in the department." He is looking hard now at moving to a startup firm that will cut him in on equity or a larger slice of the pie, speeding up the savings and rewarding him now for outsized commitment and contribution.

Although he and Paige easily deflect most consumer enticements, Paul still finds he hankers to buy a piece of rural property, as his parents did, for family vacations. He realizes, though, that their joint income of about $125,000 a year leaves little room for such luxuries if they expect to continue growing their savings. "Early retirement is my ticket to the life I want: more time with my kids and the chance to do what I want with my days," Paul notes. "It requires sacrifices, but we've made a lot of progress and just need to stay on track."

2. Frying Fast

You are in your 40s or 50s, have worked long and hard at your career, and are thinking it can't go on much longer. You've kept your nose to the grindstone and might have vested in a pension or built up a healthy nest egg. But every time you get on a plane for a business trip and realize your children will go to sleep again that night without seeing you, your heart starts to ache. Or is that the beginning of a heart attack? Office politics and corporate financial panics are starting to feel like kid stuff, and you're not a kid anymore. Early semi-retirement seems looks like the perfect solution.

FAST FORWARD

HOW TO USE THIS BOOK BEST. If this is your situation, read most of the book, perhaps with less focus on Chapter 7, which largely concerns life after retirement.

EXAMPLE: Hanging On for Two More Years

Harry is up at 5:30 every weekday morning, at his desk on a bond trading floor in New York City by 7 a.m., and doesn't leave until 8 p.m. His two young sons are in bed by the time he gets home. They make up for some lost time together on the weekends with hockey, soccer, golf, skiing, and other family activities, but Harry can see the day when this form of catch-up isn't going to work any more.

He still likes his job and doesn't find it truly painful to go into work, but feels strongly that these are the years he should be spending more time with his sons and his wife, Pat, who quit her job many years ago to raise the kids. "If I could just work 9 to 5, it would be fine," muses Harry, but he knows his employer would never countenance that. At least the pay is good, allowing Harry and Pat to set aside a tidy sum. But they wonder whether it is enough given the high costs of their lifestyle and desire not to have to downsize to make early semi-retirement work.

Harry's biggest worry about retiring early is the unknown expenses looming in the future. For example, the boys' college costs are likely due down the line. Also, Pat's parents' health is starting to fail, and Harry and Pat stand ready to chip in for their nursing care and other health expenses. Finally, Harry's family owns a remote Canadian fishing camp that he will likely become responsible for maintaining one day.

To reassure himself on the financial front, Harry has begun attempting to quantify potential future expenses—painting a range of best-case and worst-case scenarios and trying to pin them down with actual numbers. For instance, he always worried about the costs of private school for his sons, but now realizes those costs are predictable and end in a specific year. He can set that much money aside and know his commitment there is covered.

Beyond wanting more time with his family, Harry has given plenty of thought to his main reasons for wanting to early semi-retire. He and Pat already volunteer on a few nonprofit boards, which they greatly enjoy. And Harry is strongly drawn to environmental and artistic pursuits. He figures his financial skills will translate well to a paid role in the treasury or fundraising side of an environmental or arts-based nonprofit. Harry feels this sort of work, based in an office environment outside the house, will strike the right balance and keep him challenged. That would suit Pat well, too, since she is sure she doesn't want him to sit around the house—and just possibly start managing her.

With a few more years of saving, Harry and Pat feel they'll be able to fully enjoy the best of both worlds: a solid nest egg providing financial security and the benefits of spending time each day doing work about which they care deeply.

3. Early Retired, But Open to Suggestions

You're one of the lucky ones who have already pulled the ripcord. You know why you did it, but some days it seems hard to remember that initial rush of enthusiasm and to feel you are making progress toward the goals you initially had for yourself when you decided to retire early. Nowadays, you're as busy as you ever were in your worklife, and you could never go back. Or maybe you are getting bored or feeling conflicted and thinking of going back to work again. In any case, you're not sure if your investing approach makes sense—and there are whole days that disappear in which you haven't done much at all.

FAST FORWARD

HOW TO USE THIS BOOK BEST. If you are retired but feeling restless or doubtful, your best use of this book is to jump around to specific chapters you find relevant. Test your budgeting methods and assumptions against the ones in Chapter 2. And see if you can learn some refinements to your investing approach in Chapter 3. Chapter 4 will offer simple suggestions to reduce your long-term financial risk and Chapter 5 will let you benchmark your taxes against other early retirees. If you've never considered doing some work in early retirement, see whether Chapter 6 changes your thinking. And read Chapters 7 and 8 to inspire you to make full use of the opportunities you've created.

EXAMPLE: Turning the Ship Around

After a 20-year career as an investment banker being groomed for the upper reaches of a Wall Street firm, Peter stepped aside from his fast-lane career to concentrate on living his spiritual values and integrating them with his work.

Although many small things all led up to Peter's change of course, including the relentless travel and time away from his wife and children, one important event turned the tide. Peter's earliest role model, the chair of his firm who had become the president of the World Bank, died suddenly. Despite the fact that this man lived a larger-than-life existence as one of the most powerful and revered people in the world of finance, Peter realized that the fabric of his life essentially boiled down to decades of seven-day workweeks, bruising corporate battles, and millions of miles spent in airplane seats.

Today, Peter's days are filled with leading teen groups at his church, being president of his city's library, and starting projects around a passionate new interest in environmental activism. And recently, he has been working with grassroots organizations to develop local community currencies and has met with Native American elders and leading environmentalists to invent a method to properly account for the cost of today's pollution on future generations.

4. The Seasoned Pro

You've already retired early, but the books you read on the topic seem to be talking to someone else—someone with loads of money and no experience living a full life. You're always willing to listen to another person who's early-retired, though, and at least hear what he or she has to say. While you'd rather cut expenses than go back to work—in fact, you'd rather stop eating than go back to work—you admit that after years of fixing things around the house and perfecting your putt, your happiest moments come when you get out and meet some new people and try new activities.

FAST FORWARD

HOW TO USE THIS BOOK BEST. If you have already retired, but remain curious about doing it better, look at Chapter 3 on investing and Chapter 5 on taxes to see if there is something there that can help you refine your own assumptions or fine-tune the split of your assets between taxable and nontaxable accounts. Read through Chapter 6 on possible new pursuits—with an open mind, especially thinking about unpaid work—and see if the list of early retirees' passions and projects gives you some ideas for new ways to have fun and learn something useful.

EXAMPLE: God, Golf, and Trout

Jerry grew up in rural California, the son of a Spanish logger who gladly worked right up into his 70s. But after a stint in the Marines in the early 1960s, Jerry set out to move beyond his humble background by buying and fixing up rental real estate on the side. Jerry and his wife, Fran, raised their two daughters, living frugally but not with any particular sense of deprivation, and discovered that their combined savings and real estate investments would allow them to retire before they were 50.

That was nearly 20 years ago. Jerry is now a bona fide Social Security-collecting retiree, but he has become something of an expert on early retirement planning. If asked, he is generous about offering experienced counsel to the young early retirees he meets on the golf course, where he can be found any day it's not raining.

Jerry and his family downsized and moved at the beginning of his early retirement, choosing a northeastern section of California for its low housing costs and access to skiing, golf, trout fishing, and other favorite hobbies. While Jerry doesn't need advice on early retirement, he readily admits he's no finance whiz and likes to learn how other early retirees manage their finances for the long run.

B. A Quick Look at the Chapters

Each chapter in this book explains one of eight rules on specific facets of early retirement.

Chapter 1: Figure Out Why You Want to Do This

This chapter will help you understand and build confidence in your decision to leave the stress of full-time work for a decidedly different life. It describes how people in other times and places have drawn sensible work-life balances and contrasts that with the current state of the overworking American. You'll also find several exercises to help clarify your goals for what lies ahead and build resolve to make the leap.

Chapter 2: Live Below Your Means

This chapter delves into the budgeting and spending side of early retirement—from the early days of planning to the years living it. Reducing the money you spend can make the difference between a successful early retirement and 20 more years of office politics and commuting. Since Living Below Your Means can put you squarely at odds with the dominant consumer culture, this chapter offers plenty of tips and encouragement to help you resist the urge to splurge. A section on early retirement finances for parents aims to put to rest the jitters associated with paying for kids and college. Good quality of life at rock-bottom prices may be available to those who early retire overseas—and another section gives the details.

Chapter 3: Put Your Investing on Autopilot

This chapter introduces Rational Investing, a no-hassle investment approach based on the latest research in diversification, asset allocation, and long-term investment returns. The approach works on autopilot and is simple enough for anyone to use, with little intervention or decision-making required each year. This chapter also addresses pervasive investing myths that hamper long-run performance, and introduces three durable portfolios specifically designed for early retirees.

Chapter 4: Take 4% Forever

Withdrawing a safe amount from savings each year is the way most early retirees fund their living expenses. The chapter presents a rationale for safely spending about 4% of a portfolio's value each year, and outlines a simple method for adjusting those annual withdrawals to changing market conditions. New research, commissioned for this book, tailors recommendations specifically to the needs of early retirees, who must keep savings intact over the long run.

Chapter 5: Stop Worrying About Taxes

This chapter trumpets the good news that early semi-retirement is surprisingly tax-efficient—and explains why. It also compares two families spending the same amount: one in early semi-retirement, the other traditional salary-earners, so that you can understand how to fine-tune your finances for maximum tax efficiency.

Chapter 6: Do Anything You Like, But Do Something

A host of psychological and sometimes financial realities make it essential for early retirees to do more than just rest and relax. This chapter examines in detail the types of work, paid and unpaid, that fit early semi-retirees best. And if you've ever worried that you'll run out of interesting things to do once you leave full-time work, the chapter also includes a rich assortment of activities in which early retirees immerse themselves.

Chapter 7: Don't Blow It

This chapter gives tested tactics for keeping your mental equilibrium during early retirement and combating feelings of laziness, boredom, panic, and guilt—moving into a sustainable, fulfilling lifestyle.

Chapter 8: Make Your Life Matter

This chapter points to the outsized impact your life can have when you start consistently doing the things you care about and love. To help you stay on track, the chapter also includes a handful of simple rules for creating a life well-lived, distilled from years of thoughtful research on the subject by those who have gone before us. ●

CHAPTER ONE

Figure Out Why You Want to Do This

Throughout recorded history, people have recognized a fundamental change that appears, reliably, in the middle of life. Like the flu, there are a number of symptoms that identify the culprit. However, unlike the flu, this change—while sometimes wrenching—is not an illness but a normal, healthy transformation, a new orientation toward life.

You may be coming to the point at which making more money or acquiring more material goods simply isn't hooking you the way it once did—for example, the thought of owning a bigger house or a third car just feels like more hassle. You realize that your dominant mode—constantly on the go, taking charge, controlling, all-action-all-day-long—has started to feel counterproductive. Work

> *What do you want from life?*
>
> —THE TUBES (BILL SPOONER AND MICHAEL EVANS)

doesn't hold your attention anymore, and distractions can mount into something like a perpetual state of spring fever. You see signs of aging—forgetfulness, graying hair, reading glasses, or chronic aches and pains—as a rude reminder that the clock is ticking out your time on earth.

You might also be feeling limited by a life focused on the work achievements that have brought you this far. A part of you senses that the interesting projects are going to require a different approach, that you won't be able to accomplish them simply with more hard work and determination. And you feel the urgent need for much more time than you have.

Hindus have for millennia called this *vanaprastha*, the third phase of life starting around age 40 or 50 when a person graduates from studying, then working madly, raising a family, and accumulating wealth—and moves into early semi-retirement, gradually withdrawing from the fray and seeking ways to help the next generation by giving back with resources and experience. The Chinese have long identified a person's 40s as the time to pivot from the learning and career preoccupations of life's first half to a more reflective and supportive role in the second half. In the United States, the old notion of a midlife crisis is now being replaced by a healthy, engaged form of early retirement that can conceivably last for decades.

If you love your career and want to keep working in it, then you are certainly fortunate and should stay the course. And if you must keep working to make the money needed to support yourself and family, then by all means keep at it—while seeking ways to reduce your financial needs by scaling back spending. But if you don't need and don't particularly want to stay on in your fast-paced career, you can choose to stop.

Working full time until you are 65 or older is now a choice for many people, and in the coming years, may no longer be the norm. Early semi-retirement will become the accepted route for many who seek a modest amount of meaningful work that can provide financial security and challenge, combined with plenty of free time to stay healthy, develop nourishing relationships, and explore new directions.

If you have started to think along these lines, and early semi-retirement feels like it could be a fit for you, then get ready to tackle the first rule of early semi-retirement: Figure Out Why You Want to Do This.

Briefly, you'll need to start with some clear thinking on two fronts. First, begin to identify and honestly face up to aspects of your current life that just aren't working any longer. Second, start to grapple with questions such as: If you had all the time in the world and no financial worries, what would you do? What would that feel like? What could it become?

This chapter provides plenty of help with finding your own answers to these questions—giving background material, historical context, and several exercises to help clarify your thinking and build your resolve to act.

A good place to start figuring out why you might want to retire early is to look at the sorry state of the Overworked American, the subject of the next section.

THE OXYMORON OF THE AMERICAN VACATION

In addition to putting in long hours each week, American workers also take far fewer paid vacation days than workers in any other developed country. At 10.2 days per year, the United States comes in last on the list of 20 leading economies, well behind the top ten European countries that average 29 days of paid vacation per year, or nearly six weeks, tallied in addition to holidays. Giving the lie to stereotypes, even Japanese workers take 17.5 days a year of paid vacation on average and the Chinese take 15 days.

How American vacationers look and feel is even scarier, with nearly 60% of executives and professionals doing work and calling into the office at least every few days. Of those recently surveyed, nearly half were required to leave an itinerary or contact information with their employers before going away on vacation.

Sources: Bureau of Labor Statistics, Economic Policy Institute, and American Management Association

A. Why Work Seems Stale

Before making the leap into early retirement, nearly every person steeled his or her personal resolve to do it by passing through a very low period—a place of being world weary, sick of the stress and pace and compromises of the get-and-spend, live-for-work culture. Your work situation may still be pleasant and comfortable. However, if it is not, a candid look at the current state of the American working life may give you context for your feelings of dissatisfaction and help you see that leaving the rat race behind can be a mark of eminent good sense.

And in case you start feeling guilty or uncertain, realize that through history and across cultures, people have organized their lives in ways that look very much like early semi-retirement. In fact, our recent workhours, work patterns, and career arcs are atypical in human history. You have a right to a sane balance between work and life—even your ancestors had it, at least until the Industrial Revolution. Believing in your inalienable right to a balance should help as you form the resolve to make your early semi-retirement happen.

But today we live in a consumer culture, with a sense of status getting all wrapped up in our lifestyles, the things we buy, the work we do. Whether aware of it or not, we agree to be part of this cycle, in which material expectations seem to rise just fast enough to sop up income, keeping us in debt and hard at work for decades. Thanks to advertising and easy credit fueling our desires for more, the average American family has just $1,000 of savings after subtracting personal—that is, nonmortgage—debt. In fact, things have gotten so out of hand that according to a recent poll by the Center for a New American Dream, a Maryland-based consumer rights group, nearly 90% of Americans now agree with statements such as: "As a society, our values are out of whack" and "Americans are too materialistic." We are quite simply hooked on consumption, and are paying for it with long hours at work, more spending—and lots of stress.

1. More Workplace Woes

Stop by any suburban office park, downtown office building, or other workplace, and chances are you'll encounter lots of people who would rather be somewhere else. Work seems to have taken over our lives. For the middle class, according to John de Graaf, David Wann, and Thomas H. Naylor, authors of the book *Affluenza: The All-Consuming Epidemic*, the work year has expanded by 660 hours since 1970, or more than 13 hours per week, to an average of over 46 hours per week. And currently, as many as one-fifth of American workers are spending more than 12 hours a day away from the home at work or commuting.

The lucky ones at least have jobs that let this breathtaking cycle of getting and spending continue. Unemployment has been stubbornly high in recent years, and many discouraged workers eat through their savings and have even worse worries and financial anguish wishing only for the chance to leap back into the maelstrom. When they do get a job, it often comes with fewer benefits or less security as companies seek to offload risk and expensive overheads by hiring more consultants and contractors. It is a sad irony of our system that so many have no work, while others have too much.

2. More Expenses

Many Americans are working so much because they feel they have no choice: Per capita consumption has doubled during the past 30 years, according to John de Graaf, editor of *Take Back Your Time: Fighting Overwork and Time Poverty in America.* And whether they rely on credit or pay cash, everyone seems to feel a need to keep up with this escalating standard of consumption.

Even for those not afflicted with escalating needs, costs are on the rise. By early 2005, the common biggest expense, a home, nearly tripled over the preceding 25 years in inflation-adjusted dollars for those living along the coasts and Great Lakes. Over this same period, salaries in the U.S. went up an average of just 23%, according to the Bureau of Labor Statistics. So there is hard math to support the feeling that it's hard to keep up. Those who covet even more space to store the ever-growing pile of things can buy a new home and get, on average, three times the closet space of the homes built in the 1950s—and an even bigger mortgage.

PLASTICS!

Few filmwatchers could have guessed the real growth industry in Mr. Robinson's advice to young Dustin Hoffman as Benjamin Braddock in *The Graduate*. The number of those who own credit cards have gone from a few hundred original Diner's Club members in 1950 to 1.2 billion in the U.S. today. We collectively hold $1.7 trillion of consumer and credit card debt, not counting mortgages—and each individual cardholder carries an average $8,562 of debt. Each year, cardholders pay $50 billion in finance charges and fees to the credit card companies, while 1.2 million of them declare bankruptcy. Small wonder that a recent survey by Fortune/Zogby in conjunction with PBS *Wall $treet Week* found "eliminating credit card debt" as by far the most important indicator that a person was "well-off or successful."

The prevalence of easy credit may be one reason savings rates among families in this country are so low: 40% of them spend more than they earn each year. Obviously, anyone who wants to retire early will need to get this sort of spending under firm control. Consumer credit, for all its convenience and benefits, has probably kept more people tied to the treadmill of full-time work than anything else ever invented.

Sources: Motley Fool Credit Center, American Consumer Credit Counseling, BankRate.com, and DebtSmart.com

3. More Stress

From statistics on long workhours and frustrating commutes, to sky-high divorce rates and personal debt, to the vast numbers of anti-depressants and medical remedies downed, there is ample proof that Americans are feeling the pressure of life.

When asked directly, as in recent polls by Yale and the Families and Work Institute, more than a quarter of American workers felt very or extremely stressed and burned out by their jobs. But whether we are more stressed today than in previous times—often the subject of heated claims and counterclaims among political factions—is not the real issue. What matters is how *you* feel. If you feel more stress than you would like, then you need to take action.

Fortunately, there are plenty of resources available to help. While early semi-retirement offers one powerful way to reduce stress over the long run, it may not be an option that is available for you just yet. Don't despair. Many of those on the road to early retirement, living frugally and saving money, begin to feel a glow as they move toward financial independence and the knowledge that they are beginning to work by choice and not by necessity. If a job becomes too stressful, they can walk. Just knowing this can take a huge weight off.

Many simple but powerful techniques, from yogic breathing and stretching, to mental timeouts, to simply turning off the cell phone, can get you started on a saner way of life right away. Aside from clearly external stressors, such as toxic air or industrial noise, much stress is caused by the way we respond to situations, the things we tell ourselves or feel while stuck in a traffic jam, or when falling short of a goal. Changing expectations, reframing a situation, letting others share some of the burden of our shortcomings, and trusting that things will work out fine—even if not in the precise way we envisioned them—can all help reduce stress, without changing any of the actual stressors in the outside world.

Still, this approach has its limits. When it comes to juggling challenges such as parenting, paying the mortgage, keeping a client happy, caring for an aging parent, and staying fit while still keeping a marriage together, all the best techniques may start to come up short unless you are able to get more of your time back—something early retirement can clearly allow.

LIBERATING MEN THROUGH EARLY RETIREMENT?

A recent National Fatherhood Initiative survey found that 70% of fathers say they would be willing to take a pay cut to spend more time with their families, but few seem able to manage the time away from the job.

Today, for instance, only one father stays home, not working, with school-aged children for every 100 women who do so. While these roles may not always be chosen freely, or may be the result of economic necessity, studies do show that women seem better than men at finding their way to a saner work-life balance, including flexible work or home-based and part-time employment, although they bear the attendant economic tradeoffs. For instance, one recent study found that one in three Caucasian women with MBAs is not working full time versus just one in 20 men with MBAs, possibly suggesting that women who have the economic means to do so are choosing to work less.

Given the stresses of the work environment and men's proclivity to work long hours for many years in it, combined perhaps with their unique physiologies, it may be no surprise that one in five men dies of heart disease before the age of 75—and one in three are likely to die of either cardiovascular disease, stroke, diabetes, or other stress-related diseases before normal retirement age. As a result, men die, on average, more than five years earlier than women.

While early retirement offers a way for everyone to enjoy the benefits of spending less stress-filled time in the workplace, men, with few role models for saner work-life balance, stand to benefit in important ways. Because family expenses are covered by a Safe Withdrawal Rate instead of a regular paycheck, early retirement lets men sidestep their social conditioning and comfortably reduce workhours. From this simple step can come a cascade of physical and emotional benefits.

For instance, it is well understood that lack of exercise can lead to heart disease and that unrelenting stress is a killer. Best-selling author Dean Ornish, M.D., and others have conclusively demonstrated that switching to a low-fat vegetarian diet combined with regular exercise, meditation, and relaxation can reverse heart disease. But it is devilishly hard to make meaningful progress on these fronts while contending with daily commutes, demanding work obligations, and long hours under the fluorescent lights.

If enough men can find a way to take their feet off the gas pedal by retiring early, it may just help bring their life expectancies, currently 74.5 years, closer to women's 79.9.

Sources: Catalyst, a nonprofit business research organization; U.S. Bureau of Labor Statistics; U.S. Census; Center for Disease Control; National Fatherhood Initiative survey

B. Work in Other Times and Cultures

It's hard to imagine how we ended up here, with millions of people working harder and longer, only to be less happy, less healthy, and more stressed than ever. From this point of view, we may actually be worse off than at any time in recent history.

For example, 200 years ago, members of European and American upper middle classes had avocations, professions, owned businesses or property, conducted work, and bought things. But despite an active work ethic, people took plenty of time out for recreation, community activities, relaxation, and self-improvement. This balanced approach to living derived in large part from Greek and Roman values in which work was regarded as a necessary means to economic survival, but not an end in itself. As Aristotle said, "We work in order to have leisure." Improving one's mind, participating in the community, and enjoying the arts were seen as much more worthy than working to accumulate wealth—and were honored as the appropriate occupation of those who no longer had to work for a living.

While it is not realistic to propose returning to a mythical golden age or archaic economic system that consigned far too many people to short, brutish lives—often of slave labor—it is worth exploring how average people in different times and places drew the balance between work and life.

1. Leisure in the Medieval Period

Even Luther and Calvin, architects of the Protestant work ethic who viewed work as intrinsically ennobling, could hardly have envisioned or condoned the sorts of hours we now routinely work, especially when set against the paucity of time spent with our parents, children, and friends. Workhours from the 1200s to the 1700s, even for serfs and laborers, typically involved eight-hour days and five to six *months* of vacation and holidays per year. Agrarian workers tended to work longer days, but only an average of 150 of them per year.

Medieval peasants, who enjoyed much more leisure by choice, were comfortable with the balance between work and life because they did not especially need or want material possessions requiring them to earn more money. Early retirees can take the medieval peasants as guides, voluntarily stepping out of the spending for status cycle to move the dial back toward more leisure.

2. The Industrial Revolution

Sociologist Juliet Schor, a seminal researcher in the field of work and leisure, makes clear that the awful work conditions normally associated with the past began only in the mid-1800s with the Industrial Revolution, when workers were coerced or forced into working long hours.

Even at the height of the Industrial Revolution, when Americans were bent on building railroads, factories, and the infrastructure of an industrial economy, they were also busy building strong communities and a better society around new universities, libraries, museums, parks, and other institutions.

From the archetypal early semi-retiree Ben Franklin in the 1700s to Andrew Carnegie 100 years later, along with millions of unheralded folks, Americans have been actively engaged in building a vibrant public life outside the sphere of paid work and business.

3. Gentlemen of Leisure

In 1899, Thorstein Veblen wrote the delightful *The Theory of the Leisure Class,* which attempted to catalogue a sociology of wealth, consumption, and leisure back to the cave dwellers. He documents well the Gentlemen of Leisure living off inherited wealth and their tragicomical need for conspicuous consumption of goods to maintain social standing.

Veblen offers some solace, though, for today's frugal early retiree concerned about keeping up appearances. Consuming leisure has been a staple of elites all the way down to the bushpeople. It was only the rise of mobile, impersonal societies that tipped the scales toward the need for material status symbols, "signatures of one's pecuniary strength . . . written in characters which he who runs may read." Veblen assures us that as long as the community is cohesive, consuming leisure has plenty of respectability.

So hang with the neighbors, ignore what anybody else thinks about your old car, and you'll have fun and be admired, to boot.

4. A Lesson From Europe

We don't need to look back in history to find valid models of a sane work-life balance. We can find it today throughout Western Europe, available not only to economic elites but to a wide spectrum of society. Although their approach depends heavily on legislated work rules, unions, and major social spending— something Americans as a nation tend to shun—the model can still work for you as an individual. With up to eight weeks of paid vacation, numerous holidays, and full-time workweeks in the range of 30 to 40 hours, compared to the majority of Americans, most Europeans are fit and well-adjusted with plenty of time for meaningful lives outside work. European companies are vibrant world competitors across a broad swath of industries, while their arts and design set global standards. And the place looks great.

You might not love Europe or want to live there, and its economic choices are not without costs, but it is hard to fault Europeans' success in keeping work contained as a component, but not the dominant component, of a well-rounded life.

WORK AROUND THE WORLD

Here is a telling look at the number of hours workers throughout the world typically clock in each week.

Dutch, Austrians, and Swedes working more than 48 hours per week: 1% to 2%

Western Europeans working more than 48 hours per week: 5%

Americans working more than 48 hours per week: 20%

Japanese working more than 48 hours per week: 28%

Japanese dying each year from karoshi, the official term for Death by Overwork: 10,000

Sources: Jon Messenger, "Working Time and Workers Preference in Industrial Countries, Finding the Balance" (Routledge Studies in the Modern World Economy, 50); and Hiroshi Kawahito, National Defense Council for Victims of Karoshi, quoted in Yomiuri Shimbun Online

5. Slow Progress in America

America has experienced various reform movements designed to make work more meaningful and empowering. In the 1920s, that even took the form of a movement toward shorter hours, led by W.K. Kellogg of Kellogg's Cereals and the six-hour workday. But during the Depression, this trend evaporated as unions sought guarantees of a longer paid workweek.

The most recent reform arose in the '80s and '90s, when companies tried to get employees more involved in decision-making in a more congenial work environment complete with casual dress codes, snacks, and recreation spaces. But today, whether a workplace emphasizes suits and power lunches or onsite yoga classes, one trend has trumped all others: Americans are working longer hours under more stress than ever before. Or as prominent venture capitalist Fred Wilson told an audience of New York City entrepreneurs a few years back: "Sleep is optional for you guys and your teams."

In this vein, national coordinator of Take Back Your Time Day, John de Graaf, feels that some of the most gleeful media coverage of the Overwork Reform Movement has been aimed at subduing workers' calls for a more European-style work schedule. He says the underlying message to American workers has been: "You really don't have an alternative, so shut up and work more."

RESOURCES

FOR MORE ON OVERWORK REFORM. Take Back Your Time is an organization that pulls together people from business, government, and other walks of life to advocate, among other things, a mandatory three weeks of vacation for workers. It sells a great T-shirt, fittingly emblazoned: Medieval Peasants Worked Less Than You Do. You can find the organization at www.timeday.org.

C. Planning to Make the Leap

A few of my lucky early retiree friends basically woke up one day, usually while job hunting after a layoff, did a few calculations, and realized they never had to work again. For them, early retirement planning has focused on making the psychological adjustments; the earning and saving part was done. Other people inherit a large sum, radically improving their financial situations and making early retirement possible at a single stroke.

But most people don't just happen to accumulate a large nest egg in midlife. It usually takes years of diligent work to attain financial self-sufficiency. Even if you are successful in earning large amounts of income, all but the very upper crust will need to do it without acquiring a taste for multiple homes and exotic cars, shopping trips to Paris, private schools for the kids, and other extravagances that can keep people harnessed to the working world simply to support an expensive lifestyle.

This model for successful long-term saving was wonderfully validated in Thomas Stanley's *The Millionaire Next Door,* a report on the simple frugality underlying the financial success of most of America's down-to-earth millionaires. The secret is simple: Keep expenses low and save more than you ever thought possible.

These habits, developed early, can make a huge difference in your ability to retire or semi-retire early. Socking away the maximum contributions in tax-advantaged arrangements (see Chapter 5, Section B) and employer-matched funds and seeing the dramatic effects of compounding over time can put a big premium on getting started.

1. The Importance of Working Together

Unless you are single, planning and saving for early retirement crucially requires some sort of buy-in from your spouse or partner.

If early retirement is your idea alone, and your spouse or significant other is lukewarm or cold toward it, your first step will be for the two of you to work out a reasonable set of expectations. Perhaps it would help to uncover the potential benefits or compromises together. For example, you may be sick of work, but your partner may not be. However, he or she might have a strong desire to go back to school, travel, or move closer to adult children—goals which could be advanced in early retirement. Plenty of couples actually do a "one-legged early retirement" in which just on person retires early and the other stays happily working on the traditional retire-at-65 cycle. Aside from the difficulty in planning long trips as a family, this approach has obvious economic advantages, too.

Depending on how long it takes to build your savings, you may have 15 years or more to plan and adjust. This puts time on your side in terms of helping a spouse or partner get used to the idea of making needed changes to lifestyle and mindset. But it also means you have many years over which you'll need to keep the dream alive and together adhere to spending and savings discipline.

2. Moderation Is Key

Be careful not to overdo it. Early retirement is about learning to savor life and live it fully—and saving up for early retirement will take a long time. You can get obsessive about hard work for a few years, but burnout is waiting for you if you don't pace yourself. Don't rush. Saving too ardently can bring its own problems.

> **EXAMPLE:** Sean, an aspiring early retiree, is in danger of ruining a promising relationship with his girlfriend because of his excessively frugal ways. Sean hasn't taken a vacation in five years, having ascertained a delay to his early retirement due to the time and money he'd spend on a vacation. And almost any entertainment expense, aside from going to the park, is not in his budget.

Humans probably aren't meant for extreme levels of self-denial. Even the Puritans passed along the old adage about All Work and No Play, and the story of King Midas probably figures in somewhere here, too. By grasping to have it all too soon, you could end up losing the truly valuable things in your life by trying to secure them in perpetuity. There is very little you can do to hurry this planning and saving process, no matter how strong your desire to leave the world of work.

D. Moving From Work to Early Semi-Retirement

You might be starting to agree that life in the trenches of overwork may be paying the bills, but at a high price. You might also be feeling a sense of the desperate financial treadmill on which most people struggle much of their lives, resolving to move beyond it. Developing these insights is a good beginning, but there will be many more steps and challenges on your way to building and bringing newfound resolve into action.

For example, you are embarking or potentially embarking on a lifetime of maintaining spending discipline, which for some will feel like a real burden.

You'll also find that opting to live a more modest lifestyle with more free time can challenge the current dominant attitudes about status, work, consumption, and careers. Neighbors may whisper. In-laws may ask difficult questions. Friends may express concern.

Stay the course—and learn to find strength and conviction deep inside, trusting the rightness of bringing sanity and balance back to your life.

WITH FREEDOM COMES RESPONSIBILITY

Be aware that early retirement may demand something from you that feels new and different. You will have unprecedented freedom and choices to make; you'll be creating your life rather than taking one that is handed to you. As exhilarating as this may seem, many people are so used to having circumstances or other people dictate the course of their lives that the change can be a bit disconcerting.

As you plan for early retirement, you'll need to prepare yourself mentally for the freedom and responsibility of shaping your own life. Often this will mean creating new structures for your days, new obligations. Choose them carefully to support and enhance the changes you want to make. (See Chapter 6 for a detailed discussion of how to structure work and activities in early semi-retirement.)

---

1. Carrots and Sticks

There are two classic ways to motivate a donkey that won't budge: Dangle food in front of its nose to get it interested in moving forward or swing a stick on the rear to get its full attention and cooperation. Picture the image of the lateral thinking farm kid who ties the carrot to the stick, hops on the donkey's back, and hangs the stick out in front with the carrot dangling a foot away from the mouth of the now-galloping donkey.

Moving yourself away from your own status quo may also involve some combination of carrots and sticks—and a good measure of creativity. Many early retirees are motivated by the lure of unlimited time to engage in hobbies and leisure activities, the chance to pursue an avocation, get healthy, and be with family. The flip side of these, and the motivation far more effective at galvanizing a potential early retiree into action is unfortunately the negative one: the stick, the sense of deprivation or harm that makes you want to move on to a better place.

This may include the pain of being separated from your children all week, knowing they miss you, or even worse, don't really miss you anymore because you've become a minor character in their lives; the assaults on your health and emotional well-being from long stressful workhours; the deterioration in your marriage. Sticks have a way of cutting through everything else—pushing people to make changes, to fix something that is broken.

Whatever your motivations—be they carrots, sticks, or some combination of the two—plant them firmly in your mind. Figure out and remember well why you want to do this: It will help power you through weariness, obstacles, self-doubt, any number of difficulties that may arise.

OF MICROBES AND FROGS: LIFE LESSONS FROM NATURE

Scientists have now observed and confirmed that a bacterium that likes a certain environment will make regular excursions away from its location to ascertain whether life nearby is more or less congenial than the one it is in at the moment. If its chemical sensors detect things are worse, it returns on the same path to its base and heads off in a different direction. But if it detects more favorable concentrations—of sugar, or proteins, or whatever—then it sets up a new base and keeps looking again. This cycle isn't continuous, but kicks in every so often, even if the bacterium is in a comfortable location.

The lesson to be learned from the microbes is obvious. Don't just accept your current situation as destiny. Spend a little time looking around to see if there is something else you'd like better. But a word to the wise: Given that the institution of marriage is not big in bacterial cultures, don't expect to apply this approach to all parts of your life.

Another image from the world of science should be instructive to those yearning to leave the salt mines of Overwork. I haven't done this experiment myself, but have seen it reported in enough places to believe it may be true.

Put a frog in a big pot of cool water and put the pot on a hot stove. The frog, initially quite comfortable, will swim around, increasingly uncomfortable, increasingly desperate, but never feeling the trigger that will cause it to jump out of the gradually heating water. After several minutes—the reason I haven't done this experiment personally—the unfortunate frog will cook and die. However, take a second healthy frog, pop it down into the same hot water that cooked its friend, and it will instantly hop out—a bit singed perhaps, but quite clear that it wants nothing to do with a vat of scalding water.

The lesson here: Don't let yourself be the first frog. Use your brain to decide when to hop out before it's too late.

a. Understanding the carrots

You may be one of the lucky ones who is actually quite comfortable with the world of work. You see early retirement as a natural evolution arising from a simple desire to pursue new interests at a comfortable pace. For you, early retirement is motivated primarily by the carrots—the wholesome attraction to a better life.

In the long run, carrots are what you'll need to stay in early retirement and make it satisfying. While sticks may get you moving initially, once the changes are made and the problem fixed, they lose some of their motivating power. Carrots will keep you nourished over the long run with interesting projects, constructive changes, creative achievements, new directions, and growth.

While you may have daydreamed and wished for the carrots over the years, if they were out of reach, you likely set them aside as impractical or simply unachievable. Most early retirees put interests and avocations on hold in their teens and early 20s because they offered no reasonable way to start a career. In early retirement, you can rediscover and develop those interests and uncover new ones. With large blocks of free time you'll need something to fill your days or you may find yourself bouncing back to full-time work out of boredom. Reconnecting with those early interests and building some momentum in pursuing them will keep you on track while you are making the transition from career to early retirement.

b. Understanding the sticks

Not everyone is lucky enough to be motivated solely by the carrots. Those whose lives have reached toxic crisis know only that they must escape. Things as they are have simply gone on too long and if they don't change, something bad is going to happen.

The stick that finally got me moving into early semi-retirement came from a wistful old song, "Cat's in the Cradle," by Harry Chapin, about a father who never had enough time to spend with his son: *When you coming home, Dad? I don't know when . . . but we'll get together then. You know we'll have a good time then.* And of course, there never was enough time; the son who so admired his father grew up to be just like him, with a fast-lane life and no time for his dad or his own son, either.

HOW IT WORKED FOR US

My wife, Wonda, and I started planning nearly 15 years before I was finally able to leave my full-time career. One important early influence was Paul Terhorst's book, *Cashing in on the American Dream,* which I devoured, concentrating on the ideas that were relevant to our situation and discussing them often.

In preparation for the future, Wonda and I did three key things. First, we started saving more. While we were living in Japan and both employed, all our expatriate friends had cars, but we walked and took cabs or the subway. Tradeoffs such as this helped us put my entire paycheck in the bank and live off Wonda's earnings. I opted to move into sales and sales management where I earned more, then rolled those savings into seed capital for my first business.

Second, we began adapting our rather traditional expectations about how and when our careers would peak. We agreed that neither of us cared if I kept climbing the corporate ladder, and I began making plans to invest in or start a small firm and try to graduate from the world of work within ten years. This firm turned out to be far more lucrative than traditional employment would have been. Wonda, an attorney, had always assumed that she would have multiple careers. As she started to see herself burning out on law, she did not resist the idea of leaving, telling herself she could return to the profession in the future if need be.

Third, over the years, we began to focus more on the positive benefits of life after early semi-retirement—being together more, becoming more engaged in community activities, exercising regularly, buying a sailboat and having the time to take it places, and being more available to care for our children and our parents.

Wonda began her early semi-retirement in 2000, which brought immediate benefits to our family in terms of reduced stress and smoother logistics. Mine followed a year later. Failure to make psychological and practical preparations and gradual lifestyle shifts, however, would likely have resulted in either or both of us boomeranging back to full-time work.

Thinking about my two boys growing up, missing me and wanting me around more was a huge heartache during those final years before early retirement, especially on weeks filled with business travel. I am glad to say that now, when they want to play catch, tell me a joke, or ask about algebra, I am able to be right there for them, with full attention. Early retirement has taken the sting out of that old song for me, and will, I hope, help my own sons to be better fathers one day, too.

Whether toward the needs of a child, spouse, or friend, or simply to that still small part inside that needs time and care, you may be working up a healthy resentment about brushing quiet needs aside while barging along through life dealing with more pressing matters.

But perhaps you feel you are holding up pretty well to all the stresses and toxicity of modern life. You're made of pretty hardy stuff, and you've figured out how to have some fun along the way. Even so, try to imagine a life without the overwork, sleep deprivation, stale office air, lack of exercise, or overextended finances. Picture how you would feel if you could spend much more time with friends and family, or relaxing at the lake. You might have better things to do than to sit with a throbbing headache in traffic on the way to the airport for yet another midweek business trip, then sit through a series of long meetings in a windowless conference room.

In any case, think clearly about the toll that your current career and workdays are taking on your life and your reasons for keeping at it—not as some sort of depressive self-indulgence, but simply to give yourself a clear picture of just what work life has become for you. See whether any taint is holding steady or whether it is getting progressively worse and harder to stomach. And answer honestly whether you and your family members are healthy, relationships intact, with no one developing any depressive or self-destructive tendencies.

If any of these areas turn up problems, pay attention and remember them. You'll need to repeatedly draw on these feelings and resolve to help clarify your personal answer to Rule #1 of early semi-retirement: Figure Out Why You Want to Do This. Early retirement is a big step, and will involve sacrifices and adjustments—with plenty of time in the years ahead to contemplate whether you've made the right decision. A firm understanding of any stick that is encouraging you to move on from your old way of life now will help you stay the course toward permanent, positive change.

2. Getting Started

Whether you are primarily motivated by sticks or carrots, you'll need to spend plenty of time to answer the question: What do you want to make of your life once you have it back?

Chapter 2 on saving and budgeting explains concrete steps to begin the essential planning for the financial side of early semi-retirement. This section helps you get started emotionally by describing exercises to help build your initial resolve and laying the psychological and emotional groundwork to help you make up your mind to change. Once you know why you want to change, it will be easier to follow through with the saving and financial sacrifices you'll undergo to make early semi-retirement a reality.

Following are several techniques that can shake up your old thinking and get you to see that changing gears in midlife is not only possible, but a normal and healthy part of life. You can use them with equal benefit if you are at the earliest stages of planning for early semi-retirement, about to retire, or are already happily early retired and thinking about how to take advantage of the time and potential you have created for yourself.

> **TIP**
>
> **THE IMPORTANCE OF PERCOLATION.** To focus your thoughts and motivations for retiring early, try writing down your feelings about work and life, perhaps early in the morning or after taking a long walk. Talk with your spouse or partner or a trusted friend. Or sit on a rock overlooking a stream or ocean for an hour while you let your answers become more clear

a. Building your resolve

Imagine you get a call from your doctor's office. You haven't been feeling well, and a number of tests have just come back from the lab. You learn you have a rare terminal case of something unpronounceable and are likely to die within a year. Try to experience everything that means. If you need help with that, sit in a full tub, remove the plug—and stare down the drain as all the water runs out.

Now snap your fingers, pinch yourself, and look in the mirror. The dire prognosis isn't true after all; you are still alive and well. Try to carry some of the feelings you had moments earlier into a deeper appreciation of your life. What do you want to do before you die? What do you feel is crucial to do with your time? Are all the things on your calendar important enough to do if you thought you had only a limited time left to live? What would you rather be doing instead?

Most people can come out of this exercise with a few things they wish they could do, a few things they are pretty sure they could prune out of their lives to make room, and a bit more resolve to make positive changes going forward. If you're feeling uncertain about whether early semi-retirement would be right for you, imagining these What Ifs can help uncover deeper feelings about what you want your life to stand for and whether you need to make some changes to accomplish it. Most people feel they could make these changes more easily if they had more free time, which early retirement makes possible.

If nothing else, this exercise can prod you with the nagging question: "Would it take a terminal disease for me to start putting my priorities in order?"

FACING UP TO FEAR AND GREED

If Jealousy is the green-eyed monster, Fear and Greed deserve their colors, too. Many people say they would like to retire early and have the financial means to do so, but they are conflicted and unable to bring themselves to make the leap. Their concerns invariably revolve around some combination of fear and greed.

For example, Paul Anderson, now in his late 50s, has vested in a generous pension, working for more than 30 years as a unionized employee in an American company in Asia. He is single, miserable in his work, and thinks daily about retiring. He has the financial means to retire today and live well for the rest of his life, pursuing several interests he longs to devote time to. Yet he recently signed a contract agreeing to stay on for another two years, and wonders whether he might end up signing on again at the next renewal time. When it comes down to the wire, Paul can't resist the allure of vesting a couple more percentage points in his pension, adding a few more dollars to his savings. Even Paul isn't sure whether he is motivated by an irrational fear of not having enough money during his retirement or by his greed for a few more dollars a month in his pension. Meanwhile, both he and his co-workers suffer his continued presence on the job, where he clearly has no desire to be.

Human nature is all too susceptible to golden handcuffs that keep many tied to the treadmill for "just another year or two." To retire early, you'll have to become determined that when you do have enough, you will walk away from those last few dollars to get free.

If your worries are always focused on whether you'll have enough money, then it is possible that no amount will ever really feel comfortable and you will always worry about needing and getting more. But if you are able to shift your focus to a new set of activities that you really enjoy doing, and feel deeply satisfied doing them, then even if you must make financial sacrifices eventually, you'll almost surely find yourself adjusting to them with creativity and equanimity.

b. Carrying the boat

Moving into retirement is a point of discontinuity in life and requires new thinking, a willingness to change and to do things differently going forward. Imagine yourself making the shift, something like switching from skating facing forward to flipping around and skating backward.

Ram Dass, a great spiritual teacher, described the process in a 1988 lecture to a group of midcareer business people seeking the next step in their lives. His advice is particularly apt for those contemplating early retirement. Working hard and staying focused on making money got you this far, Ram Dass said, but do you need to do it your whole life? Think of your professional life and career as the boat that carried you across an ocean and landed you on the far side. Then ask yourself a couple questions and respond honestly: Now that you've come on shore, do you need to carry the boat on your back? Or can you set your old ways aside, grateful for how far they have brought you, and move into new terrain on foot with a new set of tools?

You are changing and preparing for the next big chapter in your life. With luck, this won't happen because of some traumatic event, but because of natural evolution. Signals to you that you're changing might be that the skills and attitudes that served you well in your career are starting to feel a little toxic. You sense that you're somehow addicted to the adrenaline, the thrill of the next deal, or the three-ring circus of your professional life, but a quieter part of you yearns for simplicity, calm, time to think and plan, time to relax and make new friends. Once you understand that to move forward, you need to stop much of what you've been doing, you are ready to leave the boat and begin walking.

c. Mapping out a perfect life

"If you don't know where you are going, any road will take you there," the strategy professor at MIT, Arnoldo Hax, used to tell his students. His point was obvious, but doing anything about it has long bedeviled the best corporate management teams. Those attempting to be strategic about planning their own lives grapple with the same issue: the biggest challenge is often figuring out what you want to do and why. Once you've done that and can focus your full attention on actually going there, progress comes much more easily.

In between all the work and sacrifice you are making to save and prepare for early retirement, picture yourself with a whole week, at home, free. Concentrate on what you always thought you might be interested in if you just had the time. What would make you feel you were making a positive difference in the world? What kind of person do you admire or want to become?

Many early retirees look back to the time they sat with these questions as a critical breakthrough in forming the resolve to retire early. By taking the tangible step of filling in a calendar or writing out a typical day, week, or year's blend of activities, you can create a powerful vision of the life to which you are moving.

Some of your goals may require internal changes—for instance, getting healthy, working on relationships, or developing a quietness inside that will allow your best self to shine through. Other goals will be physical and external—remodeling or building onto your home, moving to a favorite vacation spot year round, creating things. Still other changes will concern the activities that fill your day: the people and organizations in which you get involved, the places you go, or projects you undertake.

Make a list of the activities that you would find valuable in filling your time and post it somewhere visible. When you do early retire, that list will be a handy guide for how you fill those days when you drop off the kids at school and realize it's only 8:30 and you have nothing scheduled to do the entire day. Your list will keep you on track like a map and compass, guiding the small steps to create a life reflecting your dreams and values.

If you are still working full time and honestly don't have time to engage in any of these changes now, you can still begin to lay the groundwork. Collect some brochures about an organization with which you'd like to get involved, attend a weekend event with people who are doing something you're interested in, read some books or write something in a journal that helps you envision your perfect day or year in early retirement. Plant these seeds now.

This quiet gestation period may take years, but it will ensure that when your finances and circumstances allow you to eventually retire, you'll have a pretty good idea of at least some of the things you'd like to do with your days. Once you can invest large amounts of your time doing the things that inspire you, you'll find they lead to even more new interests, and some of the initial ones may even fall away; that is fine. The important thing is to get started.

d. Fitting rocks into a jar

Imagine you have an empty jar, a collection of a few large rocks, and several handfuls of gravel. Your task is to put all the large and small rocks into the jar. One approach would be to pile all the gravel in first, but doing so would leave room for only one or two of the large rocks; you wouldn't get everything to fit. Switch your approach and put the large rocks in first, and you'll find that the gravel will all fit nicely around the empty space. If a bit of gravel doesn't fit at the end, you've not lost much.

Let too many little things take priority, and there never seems to be time for the big things. Consider the Big Rocks to be the really important things you want to accomplish in life, the things that define you. Get the big things in first, work on the right projects and priorities, and let the little stuff fit in around the edges. Let your Big Rocks be nonnegotiable priorities in your weekly calendar—and learn to say "No" when other things begin to intrude. Then fit those other things in where you can.

Understand that moving into early semi-retirement is an effort to take one of the biggest rocks of most people's lives—earning a living—and demote it to being a small to medium-sized rock, making room for other priorities.

BIG ROCKS FOR EARLY RETIREES

Certain Big Rocks for early retirees come as no surprise: more time with family, getting fit, or concentrating on a hobby or interest begun years earlier. Nonetheless, plenty of early retirees find themselves unexpectedly developing new interest in something they had never anticipated.

And on the flip side, interestingly, many early retirees note that they had expected to travel extensively, but that after the first few years had found themselves traveling less even than they had during their working years. Perhaps there was not as much need to escape daily life. Or perhaps so many new interests arose that it became hard to get away.

In any case, early retirees recently surveyed offered up the following as some of the unexpected new activities in which they became immersed:

- surfing
- Tae Kwon Do
- sculpture
- environmental activism
- local politics
- homeopathy
- meditation
- sailing
- cooking
- home brewing
- hiking and fitness
- woodworking
- Native American spirituality, and
- landscaping with native plants.

Whatever work you choose, let it arise from a blend of interests and passion, a focused activity that keeps you on track, whether it is initially paid or unpaid. It may only be for a few hours a week, but it should be real—a commitment in which you fully engage your energy, your brain, and your creativity to make something happen. Perhaps others depend directly on you, perhaps you deliver something of value or create something tangible. Or it could be that everything you do for a number of years is really preparation for a second stage in which you'll have more direct responsibility in a new field. (See Chapter 6 for a detailed discussion of possible activities to take on in semi-retirement.)

RESOURCES

FOR MORE HELP IN MAKING THE TRANSITION FROM WORK TO RETIREMENT. There are a number of resources to help shake your old ways of thinking while you contemplate moving on to early retirement. Here are a few of them.

- A great workbook to help you reconnect to the artist inside— the one you might have pushed aside back in your youth as you set about having a serious career—is *The Artist's Way*, by Julia Cameron (Jeremy P. Tarcher).

- Just about any tape by former Harvard psychology professor Ram Dass will likely be helpful while you are working through the transition from your old life into something more sustaining. You can find tapes by Ram Dass at: http://ramdasstapes .org/audiobook/index.htm.

- A book about early semi-retirees engaged in public service that gives detailed examples of what others are doing to have fun and make a difference is *Prime Time: How Baby Boomers will Revolutionize Retirement and Transform America*, by Marc Freedman (PublicAffairs).

- Even if you get seasick and hate boats, reading cruising literature can help you vicariously savor the joy and freedom of life after the job. It's hard to find a group of people who better embody the early retiree spirit than casual long-term sailboat cruisers. Good magazines are *Cruising World* and *Blue Water Sailing*.

3. Keeping Going

If you are already in early semi-retirement, remind yourself frequently of your carrots—the positive reasons you chose this path, the things on your list that you wanted to accomplish with all your free time and energy. After an initial period of rest and recuperation, you will probably find a need to replace the sense of accomplishment that work rightly gave you with a new

set of challenges and commitments. Chosen well, you'll feel you are accom-
plishing something really worthwhile, not just passing the time and keeping
yourself amused.

Be tolerant and patient with yourself, though, as these changes take time.
Real, durable change will not happen in a smooth arc—there will surely be
stops and starts along the way. Interests will grip you and then fade away. And
you may find yourself trying too hard to turn an interest into something big
enough to fill the time you have available. Resist this urge, a leftover habit
from your previous way of approaching work. Be watchful and open, but
see if you can let your new activities choose you. Trust that things will move
along in their own time as long as you keep taking small steps.

FILLING UP ALL THAT FREE TIME

Believe it or not, the biggest stumbling block many people have when
thinking about early semi-retirement is how they will fill up the free
hours of the day and night.

The short answer is that if you've done your planning and follow a few
basic strategies, this never seems to be a problem. A year or so in, you'll
be wondering how your days are slipping away. Develop and keep your
list of projects and challenges posted prominently and refer to it whenever you sense yourself needing a boost. (See Chapter 6 for examples of
projects in which early semi-retirees have become involved.)

If you live by seizing each day as an opportunity to grow and learn,
you'll find plenty to keep you as busy as you want to be.

4. Maintaining a Balance

When you imagine early retirement, you'll probably focus on the first few
months—with the chance to rest, recharge, and do all the little things that
you never seem to have time to do: read books, play golf, fix things around
the house, shop, cook, or decorate. All early retirees go through this detox

stage; it is an important part of shedding the accumulated baggage from their former overstressed lives.

But after a while—as long as a year, perhaps—many early retirees start to feel a little antsy. Most people simply are not designed for a lifetime of leisure and unwinding. A task expands to fill the time allotted it and they suddenly realize they've spent all morning just moving from the living room to the kitchen, with lots of staring out the window to fill the time.

If you are starting to feel this way, you may have begun to realize that you need something that challenges you, engages you, and lets you make a difference. Daytime television, overeating, peccadilloes, all manner of unhealthy and unpleasant obsessions can start to arise when you truly have Nothing to Do. You might also start to watch the financial markets and obsess about your portfolio performance. Without the need to shower and change into workclothes every morning, you look in the mirror one day and find you've become more scruffy and unkempt than you'd realized. You begin to feel that all around you people have a purpose—and all you have is Jerry Springer and CNBC.

a. Remember your priorities

To get back on track, take another close look at your Big Rocks. (See Section D2d.) One or more of them will probably be useful places to find the things that will become your "work" in early semi-retirement. At least initially, assume that these will be unpaid. Suppose, for example, that one of your priorities is to become physically fit. In that case, dedicate yourself to it: Block out time for that purpose alone several days a week and try not to let other things encroach. Change your diet, read the magazines, study anatomy—whatever it takes to fully immerse yourself in this important activity.

Or perhaps one of your Big Rocks is to paint with oils. Schedule time for it each week, go to readings and galleries, seek out resources and teachers who can help you develop. Unhook from your old patterns and habits of thought, learn new ways of seeing, and make a concerted effort to begin building a body of work, developing as an artist. Keep errands and diversions in a tight box. Treat your creative work as the most important thing you do each day.

b. Find meaningful work

There are many different approaches to earning some work income during early semi-retirement. However, the ideal is usually to grow one of your interests into a sideline that can allow you to make a sufficient amount of money while staying true to the heart of what makes you love the activity. For example, you may find a local collective gallery that agrees to carry your artwork, or you may find a few clients who will pay you to be their personal trainer or coach.

In fairness, after years of the rat race, many early retirees are understandably gun-shy of anything remotely resembling work or employment. Their response is likely to be, "Bah! Never again!" While some early semi-retirees do return to a former employer for a few hours a week, most move into something new. In fact, for most people, it is generally not even helpful to think about a traditional job—certainly not the type that comes with a boss and a desk. Instead, think ball park usher, yoga teacher, real estate rehabber, scout leader, museum docent, fishing guide, tutor, or jewelry designer to get started generating your ideas about work. Try things that have always intrigued you. Try things that fall in your lap. (See Chapter 6 for a discussion of the entire spectrum of work options for early semi-retirees.) ●

CHAPTER TWO

Live Below Your Means

If you are planning to retire early, you'll need to spend less than you earn, building up savings over many years to provide income and financial security for the rest of your life.

If you have already retired, you may have what seems like a large sum of money set aside; but you can't wisely spend more of it than 4% or so a year—the amount you can safely draw out over the long run and still keep your portfolio value intact. (See Chapter 4 for details on Safe Withdrawal Rates.)

Whatever stage you're in, you may long for some material luxury such as a new car or a second home and you may even have enough cash on hand to pay for it. But because you are building a safe spending and budgeting plan for the long term, you need to keep that money invested and working for you, instead. This is the sort of discipline it takes to Live Below Your Means, which will become your guidepost for all spending-related matters from this day forward.

> *Oh Lord, won't you buy me a Mercedes Benz?*
>
> —JANIS JOPLIN

This chapter tackles the wide-ranging area of budgeting and spending, both during the years you are saving and planning for early retirement, and in the years following that—essential groundwork for Living Below Your Means.

A. What It Means to Live Below Your Means

Living Below Your Means is spending less than you make, less than you could, less than your peers. It is a powerful tool—combining discipline, commitment, and a healthy orneriness to stand against the tide of material consumption. It shouldn't mean deprivation, or being pennywise and pound foolish. Think of it simply as a sensible way of ensuring that money doesn't get squandered through carelessness, impulsiveness, or in keeping up appearances. Buy what you need and have some fun, but don't expect to buy everything you want.

You probably have some ready role models for this way of living and spending. Think of your parents' or grandparents' approach to spending; people who grew up during the Great Depression were often thrifty in the extreme and remained that way all their lives. You didn't see them buying a new car every three years. They recycled before it was fashionable and used things until they wore out. While you may never need to be or want to be quite as frugal as your ancestors—rewashing plastic bags and aluminum foil, anyone?—the heart of their time-tested spending disciplines can still serve you well.

There are some people who are simply good at saving. If you are one of these disciplined souls and have been thinking about early retirement for a while, or have already retired, Living Below Your Means is second nature, so ingrained over years of practice that it would never occur to you to blow the budget. Your whole life seems to be organized in such a way that keeping expenses in check feels easy and normal.

But others don't have it so easy. They see their lives as full of spending temptations—including meals in high-end restaurants, expensive hobbies, fast new cars, fine art, and luxurious hotels. Sometimes, just getting the property taxes paid, the insurance covered, and the kids to camp can blow the budget.

If you are just starting to plan for early retirement, with a modest amount of savings and a seemingly endless list of demands on your paycheck, you will need to buckle down. The bottom line during your planning years—while you are working full-time to get to early retirement—is that your savings must grow every year, with plenty of fresh cash flowing in. That will probably mean developing a new family culture of frugality, of doing more with less, cutting back on some of the little luxuries, and postponing or passing up bigger ticket items.

That admonition aside, the reality is that how much you spend and what defines "frugal" for you and your family involve very personal decisions, defying a single recommended script. What is working for Chris Tacy and Valerie Hoecke, a young San Francisco couple who escaped the city for a simpler life as early semi-retirees in the Sierra Nevada mountains, will simply not fit a frustrated senior executive who is seeking to continue an objectively lavish lifestyle while starting a little hedge fund and working part time from home. While moving to Guatemala was a perfect and economical solution for Willem and Ruth Havel, the culture shock was too much for T.J. Justin, who tried early retirement in neighboring Costa Rica. He switched to early semi-retirement in the more familiar environment of a small town in rural California and keeps up his part-time work to pay the bills. The approach you choose must fit your preferences, budget, and lifestyle.

B. Creating Your Spending Plan

Whether you have retired early or are still in the planning years, there are some proven steps for building and keeping a spending plan—some people just cringe at the word budget—that will ensure you Live Below Your Means.

1. Make It Reasonable

There is no point in setting spending and saving goals you simply cannot meet, or that put you and your family through such pecuniary anguish that they threaten the fabric of your world. Set budget targets that stretch but don't break you. Your goal is to feel good about the progress you are making, not to feel bad about how far you might have fallen short or still have left to go.

2. Make It Easy to Track

There are plenty of ways to keep track of your spending—and compare how you are faring against your plan.

Some people are avid fans of the complete control method, tracking every single transaction in software such as *Quicken* or *Microsoft* Money.

> **EXAMPLE:** Bob Lee tracks every cash expenditure electronically and also downloads all his credit card and checking transactions into the program. Then he classifies each expense into an expenditure category and measures it against the relevant monthly and annual budget for, say restaurant meals, home repairs, or utilities. Every week, Bob knows just how things stack up against their goals.

Many people find this approach the easiest way to track and keep on a budget. Others prefer a more flexible approach that doesn't require constant record keeping.

> **EXAMPLE:** The Sullivans set an annual spending target, put 1/12th of it in their checking account each month, and try not to overdraw the account too often If they do, they pay back the overdraft first and try to get back on track the next month by eliminating a few luxuries. If things seem to be getting progressively off track, they cut back on a planned vacation.

And still others prefer something in between. They have at least some categories for tracking spending, especially separating out items that are only paid once or twice a year from the regular monthly budget, such as insurance and taxes. Within the monthly budget, they break out core necessities from more discretionary spending. It is then easier to target the things that will be cut first if spending starts to swing out of whack.

> **EXAMPLE:** The Tadichis track and pay for taxes, annual sailboat expenses, insurance, and one major vacation directly from their money market account at various points during the year. The remainder of their annual spending is divided in 12, and they write a check for that amount from their money market account to their checking account each month. As long as their checking account isn't overdrawn, they know they are on track with their annual spending plan—and they spend almost no time on record keeping.

TIP

OUT OF SIGHT, OUT OF MIND. No matter how you decide to budget, during your planning years, once you've settled on your annual spending needs, try to get any excess income from paychecks or other sources direct-deposited into savings accounts immediately upon arrival; extra money sitting around in a checking account tends to be spent.

3. Make It a Group Effort

Nothing keeps marriage counselors employed like money troubles. If you are in a relationship, work out spending and saving goals together with your spouse or partner—and develop mutually respectful ways to implement them so you can stay on track together.

Give each other some slack and celebrate the progress you make. Work out solutions together when changes are needed. Above all, try not to let the roles become polarized: tightwad v. spendthrift or virtuous nagger v. irresponsible child.

RESOURCES

FOR MORE INFORMATION ON FINANCES. There are several good books devoted to helping you save money and get your financial house in order. Among them are:

- *Get A Life, You Don't Need a Million to Retire Well,* by Ralph Warner (Nolo)
- *Live Well on Less Than You Think, The New York Times Guide to Achieving Your Financial Freedom,* by Fred Brock (Henry Holt/ Times Books)
- *Retire On Less Than You Think, The New York Times Guide to Planning Your Financial Future,* by Fred Brock (Henry Holt/ Times Books), and
- *Smart Couples Finish Rich, 9 Steps to Creating a Rich Future for You and Your Partner,* by David Bach (Broadway Books).

C. Determining Your Annual Spending

Your spending needs will almost surely change in early retirement because you will need to account for additional items that will either add to or reduce your budget. Following are two simple methods—one starting with your current paycheck, the other with your current budget—for getting a close estimate of your spending in early retirement to help your planning and budgeting.

Categories of these additional budget items will be explained in detail later in the chapter. (See Sections E and F.) For now, just get a sense that your spending might go up or down from your current budget.

Compared to full-time workers, early retirees typically experience a number of changes affecting budgeting, including:

- much lower income taxes
- no more savings or retirement contributions
- no more work and commuting expenses
- no more mortgage and interest payments from the house and other debts
- possible reduced payments due to changing homes, or graduating kids, and
- possible additional expenses of new hobbies, travel, leisure.

In addition, early retirees seeking a true picture of their annual spending needs should calculate a few additional items as part of annual spending. They include deductions for:

- car depreciation
- long-term home maintenance such as painting, and
- investment management fees.

You'll also need to count in your annual budget any income taxes from work or investments, including capital gains taxes on any withdrawals of principal you use for living expenses.

WARNING

(!) **THE TAXING MATTER OF CAPITAL GAINS.** Capital gains taxes that you incur due to normal rebalancing and mutual fund distributions need not be calculated as part of your annual budget, since they vary from year to year and are essentially outside your control. On the other hand, capital gains taxes that you incur annually from selling appreciated assets for living expenses should be counted in your budget. However, at this modest level, capital gains taxes should be minimal or zero.

1. Start With Your Current Pay Stub

If you don't have a budget now and aren't sure how much you currently spend each year, estimate your spending needs in early retirement through the process described here. You will start with the amount in your paycheck and make adjustments from there. Find your current net salary in your paycheck—the amount that gets deposited in the bank after all payroll and income taxes are taken out—and make the adjustments noted.

a. Calculate annual pay

Multiply the net salary on your pay stub by 26 if you get paid every two weeks, or whatever number is needed to get to an annual take-home pay figure, including any bonuses.

> **EXAMPLE:** Net salary, paid bi-weekly = $2,567; multiply by 26 = $66,742

b. Subtract savings

Subtract the net amount of money you saved last year—that is, the amount actually deposited in savings. Your portfolio may have increased or decreased based on market performance, but here you are after the amount you actually saved and deposited. If you saved $5,000 but ran up $2,000 of new credit card debt, net these out to $3,000. Net savings are subtracted for the following reason: You didn't spend the money, so it won't be part of your annual expenses going forward.

> **EXAMPLE:** Saved $11,000; new credit card debt of $1,000 = Net $10,000

c. Subtract work-related expenses

Estimate and subtract commuting expenses, dry cleaning expenses, and other direct work-related expenses such as childcare and pet care. Don't forget expensive restaurant lunches if you think you'll eat more cheaply at home once you've retired.

EXAMPLE OF ANNUAL WORK-RELATED EXPENSES:

Laundry	$1,000
Commuting and parking	$1,600
Total	**$2,600**

d. Subtract paid debts

If your home will be paid off by the time you retire, subtract your current mortgage payment, but not your property taxes. Property taxes are sometimes included in your mortgage payment and should be kept out; you'll need to keep paying them as long as you live in the home.

> **EXAMPLE:** Mortgage will be paid off by retirement date, $1,550/month = $18,600 per year

e. Add the income tax estimate

Take the total of the four items described above—together, your expected taxable income—and add 3% to cover your expected income taxes, which will be much lower once you retire.

> **EXAMPLE:** $66,742 − $10,000 − $2,600 − $18,600 = $35,542
> Expected annual income tax: $35,542 x 3% = $1,066

f. Add fund management fees

Add .5% of the total value of your savings for fund management fees. Use the amount of savings you project you will have available when you begin early retirement. (See Section D5 for an explanation of how to estimate savings.)

> **EXAMPLE:** Total savings at early retirement: $792,000 x .5% = $3,960

g. Add car and house costs

Add $2,500 for each car you own and $1,000 if you own an average-sized house.

> **EXAMPLE:** One car, one house: $2,500 + $1,000 = $3,500

h. Adjust for spending fluctuations

Calculate any other known increases or decreases to annual spending in early retirement—through moving, economizing, additional travel, for example.

> **EXAMPLE:** Further projected budget cuts of $3,000 per year from other belt-tightening efforts such as reduced restaurant meals, lawn care service, or phone bill consolidation.

i. Sample calculations

Here is an example of all the additions and subtractions needed to get the expected annual spending in early retirement.

Initial take-home salary	$66,742
Less net savings	– 10,000
Less commuting expenses	– 2,600
Less paid-off debt payments	– 18,600
Plus income tax estimate	+ 1,066
Plus fund management fees	+ 3,960
Plus car and home annual costs	+ 3,500
Other spending adjustments	– 3,000
Expected annual spending	**$41,068**

2. Start With Your Current Budget

If you have already created a reasonable, livable budget to which you and your family currently adhere for regular and annual expenses, then you can skip the first two steps above, subtracting savings from your total earnings. (Sections C1a and C1b.) Start instead with your current budget figure and subtract your work-related expenses. (See Section C1c.) You will then be on the same track for making the needed adjustments to come up with your estimated early semi-retirement spending needs.

3. Sample Spending Plans

Tying all the spending changes together gives you an example of a spending plan that can be updated monthly to help you see where you stand relative to your annual budget and make adjustments as needed. The sample spending plans below split expenses into three categories:

- **MONTHLY EXPENSES,** such as food, utilities, and credit card bills, which generally recur and are paid monthly or more frequently, and miscellaneous expenses such as household items, music, and entertainment.

- **ANNUAL EXPENSES,** such as taxes and insurance, which are paid once or twice a year, and

- **SPECIAL EXPENSES,** such as investment management expenses and car depreciation, which all savers, but especially those who have stopped working full time, need to include to make their budgets accurate over the long run. (See Section F3 for a full explanation of these expenses.)

Two budgets are presented below: one for a dual-earner working family and the other for a family that is already early semi-retired. The budgets, while hypothetical, could even reflect the same family before and after semi-retirement.

You will notice that the working family's budget is nearly three times bigger than the early retired family's—$120,286 per year compared to just $41,088. While there certainly is a small amount of economizing on the part of the early retirees—for instance, from eating out less—most of the difference is simply due to the large structural changes that a family's finances undergo when beginning early retirement. These are changes such as losing all work-related expenses, getting rid of an expensive second car, greatly reducing income taxes, and paying off the mortgage. This sort of drop is not uncommon among those retiring early, meaning that actual early retiree budgets can be far below the oft-touted 70% of peak working income that is commonly recommended by financial planners as an estimate for post-retirement income needs.

Using a monthly and cumulative annual variance in the budget worksheets helps pinpoint which expense categories are over or under budget for the year. For instance, the spending plan shows the actual numbers from May of the current year, with the negative variance such as the one for utilities signaling overspending so far this year. Positive variances, such as for clothing, show that the family has spent less than the budgeted amount so far during the month and year.

This budgeting approach can be used by those planning and saving for early retirement as well as for those already retired. Its chief purpose is to show you the unvarnished truth about your annual spending and show you where you stand compared to your annual budget at any point during the year.

a. Sample spending plan for a working family

Noteworthy points here are the high cost of income tax and Social Security tax for the working couple, totaling nearly $25,000 per year. The family is still paying off its mortgage, which results in an additional $25,000 a year of spending.

Other work-related expenses such as child care and commuting expenses also weigh on the family's budget, though they do benefit from free health insurance through their employers. Finally, the working family is saving $20,000 a year another large item in the budget, though not a spending item in the traditional sense.

Spending Plan for a Working Family

	Monthly	May Actual	May Variance	YTD Variance	Annual
MONTHLY EXPENSES					
Groceries	325	400	−75	55	3,900
Clothing	400	160	240	254	4,800
Restaurants	450	295	155	−134	5,400
Misc.	250	200	50	−75	3,000
Gardening/home	125	190	−65	200	1,500
Telephone/cell/Web/cable	190	190	0	0	2,280
Utilities	215	75	140	−850	2,580
Charities	150	150	0	0	1,800
Gas/car/commuting	350	320	30	100	4,200
Mortgage	2,100	2,100	0	0	25,200
Child care	400	400	0	0	4,800
ANNUAL EXPENSES					
Property tax					2,450
Medical insurance					0
Income taxes					16,000
Social Security/Medicare					8,700
Auto insurance					2,000
Home insurance					976
Travel					3,000
SPECIAL EXPENSES					
Fund management fees					1,200
House repair allowance					1,500
Car depreciation					5,000
Savings					20,000
TOTALS	**4,955**	**4,480**	**475**	**−450**	**120,286**

b. Sample spending plan for an early retired family

Comparing the early semi-retired family's budget to the working family's reveals a number of important differences.

The early retired couple's budget is immediately noteworthy for its smaller size, just over 1/3 of the size of the working family's budget. The early retired couple has no mortgage or direct work expenses. They do pay a modest amount of income tax ($500) on their portfolio dividends and interest and $586 of Social Security and Medicare tax (Self-Employment Tax) on their semi-retirement work income. Because they are withdrawing each year from their savings for living expenses instead of adding to their stash, there is no savings listed in their budget, either.

Although both families spend the same amount on groceries, the early retired family has cut back restaurant dining, clothing, and a few other discretionary spending items—doing some of their own yard maintenance and not hiring a daytime babysitter. They are also down to just one car, though for very little expense they could probably purchase and maintain a ten-year-old car for limited local use if needed.

Spending Plan for an Early Retired Family

	Monthly	May Actual	Variance	YTD Variance	Annual
MONTHLY EXPENSES					
Groceries	325	400	−75	55	3,900
Clothing	200	160	40	254	2,400
Restaurants	250	295	−45	−134	3,000
Misc.	160	200	−40	−75	1,920
Gardening/home	75	190	−115	200	900
Telephone/cell/Web/cable	190	190	0	0	2,280
Utilities	215	75	140	−850	2,580
Charities	150	150	0	0	1,800
Gas/car maintenance	175	100	75	400	2,100
ANNUAL EXPENSES					
Property tax					2,450
Medical insurance					5,200
Auto Insurance					1,036
Home insurance					976
Travel					2,000
Income taxes					500
Self-employment tax					586
SPECIAL EXPENSES					
Fund management fees					3,960
House repair allowance					1,000
Car depreciation					2,500
TOTALS	**1,740**	**1,760**	**−20**	**−150**	**41,088**

D. Determining Your Means

When trying to understand this rule about Living Below Your Means, it's essential to know what "means" actually means for you. At its simplest, it is just a nice old word to describe income, or the amount of money you have to spend. For example, if you earn $50,000 a year and spend $51,000, you are not living within your means, but are going steadily deeper into debt. Means is the amount you can generate each year to make available to spend. If you live on less than your income, you are living within your means.

During early retirement, your means will consist of:

- any part-time work income
- any pension income, and
- the amount of money by which your savings can safely be tapped each year for your spending.

Note that if you have lots of savings, others may assume you can buy anything, or that you are living far below your means. You must think differently: Your assets are there to be tapped, conservatively, for a steady annual income. (See Chapter 4 for a discussion of why that amount is generally between 4% and 5% a year.) Spending more than this amount implies that, even though you may have loads of money, you are not living within your means.

Income sources are usually quite simple to calculate, or at least estimate.

1. Income From Work

Start by adding together the various sources of work income you might receive. The first type will be any pre-existing arrangements with a business or other reliable income source—for instance, regular payments or dividends from a company you started or sold, royalties, planned regular annual gifts of money from family or elderly friends, or alimony that you expect will continue over many years. For example, an engineer might know that a patent reliably pays $1,000 to $1,500 a year in royalties, or a writer or performing artist might estimate the continued flow of about $1,000 a year in royalties from a copyrighted work that seems likely to stay in print or distribution.

Next is any income you expect to earn through part-time work. While work options are described in detail in Chapter 6, it is worth noting here that many, if not most, early retirees find some pleasant or expedient way to earn income to help offset expenses. Whether walking dogs for neighbors, pitching in as a pall-bearer, or acting as a mediator for a local court, many retirees are on the lookout for innovative ways to earn a bit of extra income. While you are in your planning years, it is not so important to get the tally on your expected income exactly right, but rather to develop a ballpark idea of what is possible and suitable for your personal tastes.

> **EXAMPLE:** If you plan to earn extra income as a tutor in early retirement, estimate the number of students you could comfortably take on each week and the number of weeks each year you think the tutoring will span. Local payment rates are usually pretty clearly established, but you can never be completely sure that you will have as many students as you hope, at least at the beginning, and students do cancel. Nonetheless, you can readily calculate a conservative expected annual income as follows:
>
> Number of students: 4
> Number of hours per week for each student: 1
> Number of weeks per year tutoring: 30
> Hourly rate: $55
> **Total: 4 hours per week x 30 weeks per year x $55 per hour = $6,600 per year**

2. Pension Income

If you were fortunate to work for an employer with a defined benefit pension plan or for a government entity, this could be the mainstay of your retirement financing. If the pension will start paying from the beginning of your early retirement, include it in income. If it only starts paying after you reach a certain age, such as when you begin to collect Social Security benefits at traditional retirement age, then you can put it into your longer-term projections, but do not include it as income during your early retirement. (See Section E.)

3. Withdrawals From Savings

Your savings generate earnings and appreciate over time, which becomes a source of income that you can use for living expenses throughout your lifetime—your safe annual withdrawal from your savings. For those without a pension, or with limited sources of work income, this regular draw from savings, typically taken monthly, is the primary source of income during early retirement.

4. Examples of Individual Means

Most people will assemble their income from one or more sources, blending for instance, pension and part-time work, or part-time work and safe withdrawal, as in the following examples.

> **EXAMPLE:** Stuart, early semi-retired from a job as an electronic engineer, amassed $850,000 of taxable and tax-advantaged savings, but never worked for an employer that offered a traditional pension. Stuart's annual expenses are $45,000 per year. As a result, he also does part-time work to support his annual spending needs. Stuart's annual spending budget is:
>
> | | |
> |---|---|
> | Income from part-time work | $11,000 |
> | Income from savings | $34,000 ($850,000 x 4%) |
> | **Total annual income** | **$45,000** |

> **EXAMPLE:** Gayl, recently early retired after working her entire career for a county government, has never really had any savings aside from a state deferred comp plan that now contains $140,000. Still Gayl's inflation-adjusted pension (now $2,100 per month or $25,200 a year) and a 5% annual withdrawal from her deferred compensation savings plan covers a nice lifestyle for her that, with careful planning, includes multiple trips each year overseas. With this combination, Gayl feels no need to do extra paid work in early retirement. Gayl's annual spending budget is:
>
> | | |
> |---|---|
> | Pension income | $25,200 |
> | Income from savings | $ 7,000 ($140,000 x 5%) |
> | **Total annual income** | **$32,200** |

WHAT'S IN YOUR PORTFOLIO

Your portfolio of financial assets, also called your total savings, is defined as all your holdings of stocks, bonds, and other securities or investment holdings plus your equity in rental real estate. If you plan to move to a smaller home in the future, include the difference between your current home equity and the expected price of the new home. You might also wish to add other major liquid assets that you are prepared to sell if needed.

Include all tax-advantaged 401(k), Roth, and IRA money in your portfolio, just like any other financial assets, but don't count your home equity.

And be sure to keep children's college savings funds out of it. Assume those funds will be spent for education, not to support your retirement.

Some landlords will choose to think of their net cash flows from rental properties as income, akin to work income. In that case, they should not count the equity of these properties in their portfolios and should simply use the net income from the properties toward living expenses, tapping any portfolio of mutual funds in keeping with the Safe Withdrawal Rate for any remaining income needs.

5. Tracking Your Progress

If you are in your planning years, it might be useful for you to create a spreadsheet similar to the one below to track annual and total savings. In particular, it will help you project and track the progress as you save and earn each year, seeking to converge on your target retirement date with sufficient income. Your progress will be fueled by two separate engines: annual savings and portfolio earnings.

Specifically, your annual savings is the amount that you save from your paycheck each year. The best choice is to put these funds into tax-advantaged funds such the Roth IRA, traditional IRA, or an employer-sponsored 401(k)—up to the maximum allowable. Any remaining savings go into a traditional taxable savings account.

Once you save the money and add it to your accounts, it becomes part of your total savings, which will expand and contract based on market performance during the years ahead as your portfolio earnings—and will further grow based on the annual savings you add each year. Unless you have a sizable pension, these assets will become a major focus as you plan and work to save enough to retire early.

By projecting a reasonable rate of growth, you can see how the combination of fresh annual savings and portfolio earnings can work together to bring you to your goal. A reasonable assumption would be that the earnings in a diversified portfolio would grow by 8% a year, or 5% per year in real terms—that is, after subtracting 3% average inflation. While you have little control over how your assets perform, you do have control over your annual savings—and you should commit yourself to make them as large as reasonably possible.

Total Savings Worksheet

	2000	2001	2002	2003	2004	2005	2006 Projected	2007 Projected	2008 Projected	2009 Projected
ANNUAL SAVINGS										
Taxable Savings This Year	7,000	7,000	7,000	8,000	8,000	10,000	10,000	12,000	12,000	13,000
IRA/401(k) Contributions This Year	6,000	6,000	6,000	6,000	8,000	8,000	8,000	8,000	8,000	9,000
TOTAL SAVINGS										
Regular IRA/401(k)	35,000	48,000	55,000	79,000	98,000	120,000	134,000	148,700	164,135	181,342
Roth IRAs	48,000	46,000	39,000	47,000	52,000	54,000	56,700	59,535	62,512	65,637
Taxable Accounts A	187,000	164,000	151,000	207,000	229,000	239,000	255,950	274,748	294,485	315,709
Taxable Accounts B	124,000	112,000	104,000	147,000	161,000	168,000	181,400	196,470	212,294	229,408
Sum of Taxable and Tax-Advantaged Financial Assets	394,000	370,000	349,000	480,000	540,000	581,000	628,050	679,453	733,425	792,096
2007-2010									12/31/2009	
							TARGET RETIREMENT DATE			

Projected annual real growth 5% + savings

DON'T IGNORE INFLATION

Throughout the book, you'll see references to "real" and occasionally "nominal" prices.

Real prices mean nothing more or less than inflation-adjusted prices. Nominal means the actual price or value in dollars in a given year. As you develop your plans, your spreadsheets, or watch your progress, take the time to account accurately for inflation. Over the course of a few years, inflation won't make much difference, but since early retirement planning involves decades, it eventually makes a large difference. For instance, $100,000 in 2006, at an average inflation rate of 3% per year, will be worth just $47,760 25 years down the line. Conversely, it would take more than $250,000 today to buy something that was worth $100,000 in 1981.

To account for future inflation while making projections of portfolio earnings, subtract 3%—the long-run average inflation rate—from the amount by which you project your portfolio will grow each year. The remainder will be the rate, in real terms, at which your savings are growing toward a goal stated in today's dollars. For example, suppose you have $500,000 and would need $600,000 to retire comfortably today. You plan to add $10,000 a year in savings and expect your existing portfolio assets to grow at 8% each year, in line with historical averages.

After one year, you will have:

Initial principal	$500,000
Portfolio real earnings	
5% (8% return less 3% inflation)	$25,000
Savings	$10,000
Real value at the end of first year	**$535,000**

The following year:

Initial principal	$535,000
Portfolio real earnings (5% of $535,000)	$26,750
Savings (in today's dollars)	$10,000
Real value at the end of second year	**$571,750**

Finally, in the third year:

Initial principal	$571,750
Portfolio real earnings(5% of $571,750)	$28,587
Savings (in today's dollars)	$10,000
Real value at the end of third year	**$610,337**

According to this plan, you can early semi-retire in roughly three years. To understand how you would have been led astray if you had worked with nominal dollars—by assuming, for instance, the full 8% annual portfolio earnings—do the math and you will see that you would have mistakenly concluded that you could early retire on target after just two years, as the nominal value of your portfolio would exceed $600,000 at that point. It takes an additional year to get the real value over $600,000, your target.

RESOURCES

 FOR MORE HELP ON COMPUTING INFLATION. It doesn't take a rocket scientist to adjust for inflation, but in this case the good folks at NASA have provided a useful calculator at www1.jsc.nasa.gov/bu2/inflateCPI.html.

The Bureau of Labor Statistics provides a useful calculator for converting dollars in any year into the equivalent dollars of any other year at http://146.142.4.24/cgi-bin/cpicalc.pl.

Historical inflation rates are available in a table from the Minneapolis Fed at http://minneapolisfed.org/Research/data/us/calc/hist1913.cfm.

6. Doing the Math

Now that you know how to produce the necessary information to project your spending and means, you are ready to take a more complete look at your full income and spending picture during the first year of early retirement.

a. Savings, Income, and Expenses Worksheet

The following Savings, Income, and Expenses Worksheet ties together all the financial information an early retiree or aspiring early retiree needs to confirm that income will cover expenses once the steady paychecks stop. It is the central spreadsheet that all early retirees should create, in some form, during their planning. You can use the form below as a model and feel free to add your own embellishments.

Briefly, the worksheet consists of two sections: Section 1 gives a complete look at savings; Section 2 summarizes income and expenses. By adding up all your savings and applying a Safe Withdrawal Rate (discussed in detail in Chapter 4, Section A), you'll find the income your savings will produce annually over the long run. Use that in the income and expenses section combined with other income sources to see if your total income will cover your projected expenses.

Here are some details to keep in mind when proceeding through the worksheet.

SAVINGS. Begin by focusing on the amount of your total savings at the start of early retirement. You might want to use the estimate from a spreadsheet you generate along the lines of the Total Savings Worksheet (from Section D5). Or you may have your own projection for the value of your savings, in today's dollars, on the day you plan to begin early retirement. This is the amount of **total savings**—in the sample worksheet below, $792,000.

Next, make sure that number is clean—for example, that you have not inadvertently included your children's college savings and that you have adjusted for any personal debt that needs to be paid off and for major expenses just around the corner. Make these adjustments and you will have the **net value of savings.**

After that, you can add any adjustments you feel are warranted—for example, the value of the equity in your home that you could realize if you sold it and moved or personal property you would be prepared to sell for cash if needed. Remember that these are hypothetical additions to your portfolio—useful for planning purposes, but not the same as real cash until you actually make the changes. That gives you the **total adjusted value of savings.**

SAFE ANNUAL WITHDRAWAL AMOUNT. You can next calculate a safe annual withdrawal amount—the income you can safely take from your portfolio each year which you will use for living expenses. Withdrawals of between 4% and 5%, as discussed in Chapter 4, are generally considered the maximum safe levels over the long run. The example below uses 4.3%. The **safe annual withdrawal amount** in this case is 4.3% of the total adjusted value of savings of $842,000, or $36,206.

The second portion of the worksheet, Income and Spending, helps you align income and spending to make sure you will have enough money to spend each year—and confirm that you will in fact be able to Live Below Your Means.

INCOME. First, re-enter the safe annual withdrawal amount calculated earlier: in this case $36,206. Next add any projected income from pensions and part-time work, along with other expected income or gifts of money.

EXPENSES. Section C of this chapter explains how to come up with your projected expenses in early retirement. Fill that total in on the worksheet next. As with all the figures here, the expenses should be calculated using today's dollars.

b. Conclusions from the worksheet

The result of subtracting total annual expenses from total annual income gives the **net shortfall or surplus**—the important number that signals whether you can indeed make ends meet. Note that it is not essential that the budget balances to the penny so much as that you can confirm you are quite close to living within your Safe Annual Withdrawal Amount and various income sources.

In this example, the numbers demonstrate that spending will be just under available income—a clear indication that this early retiree will be able to comfortably live on the annual Safe Withdrawal Amount and part-time income as planned.

Savings, Income, and Expenses Worksheet

1. TOTAL SAVINGS	792,000
DEDUCT outstanding personal (nonmortgage) debt	0
DEDUCT children's college saving accounts	0
DEDUCT additional parent contributions to children's college savings	0
DEDUCT known or planned major capital expenditures	0
NET VALUE OF SAVINGS	792,000
ADD Value of personal property you would sell for cash	50,000
ADD Net Value of other planned downsizing steps (for example, smaller home)	0
TOTAL ADJUSTED VALUE of SAVINGS	842,000
Safe annual withdrawal amount of 4.3%	36,206

2. INCOME AND EXPENSES		
INCOME	MONTHLY	ANNUAL
Safe withdrawal amount (from above)	3,017	36,206
ADD pension Income		0
ADD expected work income		5,000
ADD other expected income or gifts		0
TOTAL ANNUAL INCOME		**41,206**

EXPENSES	MONTHLY	ANNUAL
Average recurring monthly spending	1,740	20,880
Annual expenses less income taxes		11,662
State, federal, and self-employment income taxes (3% of income)		1,086
Fund management fees (0.5% of financial assets)		3,960
Amortization expenses: car, house repainting		3,500
TOTAL ANNUAL EXPENSES		**41,088**
NET SHORTFALL OR SURPLUS		**$118**

IS SOCIAL SECURITY INSECURE?

There are regular bouts of sturm und drang over the precariousness of Social Security and the need to radically reshape it to preserve retirement funds for the future.

The likely reality is that those who have so much income they don't need their Social Security checks may find their benefits trimmed. Those who need it because of poor future market performance or low savings can expect to find a safety net.

Early retirees, however, have a special concern with Social Security's future. Among the many proposals aired in 2005, one that seemed to gain bipartisan support involved indexing benefits to inflation as opposed to the average growth in wages. Early retirees who stop working in their 40s, for instance, would lose ground under this system, ending up with benefits which might not have kept up with overall living standards. It would be a mistake, however, to conclude that the only way to ensure a safe retirement is to keep working full time, contributing at the maximum levels to Social Security to receive its maximum benefit. Those who have worked just 20 years, say until their mid-40s, and contributed at near the top rates during that period end up with nearly 85% of the benefits of those who work the additional 15 years to get Social Security's maximum benefit and then wait until age 67 to start collecting it. The difference amounts to only about $300 per month, or $3,600 per year.

If that difference weighs on you, then for a reasonable sum—in the range of a $30,000 one-time payment—you can purchase an annuity that should make up the gap in benefit levels. Overall, that seems a small price to pay for being able to leave full-time work 15 or 20 years early.

E. Planning for Changes

After confirming that income and expenses can stay in balance during the first year of early retirement, take the next step and try to look out several years to see if anything material might change.

Predictable ebbs and flows of life will have an impact on your finances. For example, leaving full-time work and beginning early retirement brings one set of changes, such as reducing work-related expenses and possibly embarking on a more frugal lifestyle. Another may come as children leave home and your food and other bills drop. You may decide to move to another house at some point, pension or Social Security payments will eventually begin, and you may eventually need long-term care. While you won't know today the exact financial impact of most of these changes, you should begin making assumptions, predicting the various impacts, the ups and downs of your unfolding financial future. Simply accounting for these changes, even with roughly estimated numbers, puts you well ahead in your long-run budgeting: As the actual events draw near, you'll have better numbers to plug in. But you'll never be completely blindsided by unexpected new costs. For example, if you keep an estimate of nursing care expenses in your long-term budget—starting at around age 85 and lasting for ten years—you will never be financially surprised if these expenses are needed down the line, even though the actual cost of nursing care may be higher or lower than you anticipated.

To build a solid model of your long-run finances, you'll need to move past the simple spreadsheets and single-year approach presented up to this point with the help of modeling software, some of which is free of charge, as described below.

There are two major advantages to this next level of analysis. First, you will be using actual historical financial returns to test your spending projections, giving you the probability of achieving sufficient market returns to support the withdrawals you need over the years.

Second, the calculator will give you the ability to change assets or annual income and spending at distinct points in the future. This lets you model the impact, for instance, of receiving an inheritance or buying a second home, as well as make alterations in your income or spending from, for example, pensions, Social Security, or children leaving home.

RESOURCES

 FOR HELP WITH CALCULATIONS. Look to FIRECalc at www .fireseeker.com. FIRE stands for Financial Independence, Retire Early. FIRECalc, developed by Bill Sholar, is free, but you are asked to make a voluntary contribution if you find the tool useful.

An active community of users supports and responds to questions about the tool at www.early-retirement.org.

CALCULATING WITH FIRECALC

In addition to FIRECalc, there are several calculators that will map changes in spending and asset levels in the future, but they test portfolio survival against simplistic and dangerous assumptions of steady annual market returns, producing overly rosy results. Other online calculators test a current portfolio for long run survivability, but leave no room for changes in assets or spending in the future, or else use overly pessimistic simulations which fail to incorporate markets' tendencies to return to their long-run average returns. FIRECalc alone performs the two functions early retirees need most: assessing portfolio survival against actual historical returns and allowing for changes in assets, income, and spending levels at key points in the future.

The FIRECalc input and result screens are detailed and self-explanatory, and if you have gone through the steps in this section, you should have most of the information you might need. However, FIRECalc asks for a few responses that might require further definition so that you can best to prepare to use the site.

LIFESPAN OF PORTFOLIO. None of us know the hour of our final curtain call, but unless you have particularly bad genes, it may be worth assuming you will live to be 90 or 100 for purposes of these projections. For a statistical estimate of your lifespan, compare your genetic and lifestyle factors against a longevity database at: www.agingresearch.org/calculator /quiz.cfm.

SOCIAL SECURITY. The Social Security Administration sends an annual mailing outlining your expected benefits. You can also get a close approximation anytime by entering a few pieces of data into the calculator at www.ssa.gov.

SETTINGS AND DEFAULTS. These are specific questions about your portfolio and withdrawal, discussed below.

PERCENT OF PORTFOLIO IN STOCKS. Type in 50 for a portfolio that is 50% stocks.

WHERE IS THE REST INVESTED. Finish by choosing 5-Year Treasury bonds to provide the closest, albeit imperfect estimate of the Rational Investing Portfolio. If you have a different mix of investments in your own savings, then use that instead.

WHAT ARE THE TOTAL ANNUAL INVESTMENT EXPENSES. Use the actual average expense ratio of your investments if you know it. You can find data on each of your fund's fees and expenses in its prospectus or by entering the ticker symbol at www.morningstar.com. The Rational Investing Portfolio has average annual fees and expenses of about .4%, though internal fund trading costs and brokerage expenses might push that closer to .6%

WHAT ESTIMATE OF INFLATION WOULD YOU LIKE TO USE? The Producer Price Index or PPI generates a slightly lower percentage of success than the CPI. This may be a result of the CPI's being systematically ratcheted down via "hedonic" adjustments designed to reflect improvements in product quality and features over time. Use the PPI if you would like to be more conservative or if you don't trust the CPI figures.

There are a number of other important areas to consider when attempting to sketch in some of the principal unknowns in your long-term budgeting process.

1. Health Care Costs

Plan to keep some form of health insurance to cover at least the catastrophic needs you and any of your dependents might have during your early retirement.

Most early retirees, no longer covered by their former employers' health plans, opt for a high deductible insurance linked to a Healthcare Savings Account (HSA), a sort of medical IRA. Many of these policies are available in the range of $300 to $450 per month for a couple, which is well below $800 for a traditional policy. The catch is that you pay actual health care costs each year up to the limit of the deductible; the insurance picks up for the rest of the year.

While the premiums for your insurance cannot be paid from the pretax dollars in your HSA, the annual deductible can. In 2005, contribution limits to the HSA were set at $2,650 for singles and $5,250 for families; those 55 and older could put in an extra $600 a year—with unused funds staying in and rolling over for use in a future year. Your annual insurance deductible will generally also be set at about these same rates; rules vary by state.

RESOURCES

FOR MORE ON HEALTH CARE COSTS. You can find information on setting up high deductible health plan and Health Savings Accounts at the U.S. Treasury's site at www.treas.gov.

There is also a well-organized commercial site for employers and individuals to research HSA offerings at: www.hsainsider.com.

HELP IS ON THE WAY

More help may be on the way with innovative new health insurance products designed to bring in part-time, self-employed, and others who make up the more attractive subsets of the 45 million uninsured people in the U.S.

In 2005, Anthem, now part of WellPoint, launched a popular new Blue Access Economy Plan in a handful of midwestern states that includes three annual doctor visits, a generic drug plan, and a relatively low $1,000 deductible—all for less than $65 per month for an Ohio male. Other firms, such as UnitedHealth Group and Aetna, have begun targeting the uninsured, attracted by the large market of middle aged, middle class, relatively healthful people without corporate health insurance, which should generate more sensible and affordable solutions to the health insurance conundrum for early retirees.

A current federal push to make health insurance products available in all states simultaneously, instead of state by state, will also increase choices for early retirees.

Once you reach regular retirement age, if you continue to live in the United States, you will likely be eligible for Medicare. This will save you much of the cost of health insurance and can provide an overall drop in health care expenses during the 25-year period from age 65 to 90, though you may still find you need supplemental Medigap coverage. After that, you might want to budget for the possibility of nursing and long-term care, which currently can be expensive, and much of it is not covered by Medicare.

2. Long-Term Care

A number of early retirees, typically those who have enough money to pay the premiums but not enough to self-insure, have chosen to purchase long-term care insurance to help foot the cost of this care. Be aware, however, that this coverage is expensive, and like long-term disability insurance, has had more than its share of possible pitfalls for consumers.

Although premiums may be locked in for a number of years, when they do unlock, their costs can jump dramatically, as they did industrywide in 2005 with 40% increases. One way around this is to prepay the insurance for life. For example, Bob Smith and his wife prepaid their long-term care policies in 2004 with a single $35,000 premium, though that premium would also be higher today. Again, this may be risky if the insurer is on shaky financial footing or later becomes that way.

The high costs and uncertainty about benefits has led many other early retirees to buy a gym membership and start eating healthy foods instead—convinced that dedicated efforts to stay fit are the only real solutions to the long-term health care issue.

RESOURCES

A number of websites offer consumers information on evaluating long-term care insurance.

Among them are:

- "Do You Need Long Term Care Insurance?" *Consumer Reports*, November 2003, at www.consumerreports.org, located behind the Personal Finance tab, and

- "Avoiding Fraud When Buying Long-Term Care Policies," available at http://consumerlawpage.com/article/insure.shtml.

3. Taxes on IRA Withdrawals

Most early retirees will have stashed at least some of their savings in a tax-advantaged account: a 401(k), IRA, SEP-IRA, Roth IRA, or Retirement Savings Account (RSA).

These fall into roughly two groups:

- the Roth type, in which funds can be withdrawn without paying taxes, and

- regular IRAs, in which income taxes are due on all money withdrawn.

For both types, withdrawals are subject to certain rules. Minimum distributions start at age 70½ for regular IRAs. Roth IRAs, however, do not mandate minimum withdrawals—although taxes must be paid on funds when they are put in, basically depositing after-tax dollars.

Despite the common nostrum to avoid paying taxes as long as possible, many savvy early retirees prefer to keep their funds in Roths, converting regular IRA funds to Roths on advantageous terms whenever possible and paying the taxes due with other taxable funds. The reason: Over decades, IRA balances can grow quite large and taxes due on them can become staggering. What is more, regular IRA holders must plan to liquidate their IRAs over their lifetimes, ensuring that their income taxes are paid. A Roth holder can keep an IRA intact and even pass it along to beneficiaries, who will need to liquidate the Roth IRA over their own lifetimes—again, without paying income tax on withdrawals. This may be one case where "taking your medicine early" holds a big reward over the long haul.

This issue matters here since, if you still hold a regular IRA, you will have to withdraw its funds—starting no later than age 70½—and will pay regular income taxes on those withdrawals. As a result, your taxes are likely to increase from the low levels you've been paying as an early semi-retiree and your required minimum distribution (RMD) may be extra income you'd rather have left alone, untaxed and compounding. (See Chapter 5, Section B5 for a step-by-step tax-wise conversion strategy for converting regular IRA funds into a Roth IRA.)

EXAMPLE: Fiona contributed $100,000 into a traditional IRA over the course of her working years, which grew to $200,000 by the time she was 45 years old. A 7% average annual return, that IRA can be expected to grow to some $1,080,000 by the time Fiona must begin required minimum distributions at age 70½. Under current regulations, she will need to withdraw about $40,000 when she is 71, growing to $150,000 in her late 90s when the required minimum distribution begins to taper.

Added to the dividends, capital gains distributions, and interest, the rest of her portfolio is earning at that point, along with her Social Security and any other pension income, the extra RMD will almost surely be entirely taxable—at a rate perhaps as much as 30% or more with state and local taxes, and even higher as the withdrawals mount. Thus, Fiona can count on taxes increasing at age 71 by as much as $12,000 per year, and later, by as much as $50,000 per year, albeit in inflated dollars.

DON'T TOUCH YOUR IRAS AND 401(K)

Unless the tax code changes dramatically, assume annual spending should always be paid out of taxable accounts if possible. (See Chapter 4 for details on which assets to spend in which order.) The goal is to let tax-advantaged money compound as long as possible, preferably in a Roth IRA. But any tax-advantaged savings plan is better than none. If you must take your IRA or 401(k) money out before you reach age 59½, there are rules that permit this without penalty, though you will be taxed on the withdrawals as always.

For a complete discussion, see "Getting Your Retirement Money Early —Without Penalty," by Twila Slesnick, at www.nolo.com, under the topic Retirement Plans.

RESOURCES

FOR MORE ON RMDS. You can find a good calculator for required minimum distributions online at www.hughchou.org/calc/mdib.cgi.

4. Inheritances

While it may seem presumptuous or uncomfortable for you to consider it, many of today's early retirees are likely to receive some sort of inheritance from their parents around the time they hit traditional retirement age. If your family is a close one and your parents are sufficiently affluent and insured so that there will almost surely be a sum to pass along, it makes sense to include the likelihood of an inheritance in your long-run financial planning.

However, relying on circumstances outside your control and the estate planning wishes of your parents comes with risks: The funds might skip a generation and go directly to your children. They may end up being shared with charities or a late-life spouse and family. Or they may simply be used to pay for your parents' own long-term care.

ADDITIONAL READING

FOR MORE ON INHERITANCES. For a discussion of these issues and advice on how to discuss these matters with your parents, see *Get a Life: You Don't Need a Million to Retire Well*, by Ralph Warner (Nolo).

A NEW LOOK AT RISING STANDARDS OF LIVING

Another point for those just now switching gears into early retirement to remember is that human nature seems wired up to expect a gradually increasing standard of living over the years. Real incomes have, for decades, risen about 1% a year and our personal and societal expectations about lifestyle seem to have built-in escalators, too—at least until we become too old and frail to get out and about.

For instance, eating at restaurants was a rare treat for most people in the 1950s, but commonplace today. Vacations today are more likely to involve flying and exotic locales—and hotels have improved from basic to clean and modern to boutique and luxurious.

Planning to keep the real value of your portfolio and the income you withdraw from it merely stable over the long run may mean you slip gradually behind peers and your own rising expectations. That may be just fine for an independent-minded early retiree who is prepared to either take chances on favorable market outcomes or else unhook from upscale consumption.

Then again, that may be a future that makes you queasy. In that case, if you are able to keep Living Below Your Means, you might want to spend less than your Safe Withdrawal Rate, say 3.0% to 3.5%. (See Chapter 4 for a complete discussion.) This will leave more in your portfolio each year, harnessing the power of compounding and ensuring the portfolio value increases in real terms over time. This will then support withdrawals which will themselves grow in real terms over time, giving you a sense of keeping up with a gradually rising tide.

F. Shifting Your Thinking to Reduce Spending

If you are like most people when you first begin early retirement, you will follow one of two paths: Either you'll make a dramatic downshift, moving to a new location and adopting a new frugal lifestyle. Or you'll stay put, making only minor changes in your living circumstances.

If you stay put and make few changes, it is generally not safe to assume your core spending will drop dramatically just because you have stopped working. In fact, some new early retirees find their spending actually increases as they have more time to travel, pursue hobbies, or possibly take some long-delayed classes. You might even kick off early semi-retirement with a large purchase—a boat or second home—now that you have the time to enjoy such things. And you'll probably need to start paying for health insurance that an employer used to cover.

To make it all work, you are back to Living Below Your Means, the touch-stone of all those seeking financial independence. To compensate for the few areas in which your expenses may climb as you start early retirement, you'll need to use some of your new free time applying your best frugality skills to find places to cut expenses, too. The following sections give you tips and strategies for identifying and then reining in your spending.

Many of these techniques will be equally effective for those in their planning and saving years and those who have already retired. Saving money, however, takes on a whole new importance for early retirees, who do Ben Franklin one better. For them, a penny saved is more than just a penny earned: It can mean the difference between retiring early successfully and having to go back to full-time work.

1. Cutting Back on Small Expenses

Day to day, you'll have plenty of chances to cut minor expenses once you start early retirement. The biggest among these is likely to be your actual direct work-related expenses—money spent on commuting, parking, business clothes, restaurant lunches, dry cleaners, and importantly, those stress-busting treats you rewarded yourself with after a frazzled day in the trenches. These can really add up, easily amounting to hundreds of dollars or more per month.

Other savings come about more slowly and subtly. You eat in restaurants, but after padding around comfortably at home in fleece and slippers all day, you don't have the same desire to go out to the chic restaurant with the $15 shots of single malt whisky and $28 main courses. You go out to a great pizza place instead, feeling even more comfortable, and the whole meal costs you the price of two drinks at the upscale restaurant. You might even pour yourself a wee drop of the same single malt when you get back home, costing you all of a dollar or so. And the view from your garden is likely far superior to the restaurant's, anyway.

Here are other areas in which to look for small savings that can add up.

- Pore through your bills and credit card statements for recurring monthly or annual charges that you no longer need—including old dial-up accounts, Internet accounts, and news subscriptions.
- Consolidate phone services to drop a fax line, mobile, or dial-up line that can be combined into a better package.
- Challenge billing errors that you never had time to deal with before.
- Return items you don't need, but previously wouldn't have bothered to return.
- Join a buy-in-bulk warehouse store or buying club.
- Research purchases online to shop for specials and best prices, using the information to negotiate with a local or preferred vendor.
- Submit and track rebates, and remember to cash the checks within the allotted time.
- Find thrift shops in upscale neighborhoods—often in church basements. The diligent can find top quality, lightly used items at unbeatable prices.
- Research and re-evaluate insurance or other major contracts to be sure they still make sense.

TIGHTWAD SHORTCUTS

I am by no means an expert at tightwaddery, but I do try to follow two simple rules to keep spending in check.

First, I have developed an attitude best described as "Proud to Be Frugal." I've broken through the feelings of shame or fear and am now comfortable pushing back on overpriced products and services that I view as a sort of ambient threat to my efforts to achieve and maintain financial independence.

Second, I follow a rough equivalency test that $100 spent on one part of the family budget should bring about the same value or benefit as $100 spent on something else in the budget. Where the money spent does not deliver equivalent value, I try to see whether we can live without that item or find some way to reduce its place in our spending. Not always possible, of course, but it can reinforce changes over time. For us, for instance, it has meant that we keep our cars longer, eat at less expensive restaurants, shop for travel much more carefully, donate primarily to local charities in which we are actively involved, turn down the thermostat more conscientiously, and often use the library for books and DVDs. If things ever got really tight financially, we would move to a smaller house.

Other early retirees have suggested their favorite methods to keep spending in check. For small expenses, Nords follows the "$10 Rule"—paying attention to any expense over $10 and asking himself if he really needs it. Anything under $10 that he feels he needs, he just gets, figuring that his overall budget won't be much affected by these smaller expenses. Nords feels the psychological wear and tear of watching every penny for the rest of his life would simply be too much—and that early retirement could become just plain dour if he had to feel like an impoverished grad student every time he walked into a grocery or hardware store.

Another couple that has retired early has developed a "Sell Me Rule." One of them must "sell" the other on any proposed expenditure greater than $100—a useful safeguard from racking up too many budget-busting items.

RESOURCES

FOR MORE ON LIVING FRUGALLY. Frugal living has launched its own mini-genre of magazines, books, and online support groups. A few you might want to look into or borrow from the library include:

- *Budget Living* and *Organic Style* magazines—surprisingly large circulation and mainstream appeal for simpler, natural lifestyles with less hype and consumerism.

- *The Complete Tightwad Gazette*, by Amy Dacyczyn. Dacyczyn was the editor of *The Tightwad Gazette*, a newsletter that ran for about seven years and catalogued, in a delightful and authentic style, every way devised to save money. Publishing stopped when they felt they had found and published every tip and compiled them all in this book, so you know it's complete. *The Tightwad Gazette* did more than anything else to bring the frugal lifestyle into the limelight and give it a credible spot not too far from the mainstream.

- Pat Veretto has a collection of links to frugal living resources at www.folksonline.com/folks/hh/tours/frugal.htm. She also hosts the frugal living section at About.com, http://frugalliving.about.com.

2. Cutting Back on Large Expenses

While looking at the smaller scrimps and saves you can make, pay attention to the big expense categories in your life: the Money Pits. Many believe this is where the real battle to save is won or lost. Manage these potentially budget-bruising pits carefully or they will quickly soak up vast amounts of your earnings. That doesn't mean you must do without these more expensive items and services. Just shop and plan for them more carefully and look for creative alternatives.

a. Cars

The car basically moves you around—unless you live in L.A. where your car doubles as your home, and then you're just going to have to pay up to have a really cool car. If you buy a new car every few years, especially an upscale one, then you're pouring away a solid flow of depreciation every year.

Cars are much better quality today than ever before—safer, more dependable, and longer lasting. Buying something tasteful and functional, and keeping it ten years or more, delivers huge savings. For example, the annual depreciation on a new $30,000 2006 VW Passat kept ten years and sold for $5k will be just $2,500 per year. A new $60,000 Mercedes traded up two additional times over the same period and sold each time for ⅔ of the original price—generous assumptions according to local market prices—will fritter away at least three times that amount in annual depreciation or lease expenses, to say nothing of the higher amount of capital it ties up all along.

Buying a car that is two or three years old is even smarter. Many early-retirees find the quality of a manufacturer-certified used car is essentially equivalent to a new one, at a significant discount in price.

A thriving online exchange in used cars from websites such as eBay, Craig's List, and CarsDirect can provide great values, though you should have a good mechanic check out any car you plan to buy through these channels.

Consider having just one car for a couple, or if you are really serious and live in a suitable environment for it, consider not owning a car at all. Iconic early retirees, Vicki and Paul Terhorst, sold house, car, and the lot and travel the world via public transportation, renting apartments in major cities or staying with friends and family. If you live in a city with reasonable public transportation, this can even be the norm. Some cities have fleets of cars for dues-paying members to borrow on short notice. And cabs and the occasional rental for out of town trips can still be more economical than owning, maintaining, and insuring your own car.

LEASING V. BUYING

Leasing a car is never a good idea for anyone serious about saving. Since you plan to keep your car for the longer haul, it is wise to own it, as the annual cost of owning drops each year you keep the car—at least until maintenance costs overwhelm any savings. Your monthly lease payments give you nothing but the right to use the car for that month and the right to buy the car at the end of the lease, but no ownership rights.

A look at the math makes the concept clear.

LEASING A CAR WORTH $30,000

Lease terms: No money down, 3-year term, 5% interest rate, lease payment of $500 per month

Payments after 3 years: 36 x $500 per month: $18,000

Option to purchase car at end of lease for $16,000

Assume you lease a new car again on the same terms

Assumed lease payments after 10 years: 120 months @ $500 = $60,000 or $6,000 per year

PURCHASING A CAR WORTH $30,000

Ownership terms: Pay cash, keep car 10 years

Payments after 10 years: $30,000 (initial purchase price) less $5,000 (resale value of car after 10 years: $5,000)

Net cost of owning: $30,000 – $5,000 = $25,000 or $2,500 per year

TIP

REMEMBER TO BUDGET FOR YOUR CAR. Because you purchase a car only once in several years, but "use up" a bit of the car's value each year, you'll need to add something into each year's spending to reflect your true annual cost of owning it. If, for example, the car depreciates $25,000 over ten years, then assume you use up $2,500 worth of the car's value each year if you keep it for a decade. Add that $2,500 to your annual budget during early retirement, and if you like the added security of knowing exactly where you stand, fund a separate savings account with that money, which you can then use to purchase your new car when the time comes. Pay car maintenance from your regular monthly budget, and dump the car early if it starts to need a flurry of repairs.

b. Vacations

If you are like many early retirees, vacations will become a key perk of your lifestyle now that you have more free time to plan and enjoy them. But vacations can be another spending hole if you aren't careful. In fact, they may be one place you will be looking to cut back if your portfolio has suffered a few bad years and you find you need to trim spending.

Don't despair. You can come to enjoy camping in the state park instead of staying in a villa in Provence—and the kids are likely to have even more fun. But in good times or bad, careful vacation shopping, creativity, and good planning can save you a lot of money.

For instance, consider a working vacation. An active informal network can help you find low-key resort management openings where you can tend bar for three or six months in paradise while receiving free room and board with plenty of time off to explore and meet the locals.

Or if you prefer more freedom, try house sitting. Typically you'll have the run of the property and use of cars in exchange for taking care of plants and possibly pets.

Maybe you have family and old friends who would welcome you, giving you a chance to renew relationships that have fallen off.

Or try house swapping. You can try listing your house yourself; the Internet is a real boon to doing this. Or you can pay a small fee to an exchange listing service that can connect you with digs in a foreign or distant location, complete with car and occasionally other amenities.

EXAMPLE: The Sederowsky family exchanged their home in Sweden with three different Californian families one recent summer, spending time in San Francisco, Modesto, and Los Angeles while three American families spent a month each in the Sederowsky's Stockholm house.

RESOURCES

 FOR MORE ON HOME EXCHANGES. There are several services that help arrange home exchanges. Colleges sometimes provide the same services for alumni, as do some major corporations. Commercial services include:

- www.homelink.org, and
- www.homexchange.com.

If none of these possibilities suit you, there are more choices besides booking a traditional hotel, which increasingly seem to be aimed at those on corporate expense accounts. European and American convents and monasteries often rent lodgings, which can be charming if a bit complex to book. Pay for them in cash and don't expect a confirmation of your booking.

RESOURCES

FOR MORE ON STAYS IN CONVENTS AND MONASTERIES. Guidebooks for staying in European convents and monasteries include:

- *Europe's Monastery and Convent Guesthouses*, by Kevin J. Wright (Liguori Publications), and
- *The Guide to Lodging in Italy's Monasteries,* by Eileen Barish (Anacapa Press).

A detailed list of convents accepting guests in Rome, a city notoriously expensive for hotel rooms, can be found at: http://santasusanna.org/comingToRome/convents.html.

If you are traveling slowly, try renting a house or apartment—usually for at least a week. The place will likely have more space, charm, freedom, and privacy at a lower cost than a hotel room. Country-specific agents in the U.S. can hook you up with European and other overseas rentals, providing you a measure of confidence in the property and terms. Or troll for properties directly on the Internet and conclude negotiations by phone or email.

RESOURCES

FOR MORE ON TRAVEL GUIDES. I used to buy travel guidebooks until I realized the libraries are full of them, and a person rarely needs the guidebook after the trip is done.

The best book for you will depend on your budget, with *Rough Guides* and *Lonely Planet* aiming at the budget end, *Let's Go, Michelin,* and *Insight* aiming at the middle, and *Fodor's, Eyewitness,* and other more specialized guides aiming higher.

Talk with friends who have made a trip to your intended locale for their recommendations and their favorite guidebooks; with luck, they'll offer to lend them to you.

Finally, bookstores specializing in travel are delightful places to while away your early retirement leisure hours, and can offer targeted guidance.

USING FREQUENT FLYER MILES

You may have a pile of accumulated Frequent Flyer Miles left over from your fast lane days, all but forgotten now, given that the standard mileage programs typically make you travel at times that aren't convenient for the normal working family. Dust off those statements. As an early retiree, you have the time to plan and go at mid-day or other off-peak times when miles are more likely to be redeemable, with the side benefit of beating the traffic and airport crowds.

And with the airlines frequently in financial trouble and looking for ways to reduce the ability to use unredeemed miles, it is worth trying to use them before the rules change again to make them less valuable.

Sometimes you're still better off just paying cash for the tickets. A rough guide is to value miles at a penny apiece and see whether the flight would be cheaper to buy outright. Longer trips usually end up a better deal under the miles programs.

c. Home improvements

Bare-bones early retirees and the generally frugal can skip this section; since you have never succumbed to this particular insanity, there won't be any major savings waiting for you here.

The housing-on-steroids arena can rapidly absorb vast amounts of money. Landscaping and decorating among some of the upwardly mobile seems to have taken on the quality of some sort of ancient ritual sacrifice or potlatch, with huge sums of money being thrown onto the pyre of décor.

Of course, you'll need to maintain your home and, since you may be spending more time there, making it a pleasant place to spend time will be worthwhile. Much can be accomplished on a far tighter budget, and be fun and satisfying, too. Watch the design shows on TV, which double as great free entertainment. Creativity and a bit of sweat are what you need.

EXAMPLE: Wendy bought wallpaper off the Internet, saving about 75% off normal prices. She had a local painter, moonlighting after hours, hang the paper professionally for a fraction of his employer's normal fee. She does some interior painting herself, especially the stippled sponge painting effects. She finds it fun and if she doesn't like the look, she doesn't mind doing it over. Wendy also finds lots of quality décor items at rock-bottom prices by frequenting church thrift shops and estate sales.

EXAMPLE: Ted has teamed up with his local environmental society to get three hardwood trees planted on the street side of his property at no cost. In exchange, he has helped out on three separate days planting trees with the society on public and private land. He enjoyed the social aspects of meeting new neighbors with similar interests, and now loves watching not only his own trees growing up, but also the ones he helped plant around town.

DON'T EVEN TRY TO KEEP UP WITH THE JONESES

One way to curb grand or unnecessary purchases is to think of expenses in terms of the portfolio needed to support them. It takes an additional $50,000 in the portfolio to support new spending of $2,000 a year. At that rate, keeping up with the neighbors will be expensive.

Reframing consumer goods into "reverse status symbols," if only in your own mind, can help. For example, my old car says, probably only to me, that I am detached enough not to be sucked in by the flashy ads or the need to impress.

Find your own motivations and balance, but realize that as you move into early retirement, your neighbors, even if they are saving, will probably be able to outspend you.

Learn to be happy for them.

They might even invite you over to share in the largesse.

d. Spendthrift tendencies

If you've ever been shopping with a shopaholic, you might notice that it's kind of fun. Shopoholics seem to be able to head straight to the racks of the most expensive items, guided by some inner navigation system, and produce a trail of credit card receipts while you are still debating whether you really need another new shirt after all.

If you or your spouse or partner has a shopaholic gene and you wish to retire early, you'll need to work together to understand and manage the habit. In fact, if one of you has this affliction, you may simply need to keep working. The annual budgets of families with a shopaholic member are jaw-dropping; the money seems to fly out to support the pleasure of spending, rather than for things that are actually needed.

Start working on the problem with simple knowledge. Ask the shopaholic to accumulate and add up all the receipts at the end of each week or month, then categorize the purchases as necessities or discretionary items. That may help illustrate how a few moments of weakness at the cash register or on a retail website add up to big dollars at the end of the month.

Some psychologists talk about shopaholics needing to fill a void inside themselves. Once you are retired, the pace should help you get regrounded and better able to fill your days with more meaning and balance, so if you have a passion to spend it will wither away. If the shopaholic is your spouse or partner, perhaps spending more time with him or her can address an underlying need to feel loved and needed.

e. Property taxes

Property taxes seem to be high or at least rising quickly all over the country. If you live in an affluent area with a good school system, or your local government has buckled to municipal unions, property tax rates may be over the moon. Still, moving to a low-tax area may not offer all the answers if you end up in a soul-less neighborhood without much public infrastructure or sense of community. If you want to stay put, work with your local government representatives to make sure they know you are concerned about runaway taxes. A few letters and voices speaking up in town council meetings can do wonders to galvanize budgetcutters to shake their fists and at least rein in the excesses a bit. You may also be able to successfully file to reduce your assessment.

Otherwise, it may be possible to move to a town nearby with a bigger corporate tax base or with less-than-stellar schools if you have no kids or they're grown. You would still be able to keep your community involvements. You'd just need to travel a few minutes longer to join in.

Also, moving to a smaller home within your community—even more practical if you have grown children—can deliver a triple benefit: lower taxes, reduced maintenance and upkeep, and freed-up home equity to boost earnings from your expanded portfolio. Use your local knowledge to snatch a prize smaller property at a good price, perhaps even before it gets to market, giving you the chance to share the seller's savings from not paying a realtor. (See Sections H and I1 for information on moving to another state or country, which can also help beat high home costs.)

RESOURCES

FOR MORE ON LIVING IN A SMALLER SPACE. A growing trend toward high quality, but not-so-big homes suggests that the McMansion ideal may be fading—and there are resources aimed at the new cottage dwellers.

Susan Susanka has a number of books and resources under the theme of The Not So Big House online at www.notsobighouse .com. These homes are intimate, beautiful, and functional without being big. They aren't always cheaper, though, as quality design and materials can add up.

Cottage Living magazine, a visual feast every month, is filled with great design in small packages, convincingly demonstrating that, when it comes to houses at least, less can be more. For information online, go to www.cottageliving.com/cottage.

One way to step into the downsizing waters or simply meet a yearning to try living elsewhere is to rent out your home for a few years while you try life in a cheaper location or a smaller home. It can not only make you a bit of income, but can also give you a chance to try out another lifestyle without permanently committing.

EXAMPLE: When the kids are grown, my wife Wonda and I may decide to rent out our house and spend a few years in Italy, living simply, learning Italian, and exploring the countryside. I will study sculpture while Wonda studies cooking under a celebrated chef. There is wine involved in there somewhere, too.

TIP

BUDGETING FOR HOME MAINTENANCE COSTS. Remember to budget some annual expense for necessary major upkeep costs of your home. If you know you need to paint the house every seven years and it costs $7,000 each time, then figure you are incurring $1,000 of expense each year even in those years you aren't painting. This is known as amortization—allowing you to see a steady annual expense as opposed to large lumps in those years you actually do the painting. Add the annual amortization cost, in this case, $1,000, to your annual budget.

To be even more clear on where they stand, some early retirees like to fund a separate account each year with these amortization expenses, withdrawing from it to pay for major purchases or repairs. Since other repairs and expenses come up unpredictably whenever something breaks or wears out, it is probably best to just pay for those as they come along out of your normal monthly or annual spending.

3. Expenses Requiring Special Consideration

Early retirees need to focus on two areas of expenses that may be easily overlooked or estimated incorrectly. There is good news for early retirees when it comes to taxes. (See Chapter 5 for a detailed discussion.) Investment fees, on the other hand, easy to ignore, carry some challenges for those who have substantial savings.

a. State and federal income taxes

Compared to the amounts levied during your working life, state and federal income taxes in early retirement will be almost guaranteed to be lower. Small as they are, you should include these taxes in your annual budget.

An early semi-retiree earning up to 20% of annual spending through self-employment and realizing the remainder through interest, dividends, and capital gains should be able to keep taxes down to 3% to 5% of annual spending or less—perhaps .2% of portfolio value—due to the structure of the tax code. In effect, you will be taxed like the working poor, whom the tax code is designed to help.

b. Investment fees and expenses

Your investments should be built around tax-efficient and fee-efficient funds. Fees from even these low-fee funds add up and need to be in your budget to give an accurate picture of your spending each year. Assume that expenses will be about .5% of assets each year. While this will be a bit high if you are invested in just a few low-cost index funds, it should be accurate if you allocate assets broadly. (See Chapter 3, Section E2 for more detail on this.)

In all cases, your actual fees will be higher than those listed in fund prospectuses and published materials, since all funds incur trading expenses and commissions while buying and selling securities that are never clearly reported. The .5% figure for your budget attempts to capture those trading expenses and give you a clear and accurate picture of your costs. As a reference point, John Bogle, the founder of The Vanguard Group, a low-fee mutual fund firm owned by its shareholders, estimates that the fund management industry as a whole absorbs about 3% of asset values each year in investment management fees and commission. You will be far ahead of that average, keeping more of your money at work and growing in value for you every year.

G. Children and Early Retirement

Many parents believe that the mere existence of children makes early retirement impossible. Parenthood becomes an ironclad excuse to put off early retirement while waiting for the kids to grow up. The only problem is, growing up can take a long time and your kids need you now. Continuing to work long hours and telling yourself you are doing it for the children becomes a seductive trap.

With a little extra effort and a little more frugality, you can be an early-retired parent—and also be more available to your children during their brief childhoods. The step most parents seem unwilling to take is to calculate a relatively complete and accurate figure for the costs of raising and educating children. (See Section G1 for tips on how to do this.) Set that amount aside or otherwise provide for it; that way, you'll have no need to keep working full-time solely to address a vague dread about the high cost of providing for your children.

Then move forward with early retirement as normal—if possible, while the children are still relatively young. It may take a bit more money to retire early with children, but the parents who have done it regret only that they didn't start sooner. Here are a few of the tips and techniques early-retired parents have found to work.

1. Education Expenses

As mentioned, paying for children's education is the biggest hurdle for most parents' financial planning and it can be a tough one. Mercifully, schooling costs are finite. They may seem large, but they don't last forever. Put a dollar number, even a firm upper limit, on school expenses and then plan around it. You may be relieved to find out that the number is manageable.

For K through 12 schooling, a dilemma may arise if you feel that the public schools in your area are inadequate and you must consider private schools. Large as the tuition fees may be, they too are finite—and scholarship money may be available for early retirees with low annual incomes. However, you may also want to consider moving to an area with better public schools, if only until your children are grown. While real estate values in those areas will doubtless feel expensive, you can often find reasonably priced quarters in apartments, townhouses, or smaller homes within the school district. Since you only need to be there a limited number of years, you may be able to justify living in less-than-optimal conditions, then moving on to your dream house later.

When your children are ready for college—and not every child opts to go to college—bear in mind that many state universities offer solid value for undergraduate educations, and between kids' own summer and part-time jobs, scholarships, grants, loans, and tuition discounts, a four-year education for your kids need not be a portfolio-killer. An average state university in 2005 cost about $11,400 a year in combined tuition, supplies, and room and board for in-state undergraduates living on campus. Top state universities and private schools are higher, especially for those from out-of-state—from $17,000 for residents to $35,000 for nonresidents at such schools as the University of Michigan and University of California, Berkeley. Among the elite private schools, expect to pay north of $40,000 today for all the expenses of a year of undergraduate education.

> **TIP**
>
> **CONSIDER FASTER LEARNING.** Considering the high costs of higher education, high school advanced placement courses take on a whole new dimension. A child who passes enough of them might even be able to move through his or her undergraduate degree in three years.

However, there may be help available for these expenses, even if your child does have the desire or talent to attend one of the more expensive schools. First off, eligibility for federal financial aid as calculated in the standard Free

Application for Federal Student Aid (FAFSA) is largely based on parents' current income as opposed to their retirement savings, though other taxable assets do eventually disqualify you for aid. This can help early-retiree parents, who generally have relatively large assets but low incomes, but might otherwise look rich to college financial aid departments. More expensive schools also tend to have more money to hand out, and your so-called demonstrated financial need, the number the financial aid office will be trying to cover, will be higher. So don't automatically steer your child to a less-expensive school assuming it will be easier to finance.

Early retiree parents with time to take children on adventures—a year living in India or a two-year home-schooled circumnavigation of the Pacific in a small sailboat—may also find they have given their children a defining edge in the college admissions process due to their unique life experiences. And parents who follow the classic early retiree strategy of moving to a rural area often find their kids gain strong appeal with elite college admissions departments. The joke among admissions officers now is that an Iowa address beats 2,400 SAT Scores in terms of eligibility; schools want a geographically diverse student body and have trouble getting enough qualified applicants from rural states. In any case, grants and even scholarships can more readily materialize for students whom the admissions departments covet.

So piecing together a patchwork of scholarships, grants, loans, and work-study sources of aid may bring your parental contribution down to a manageable level. If grandparents help out with additional tuition payments, then the kids might be able to graduate debt-free and maybe even have something extra left over to buy their first apartment or start a business.

If your children go on to graduate school, they should be able to get a fellowship—being a Teaching Assistant or Research Assistant—to cover many of their expenses. If they go to professional school, a fellowship is less likely. But by that point they can borrow against their own elevated future earnings through student loan programs offered at subsidized interest rates.

Once you know the upper dollar limit you feel obliged or prepared to contribute to your children's education, see if it is possible to set it aside, at least mentally, outside your portfolio. Earmark the money and do not factor it into your own calculations of funds you hope to tap to finance your own early retirement.

WARNING

SCHOOL COSTS INFLATE AT THEIR OWN RATES. Many parents use the shorthand of setting college savings aside as if they were being used to pay for a student attending college today, at today's prices, and then assuming these funds will grow over time at roughly the same rate as tuition increases. This may appear highly conservative, but college costs tend to escalate faster than inflation—so be sure to budget for that accurately.

RESOURCES

ADDITIONAL RESOURCES FOR FINANCIAL AID. Avoid services that charge up front for help locating scholarship funds. The site at www.fastweb.com offers free search resources to over a half-million scholarships and www.collegeanswer.com lists more than two million scholarships.

Online calculators and related information is also available to help in college planning.

- T. Rowe Price has several good resources at www.troweprice .com. Look under the Individual Investors and the Investment Planning and Tools tabs on the site.

- Vanguard also has several useful tools and good investor education on complex topics such as the impact on financial aid eligibility of having a grandparent pay your tuition directly. You can find it at www.vanguard.com at the College tab within Planning and Education, available from the main menu for Personal Investors and available to nonclients.

THE IMPORTANCE OF JUST SAYING NO

Many parents assume that kids need unlimited amounts of goodies requiring large amounts of spending, and continue with their nose-to-the-grindstone Overwork to provide them. In fact, early retiree parents uniformly report that kids don't really need that much, and a bit of relative deprivation is probably good for character-building. After a pretty young age, kids don't seem to want that many toys, though as they get older their appetite for electronic goodies can be unlimited.

Encourage kids to earn money to buy these sorts of extras. Babysitting, doing website design or yardwork, or giving lessons in a musical instrument or sports skill are all reasonable ways for young people to earn money and learn how to spend it wisely.

For parents, just saying "No," or postponing a major purchase until the next birthday or holiday has the remarkable power of turning a dire need into a long-forgotten want. Talking with your children frankly about the family's need to shepherd cash to allow the family budget to balance and Mom and Dad to be able to be more available than they were back during their full-time work days also seems to resonate.

2. Learning Opportunities

Early retiree parents have the flexibility to make many choices that are kind on the family budget while providing unique learning and growth opportunities for the children. For example, many early retirees send their children to public rather than private school, but then use their additional time and energy to supplement the school curriculum with home schooling and other concentrated activities aimed at helping their development.

Early retiree families also tend to provide kids with learning opportunities by taking plenty of vacations. To make that affordable, they stay in budget accommodations when they go—camping, staying with friends, or in home-stays with local families arranged through a service. These save money and often give children more meaningful experiences than staying in a hotel or resort.

EXAMPLE: Tom and Susan Chittenden take their girls out of the local public school for an annual two-month-long caravan trip around different parts of the country every spring, making use of state and national parks and other local attractions to educate the girls about different ecosystems, people, and history. Meeting different types of people and mixing it up with other kids is also valuable at broadening their horizons.

3. Savings and Work Ethic

Some parents who have retired early are concerned that they are not setting appropriate examples for their kids, who may grow up to think of work as optional or somehow unattractive. But experience often shows that parents who develop a passionate interest in community work or an avocation, as a result of having the extra time in early retirement, send a powerful message to children that work has tangible fruits and is respectable and engaging.

This is especially true if the work is done in the home or in the local community where children can more directly observe and understand the impact of the work, compared to parents who work in remote offices doing mysterious tasks for anonymous companies.

Many early-retiree households also model great savings habits, and kids understand at least one reward of saving: Lots more time with Mom and Dad than most of their peers enjoy.

RESOURCES

FOR MORE ON CHILDREN AND MONEY MATTERS. The Motley Fool has good book for older children, *The Motley Fool Investment Guide for Teens: 8 Steps to Having More Money Than Your Parents Ever Dreamed Of.*

The Kid's Guide to Money: Earning It, Saving It, Spending It, Growing It, Sharing It, by Steve Otfinoski (Scholastic Reference), gives good guidance for the middle years, grades four through eight.

Money $ense for Kids, by Hollis Page Harman (Barron's Educational Series), is aimed at kids younger than age eight and is a very gentle introduction to money and investments.

H. Retiring Outside the U.S.

The pull for early retirees to move and live overseas is growing. The cost of living in many desirable locales is just a fraction of what it is in America. Internet DSL lines, cheap cell phones, and direct dial area codes to and from the United States make staying in touch with home easy. Hospitals, roads, budget airline access, and cars are all improving—and other signposts of progress make these places much easier for an American to live in comfortably. If only as a backup Plan B to give you confidence that you can stay early retired over the long run even in the event of a sustained and severe financial reversal, it may be worth looking at this possibility.

And in addition to the attractions of a life overseas, many Americans feel the need to distance themselves from the U.S. for a myriad of personal reasons. Consider the looming liabilities being created in unfunded Medicare commitments, the enormous rise in property prices and property taxes, the costs of health insurance and nursing care—all of which add to the cost of retiring in this country. Security concerns are a fear of many living near a major city or target, while others merely feel frustration with traffic-clogged roads, bad weather, or politics. For whatever reason, plenty of Americans have begun voting with their feet. The State Department estimates that about a million Americans are currently retired abroad—and it's a trend that is likely to grow.

1. Advantages

Cost of living and quality of life seem to be the main drivers for people who leave the country. For example, Lance lives well in Bangkok as an early retiree on $1,000 a month, which he uses as a base to travel throughout Asia. Duarte is finalizing plans to early retire from the U.S. to the Dominican Republic, where $100,000 will buy a beautiful 3,000-square-foot home near the water, $60,000 will pay for a nice new bungalow on the beach, and $1,500 a month can buy a near-luxurious lifestyle including two or three full-time domestic staffers. An historic Spanish colonial home, livable but ready for restoration in downtown Cuenca, Ecuador, would cost less than $75,000.

Good health insurance for overseas residents costs about a quarter of the price of health insurance in the U.S., with evacuation coverage to fly to regional specialists if needed. Many expats remark on the high quality and low cost of at least routine health care in foreign countries, even those we think of as poor.

Even though moving to rural parts of the U.S. may still be the most familiar way for Americans to find simple, inexpensive living, our horizons are widening. Americans are more likely to go abroad for vacations and eco-tourism than ever before, making them familiar with exotic destinations.

Less exotic but a comfortable fit for many Americans, New Zealand and rural parts of France or Portugal can still offer attractive housing prices—and a simple, inexpensive way of life might not feel like deprivation if everyone around you is doing the same thing and enjoying themselves. Even rural England or Ireland, while no longer inexpensive, draw plenty of American retirees and early retirees because of their language and cultural appeal. Many early retirees are also now moving to Prague, where they can live in a stunning European capital at a fraction of the cost of Paris and London—and to Croatia, where properties in inviting historic waterfront villages are going for a fraction of the costs in other parts of the Mediterranean.

Certain countries, such as Panama, Belize, and Ecuador, have started to become magnets for a next wave of American retirees—and the process tends to reinforce itself, though land prices start to climb and the best bargains become harder to find. Having a critical mass of expatriates in an area creates a sense of home, which makes it easier for the next wave to come. And if you make the move there, offering real estate and services to cater to other displaced Americans might even turn into a lucrative and early-semi-retiree-friendly business. When you qualify to get Social Security checks, they can be direct-deposited in your foreign or U.S. bank account, no U.S. residency required.

MAY TO SEPTEMBER AT FOUR KNOTS

Sid and Mary Witherspoon left their native Australia for England in the 1970s, where Sid had been a successful real estate developer. Early retiring in their 50s, Sid and Mary bought a home in La Rochelle, on the Atlantic coast of France, where they live most of the year.

But about ten years ago, they bought a 70-year-old canal barge, *Anisette*, for a song, and have been lovingly restoring and modernizing it ever since. Now, from May to September every year, the Witherspoons take the 70-foot *Anisette*, bigger than a small house, on a leisurely circuit around the French, German, and Dutch canals. Friends from England or Australia come and join them for a week or so, giving them the chance to keep old friendships alive and have company on their tours. They stop in small rural villages along the canals, bicycle into town, and enjoy a fabulous lifestyle—at a very low cost.

2. Disadvantages

Retiring in a far-off or developing country won't be right for everyone and is not without its risks. For many, the distance from family and friends will be too great to even consider. While moving to North Carolina puts you just a few hours away from friends and family by plane, moving to Portugal means you probably won't see people unless you make the effort. For others, simply living in a foreign culture for more than a week's vacation would be uncomfortable beyond comprehension.

Although plenty of expats quickly get the hang of the language in their adopted country, others are intimidated and remain insecure about operating outside the English-speaking enclaves.

EXAMPLE: "Not my culture" is how T.J. Justin summed up his decision to forgo early retirement in Costa Rica. Although he and his family made a genuine effort to fall in love with the place and felt warmly welcomed by the local people and expats there, in the end it was just too different and a sort of homesickness for things such as American hardware stores, American plumbing, and American bookstores took hold.

In countries with the lowest costs of living, those who live too richly might become crime targets. Even those who could live much more richly abroad report that they find it best to keep low profiles, blending in economically with homes, cars, and other visible consumption in line with the local norms. Nonetheless, early retirees are advised to avoid countries such as Colombia or the Middle East in which war, civil unrest, drug cartels, and the like subvert the normal safety and rules of law.

RESOURCES

MORE RESOURCES FOR EXPATS. Health insurance from the British nonprofit BUPA has been a quality provider and a pillar of expatriate lifestyles for several decades. You can estimate your premium at www.bupa.com.

IRS Publication 54, *"Tax Guide for U.S. Citizens and Resident Aliens Abroad,"* gives comprehensive information on tax matters for Americans living and working abroad.

Weed through the hype on the following two websites and you'll find plenty of useful advice, real stories, and inspiring information for planning a retirement abroad: www.escapeartist.com/international/00_us_taxes.html and http://internationalliving.com.

Finally, Britain's *Daily Telegraph* has a special online edition for expatriates, filled with resources from the people who have been moving overseas to live for hundreds of years. You can find it at www.expat.telegraph.co.uk.

> ## WORRIED ABOUT HEALTH CARE
>
> Bart, originally from England, and Jill, an American, are early semi-retired in suburban Chicago, where Bart, a former advertising executive, has developed a small part-time business doing landscape design. While drawn to the charms of rural England, they won't consider it as a retirement destination because they feel that health care within Britain's National Health Service is not up to the same standard as America's.
>
> Even though they are both in good health, having instant access to what they consider the best health care in the world is their primary determinant of where they will live in retirement.

I. Deciding Whether It's Possible to Retire Early

Depending on their assets and personal inclinations, many early retirees have been able to pare annual expenses quite low. Plenty of couples report spending as little as $18,000 a year, though when pushed these numbers often fail to include essentials such as health insurance, investment expenses, or a proper accounting for car depreciation. But living truly frugally is possible and realistic. Ted Baker, for example, a retired government scientist from Oregon who started early retirement in his mid-50s, lives comfortably with his wife on $1,300 per month—that's $15,600 per year—for basic household spending.

Although average budgets for generally well-heeled early-retired couples are around $40,000 to $45,000 for a properly calculated annual budget, early retirement message boards are full of people living comfortably, often in rural parts of the country, on around half that amount. Annual spending of $24,000 puts them squarely in line with their neighbors who work full time, particularly since the early retirees own their homes and pay no mortgages. Then again, plenty of quite well-off people are early semi-retired, too—with budgets in the hundreds of thousands of dollars per year requiring few real material sacrifices.

You and your family have personal choices to make: deciding what is an acceptable cost of living and lifestyle and how much you are willing to sacrifice materially to make early retirement possible, either now or in a reasonable number of years.

A look at two couples—a high-earner couple in Silicon Valley and a couple with more average earnings in Missouri—illustrates the numbers and unique circumstances that can direct the timing and possibilities of early retirement.

1. Considering When, Where, and Whether to Retire Early

Brendan and Robin are in their early 40s, both toiling away at full-time jobs in Silicon Valley. While working as a software engineer years ago, Brendan had the foresight to buy a home, which the couple traded up for a bigger home when they got married ten years ago. Brendan still does software engineering, earning $135,000 per year, with additional promised stock options that never seem to be coming into the money. Robin does human resources work, earning $65,000, on a flextime four-day/week schedule. She has been taking art classes in that extra day off.

Brendan is burning out on work, but has many ideas for improving some widely used shareware, if he only had the time. And he has recently discovered a passion for surfing.

Both Robin and Brendan are ready to look at their options for retiring early. Here is a look at their annual earnings, spending, and saving, along with the value of their home and assets.

Combined income	$200,000	
Savings	$500,000	
Home value	$1,250,000	
Home equity	$950,000	
Home cost basis	$600,000	(for capital gains taxes)
Property taxes	$15,000	
Total spending	$175,000	(including 35k income taxes and 20k a year mortgage payment)

Total net worth:
(Savings plus home equity) $1,450,000

Brendan and Robin are considering three possibilities: moving to the west coast of Puerto Rico, moving to North Carolina, or staying put and living as early retirees in Silicon Valley.

PUERTO RICO. Life on the beach would be good, but not free, especially with a few trips home to California each year during hurricane season to see relatives and friends. Food and housing there are cheap, and English is widely spoken. When Brendan and Robin talk to early retirees in Puerto Rico, they realize they can live well on $20,000 a year and fairly lavishly for $40,000 per year; they assume an average of $30,000 per year.

An airy home within walking distance to a surf break with nonexistent heating bills, would cost them $90,000. Although plenty of work options are available, Brendan and Robin initially assume there will be no work income. So using a handy rule for determining a required savings amount, simply multiply their spending needs by 25, for a 4% safe withdrawal. In the future, they might invest in real estate, developing properties, and services for other expatriates, or Brendan might be able to take on some freelance programming delivered online, so they consider that they may have some other income sources down the road.

The amount required to cover their needs would be: (25 x $30,000) + $90,000 (home) = $840,000.

Note that this locale and estimate is at the high end for expenses abroad, similar to those that might be needed for a simple lifestyle in New Zealand or rural parts of Europe. Early retirees who move to places such as Thailand, the Dominican Republic, or Central America can still do it with liquid assets of around $500,000—although it is more of a stretch than in the past.

Brendan and Robin realize with a happy jolt that they could sell their house and take off to Rincon Beach tomorrow. Not wild about the cuisine, and wondering if they would get bored of the beach, however, they look at other options.

NORTH CAROLINA. Living in semi-rural America would be a bit pricier than Puerto Rico, as both living expenses and home prices are higher there. But

Brendan and Robin also feel they would have a reasonable shot at finding well-paid part-time work in North Carolina.

They believe that with a commitment to living more frugally, they can easily manage on $70,000 a year—a number inflated by properly accounting for $19,750 of easily overlooked annual spending needs, which include:

High-deductible health insurance	$6,000	
State and federal income taxes	$2,000	
Fund management fees	$5,750	($1.15 million at .5% per year)
Allowances for regular home repair	$1,000	
Car depreciation	$5,000	(two cars @ $2,500 each)
TOTAL	**$19,750**	

They also plan to travel a fair amount with their newfound freedom. They hope to purchase a pleasant home for something close to the average U.S. new home price and budget $300,000 for that.

Together, they plan to work part time to earn $14,000 per year, which they will apply toward annual spending needs. This will allow their withdrawal from the portfolio to be capped at $56,000 per year. Working with the simple 25x spending rule, (See Chapter 4) their total savings and home would together need to sum to: (25 x $56,000) + $300,000 (home) = $1.7 million.

Not bad. With a pinch here and a tug there, Brendan and Robin could probably make this move today, given that their total savings and home equity are already $1,450,000.

SILICON VALLEY. Since Brendan and Robin have many friends and family members nearby in Silicon Valley, they also consider the financial pros and cons of staying put and retiring early in their current home. Assume that even if they stay in the same house, their expenses would drop: First they will make basic 10% spending cuts as they work to simplify their lives and cut spending. More importantly, by earning capital gains and dividends, creating a sole proprietorship, and withdrawing funds from their portfolio for living expenses, they would pay dramatically lower Social Security, Medicare, and income taxes, with total taxes as little as 3% of their annual spending.

They calculate they can drop their annual expenses to $95,000, assume they would not immediately pay off the remainder of the mortgage, and earn $15,000 a year from part-time work. Their net worth requirements (savings plus home equity) would be: (25 x $80,000) + $1,200,000 (home equity) = $3.2 million.

Since Brendan and Robin currently have a total net worth of $1.45 million and are saving just $25,000 a year, they would probably never be able to retire early in this region—unless a whole raft of stock options suddenly go into the black or some other dramatic earnings improvement exploded into their lives. If they are sincere about their desire to early semi-retire, they might seriously consider the merits of moving to a smaller home or to a low-cost semi-rural area, putting their home equity to work.

2. Continuing Life in the Middle Lane

Eric and Hope never had a fast-lane life and their interest in early semi-retirement is not about salvaging health or marriage, but simply about having more time for the things they like to do.

Eric worked as a state government employee for his entire 25-year career, and while his earnings were relatively modest, he and Hope still managed to save diligently, salting away $10,000 or more each year in index funds which appreciated nicely throughout the '80s and '90s to a grand total of $420,000. This includes the vested employer matching contributions from Hope's years working as a production supervisor at a large brewery and Eric's government-sponsored savings plan. All together, Hope accumulated $70,000 in her 401(k) and Eric added $50,000 to his tax-advantaged savings balance. Importantly, Eric's 25 years in government service have made him eligible for an early-retirement benefit—and he can also expect a full good old-fashioned inflation-adjusted defined benefit pension, albeit smaller because of the early retirement option, when he is 65.

Eric and Hope have two teenagers—one of whom has just started college, the other will enter next year. Tuition plus room and board at the local university and all fees and transportation expenses come in around $12,000 per year per child. Four years of college each for two children would cost about $100,000, though one child may want to go to a more expensive school in a neighboring state.

Although Eric and Hope have set aside less than half of the full tuition bill (separate from their $420,000 retirement savings), they feel that between the children's earnings from work during the summer and part-time during school, plus modest grants and loans, they should graduate on schedule with less than $10,000 of student loans each. Some extra campus work or unsought help from grandparents may wipe even that out and give them a clean start.

Eric has for some years now been at the top pay scale for his area, earning $60,000 a year, but Hope stopped salaried work ten years ago. She currently runs a home-based business making and selling home décor items that brings in a steady $4,000 a year. Their house, now worth about $250,000, has recently been paid off, and property taxes in their rural Missouri area are just $3,000 per year.

Eric and Hope have always watched their spending and get by on $40,000 a year in overall living expenses. They figure that any savings from their recently retired mortgage and their prodigious teenage eaters moving away will be taken up in part by some of the extra travel they hope to do in early semi-retirement. In addition, they realize that as early semi-retirees, they would need to count some additional annual expenses such as cars and house painting allowances, portfolio management expenses, and taxes on portfolio earnings and work income in their annual budget. So although there will be some savings on work and commuting expenses, they decide that staying with $40,000 a year is about right.

The couple view their financial challenge as having enough income to last the 15 to 20 years until Eric's traditional pension and Hope's Social Security kick in. Hope is now 47 and can collect full Social Security at 67; Eric can draw his early retirement benefit ($18,000 a year with an inflation adjustment built in) with basic medical benefits now after his 25 years of service and will receive full pension ($30,000, inflation-adjusted) and full medical benefits in 15 years at age 65. Of course, Eric could have an even bigger pension if he stayed at work, but he has the itch to retire early and is ready to move on if he can maintain his current lifestyle.

Here is how they plan to cover their annual expenses:

Eric's half-pension	$18,000
Hope's part-time work	$4,000
Withdrawal from savings, 4% of $420,000	$18,000
Total	**$40,000**

At traditional retirement age, Social Security for Hope should be about $10,000 per year in today's dollars, which combined with Eric's $30,000 pension will just cover their annual spending. So they expect to need little or no income from their portfolio earnings 20 years from now. They may even find themselves scaling up their living standards in retirement, helping grandchildren with college, or simply living comfortably in complete financial security.

While not everyone has the benefit of a defined benefit pension plan with early retirement and medical benefits, many could live as comfortably as Eric and Hope on $40,000 a year by making some lifestyle changes. Eric and Hope have the option to retire early in financial security, in large part, because their annual living expenses are low enough to be comfortably covered by even modest pension and benefit levels. ●

CHAPTER THREE

Put Your Investing on Autopilot

It's tough being an investor these days: so many choices, so much information, gyrating markets, and the chance to buy or sell anything in the world within seconds at the click of a button. It's no wonder investors feel stressed—uncertain whether they have done the right thing or could be doing better.

If you are an early retiree, you have it especially hard. Your portfolio must provide a steady income and hold its value over the long run or you face the specter of returning to full-time work. And you may end up

> *Don't Worry. Be Happy.*
> —BOBBY MCFERRIN

spending your newfound extra time watching the daily ups and downs of the stock market, doubting your decisions, changing course, and worrying yourself sick. You need an autopilot you can trust to steer through the maelstrom. And this chapter explains how and where to get one.

A. Help for the Beleaguered Investor

Those in the investment industry play on genuine concerns and fears, often offering high-priced advice and products that can seem better suited to lining their own pockets than to meeting investors' long-term needs.

Fortunately, in recent years, an investing paradigm has emerged that can be especially useful to early retirees and other long-term investors: buy-and-hold index investing. A growing body of credible research now supports this investment approach. At its heart, index investing is based on data confirming that simply matching the performance of the overall market, without attempting to beat the averages with superior timing and insight, will generally win out over most other investing approaches in the short run and almost invariably over the long run. While superior stock-picking skills give some investors an index-beating year or two, on average the indexers edge ahead, especially against the large widely followed indexes.

While most investors have heard the merits of buy-and-hold index investing, what is only beginning to be appreciated and is especially relevant to early retirees are enhancements and research that build on the basic index investing paradigm. I term this approach Rational Investing—and believe it offers early retirees profound benefits over the long run.

Rational Investing is discussed in detail later in the chapter (See Sections E and F.) But here are some of its basic tenets.

- **ALLOCATE YOUR INVESTMENTS.** By allocating investments across several carefully chosen asset classes, not all of them stocks and bonds, you can reduce the volatility—that is, the gyrations in value—of your portfolio without giving up investment performance. This will not only reduce your stomach-churning, but will also preserve your portfolio longer in the face of steady annual withdrawals.

- **REBALANCE YOUR PORTFOLIO.** By rebalancing your portfolio back to target allocations for the various asset classes in a disciplined, systematic manner, you will not only take the anguish and deliberation out of investment decision-making, but also assure yourself superior performance over the long run. (See Section G.)

- **KEEP MANAGEMENT FEES LOW.** While for years investors seemed not to care much about the fees they paid to fund managers and investment advisors, research has now irrefutably established that fees can wreak havoc on long-term investment performance. Fortunately, in response to the resulting investor backlash, more funds have recently joined a few pioneering firms and are lowering their fees, giving individual investors low-cost ways to implement more nuanced strategies.

In addition to being effective, Rational Investing is also simple, requiring little time or emotional effort. Combining this investing approach with the Safe Withdrawal Method presented in Chapter 4 can give an early retiree confidence and success in meeting long-term financial needs. It is the closest thing to a trustworthy autopilot for your investing. That means you can stop worrying about finances—and spend your time in early retirement doing what you want to do: getting a life.

HITTING ROCK BOTTOM—AND FINDING GOLD

My investment style for 20 years could be kindly described as intuitive. I would buy or sell whatever I wanted, whenever the mood gripped me. I did buy low-cost funds and was well-diversified, with some good long-term successes, but I was particularly good at one aspect of investing: picking stock market bottoms.

Once every few years, I'd have a day in which I became completely convinced that the stock market was falling off a cliff and that if I didn't SELL NOW, I would face financial ruin. Other shortsighted investors inevitably came to the same conclusion at the same time: We created the cataclysmic troughs, the market bottoms. In this way, I sold my only two shares of Berkshire Hathaway stock at the 15-year low of $5,500 in 1990. It trades around $85,000 today.

Using these same unique skills, I knew on the evening of October 10, 2002 that I had done something very bad that day: selling $100,000 of stock in a near panic. Something inside me knew that the market, having found its way to a seven-year low, was surely bottomed and on its way back. Naturally, I failed to purchase any new stock the next day on the strength of this understanding. That would have meant I was flip-flopping.

Between the sharks at my brokerage firms and Harry, Larry, and Moe carrying on inside my own head, I clearly needed a better way to invest wisely for the long run. I needed a system that I could understand and stick to, one that generated consistent results, and would give me the time and mental energy to spend having a life instead of being glued to the financial market screen. This led me to uncover and clarify the merits of Rational Investing.

B. Where Wall Street Goes Wrong

Despite the warm and fuzzy ads exuding affinity for your financial safety, brokerage firms and securities houses are set up as selling organizations, pitching a product for a commission. It is rare to find a broker or dealer who can look at the big picture and create the low-cost buy-and-hold investing autopilot an early retiree needs. Most would much rather sell you on the merits of keeping a hand firmly on the wheel, then charge you for frequent course corrections.

Those who handle most mutual funds are only a little better. Not only do they see your assets as their source of steady annual fees, but many then vigorously trade your money at inflated commission levels to receive soft dollar kickbacks from cozy corporate partners.

Inserting these companies into your investing process eats into your returns and still fails to meet your needs for an autopilot—an overarching strategy and system to ensure safe, reasonable returns over the long run. It is easy and inexpensive to manage your portfolio yourself with Rational Investing principles. (Sections D and E explain how in detail.) And you don't need expensive help to do it.

RESOURCES

HELP WITH FINDING A SOLID INVESTMENT FIRM. You will need to buy financial products such as mutual funds, brokerage services, or Certificates of Deposit (CDs). Several quality firms exist to supply you with these building blocks for your strategy at reasonable costs. If your favorite firm is not listed below, try comparing its offerings with those of the firms that are mentioned and see if it is worth making a switch.

Vanguard is one of a small number of investment firms that I trust to generally give investors a fair shake at long-term investing, perhaps because it is run as a co-op in which shareholders own the management company and run it on a nonprofit basis. You can find it at www.vanguard.com.

There are a few other high-caliber firms that view managing your money as a sacred trust. They offer plenty of sensible index, tax-efficient, and low-fee funds. They include:

- Dimensional Fund Advisors (DFA): www.dfaus.com
- T. Rowe Price: www.troweprice.com
- Dodge & Cox: www.dodgeandcox.com
- Pacific Management Company (Pimco), fixed income specialists, online at www.pimco.com
- Capital Research, managers of the American Funds mutual fund series at www.americanfunds.com, and
- Schwab, a low-cost brokerage firm that can help you purchase DFA, Pimco, and other funds you might need to allocate your assets effectively at www.schwab.com.

INVESTMENT TERMINOLOGY EXPLAINED

For many people, one of the mystifying things about the investment world is the strange language spoken there. Here are some simple definitions for common terms and strategies, along with some basic advice for building your own autopilot along Rational Investing principles.

ASSET CLASSES are types of financial instruments broken into logical groups—for example, small U.S. stocks, large U.S. value stocks, foreign medium-term bonds, commercial real estate, commodities.

DIVERSIFICATION means owning different securities within an asset class, as well as owning several different asset classes. When one asset class tends to go up when another generally goes down or sideways, this pair of asset classes are said to be *less correlated*. Including both in a portfolio will make it less volatile—its value will move more like an ocean liner than a speedboat.

FEES. This is money your brokerage firm or fund management firm charges for its services. The average investor pays about 1% annually for investment fees across an entire portfolio and possibly the same amount again for hidden trading costs that active mutual funds incur as they seek to beat the market. As mentioned earlier, John Bogle, founder of the investment firm Vanguard, has calculated that all fees, spreads, and commissions taken together on U.S. stock funds now cost investors 3% a year. By contrast, Rational Investors find solid funds with low fees, keeping their costs far below the average, to around .4% to .6%. By keeping more of your money and keeping it invested, you come out way ahead in the long run and don't do too badly in the short run, either.

MUTUAL FUNDS OR EXCHANGE TRADED FUNDS (ETFS) are pooled investments that allow owning a piece of many different securities, far more than you would likely be able to buy on your own. *Actively managed funds* are led by a manager who uses expertise to try to beat the index—that is, the average of the securities in the asset class. *Index funds,* however, own nearly every security in an index and thereby match the returns of the asset class. Because they do not try to decide what will go up and down but simply buy the securities in the index, index funds run with less expensive people behind them. The average mutual fund charges its investors 1.75% per year to manage its assets, whereas many index funds or ETFs run at around 1/10th of that amount, or under 0.2%. ETFs, which tend to be index funds, are bought in a brokerage account and trade during the day on the stock exchanges; mutual funds are bought at the end of the trading day from the mutual fund company. Although ETFs do distribute dividends and interest just like mutual funds, they can still be more tax-efficient because no capital gains are generated when fellow shareholders redeem shares in the fund.

REBALANCING requires starting with broad and conservative allocations and staying invested, trading just annually to sell a bit of your winners—and buy a bit more of the things that are beaten down. This keeps trading expenses low. (See Section G for more on this.) Since you are broadly diversified, even a meltdown in one area won't hurt your portfolio much overall. And by using a rigorous annual rebalancing approach, you will be sure to Buy Low and Sell High—something that is devilishly hard to do when you give your emotions free reign.

TAX-EFFICIENT INVESTING OR TAX-EFFICIENT FUNDS seek to lessen taxable capital gains distributions, especially short-term capital gains on which investors would need to pay taxes. Generally, this is accomplished by trading less, as in an index fund, which has the added benefit of lowering trading commissions. These funds may also discourage investors from hopping in and out, since these exchanges necessitate taxable buying and selling. Long-term investors benefit in tax-efficient funds, which seek to simply accumulate capital gains within the fund indefinitely, delaying taxes.

VALUE STOCKS OR BONDS are priced in the bargain bin. The idea is to buy these riskier, less-known, or out-of-favor investments in ways that reduce the chance that if any one of them fails, it will hurt your overall results. This lets you capture outsized benefits over the long run. Adding value stocks to a portfolio in proportions larger than their presence in the overall universe of stocks is called giving the portfolio a *tilt toward value* or *value tilt*.

C. Myths About Investing

The market, The Great Humiliator, has been a dutiful teacher for generations of investors, exposing the many mistaken notions about how to invest, some of which are particularly seductive traps for early retirees. To fully appreciate or adopt the Rational Investing Method, you must move past a number of pervasive but counterproductive myths.

1. Find a Hot Fund Manager

MYTH: "You and I may be investment amateurs, but this fund manager I heard about is a genius. He has outperformed the market now for eight years, through up markets and down. Your best move would be to just invest with him, beat the market, and grow rich."

REALITY: While there is nothing wrong with looking for fund managers with good track records—assuming their fees are reasonable, which they usually are not—expecting to actually find ones who will outperform in the future is nearly impossible. On average, only about a quarter of fund managers outperform their relevant index, after fees, in any year; and only one in ten outperforms for three years running. One study shows the average mutual fund underperforms the market by 1% and Vanguard's John Bogle recently calculated that the average stock mutual fund achieved just 9.9% in annual returns from 1984 to 2004, falling 3.1% short of the S&P 500 Index, which returned 13%. He argues that fees and trading costs make up the difference in this zero-sum game. With thousands of funds out there, a few can always be found that outperform for several years running. But you can never be sure if this year will be the last.

As a Rational Investor, you aren't trying to find the perfect manager, the perfect stock, or even the perfect fund. Instead, spend your time studying how your portfolio as a whole responds in different market environments, how the various asset classes interact, and the optimal amount of each asset class to own. Then find managers who will deliver that asset class to you consistently, intelligently, and cost-effectively.

2. Bonds Are for Wimps

MYTH: "If the average rate of return on stocks is 12% per year and the average long-run rate of return on bonds is 6%, then why would I ever want to own bonds? I am a long-run investor, so I'm going to load up 100% on stocks and trounce the balanced investors over the long run."

REALITY: Sure, you can load up on stocks if you don't need to withdraw money for a very long time. And if you have a stomach made of cast iron. But as an early retiree, you will likely need to make annual withdrawals for decades, so you'll be selling some assets every year. You'll need to sell some of the stocks in your portfolio even if the market has dropped like a rock, which can wreck its chances of bouncing back. In short, this myth ignores volatility: An asset class that has a high expected rate of return over time is almost invariably riskier. That is fine as a small portion of a balanced portfolio, but if the volatile asset is your only asset and you need to sell some of it for living expenses every year, you can be wiped out.

> **EXAMPLE:** A person who invested $1 million in a portfolio of high-return but volatile emerging markets stock at the end of 1993 and withdrew an inflation-adjusted 5% per year from it would have a portfolio reduced to nearly a quarter of its real value over the next nine years, to just $261,600 at the end of 2002. This would mean that far too little of the portfolio would have remained to enjoy the nearly 70% surge in 2003 that brought the ten-year average rate of return for emerging market stocks back close to 10%, the impressive long-term average for this volatile asset class. The same million-dollar investment and annual withdrawals from the Rational Investing Portfolio, which includes a modest amount of those same emerging market stocks, would have still been worth nearly a million in constant dollars nine years later and $1,150,000 after inflation and annual withdrawals in 2003.

3. All-Bond Portfolios Are All-Safe

MYTH: "I know how to retire early and be really safe. I'll buy a portfolio of 20-year AAA municipal bonds with enough tax-free interest every year to support me in fine style. Who needs to think about asset allocation or risk? All bonds means no worries."

REALITY: This myth neglects to factor in inflation. Enticing as this approach is on the surface, this strategy will safely and securely decimate the real value of a portfolio and its withdrawals. Whether the bonds are municipal bonds, long-term CDs, or regular taxable bonds, the dilemma for the investor is the same. First, what the bondholders receive each year from this portfolio is a fixed coupon that diminishes in spending power each year. Second, what the investor gets back at the end of 20 years is the original principal, which, at 3% inflation rates, will be worth about half of its original value in real terms. The investor now has just half of the spending power he or she had at the beginning of retirement, permanently eaten away by inflation. And note that the popular strategy of building a bond ladder—an array of bonds with varying maturities—won't solve this problem.

There is nothing inherently wrong with bonds or tax-free municipal bonds, though most early retirees will be taxed in such low brackets that the tax advantages of munis will be wasted. The problem is not properly setting aside the first 3% or so of yield each year for inflation. After you have done that, you can withdraw safely and know the real value of your portfolio will remain intact, though there may be little left—far less than the desired 4% Safe Withdrawal Rate. (See Chapter 4, Section A for a full discussion of Safe Withdrawal Rates.) All-bond portfolios generally won't survive this dual assault; the average real return on bonds historically has been around 3%. Inflation-protected bonds (TIPS and I-bonds) have real returns of just 2% or so, and money market investments for many years have safely and reliably delivered a real loss of capital. Equities or stocks, with all their risk and variation, are really the primary liquid asset class that gives you long-term protection against inflation with enough return left over for withdrawals. Supporting a 4% withdrawal rate requires a diversified portfolio of these riskier but higher returning assets.

4. Good Companies Make Good Stocks

MYTH: "This stock-picking business isn't so hard. I can just buy the shares of good, profitable growing companies whose products I really like and hold on. I'm bound to do well."

REALITY: Of course, quality companies with strong growing revenues, steadily rising profits, well-known brands, and solid managements can provide investors with good stock returns. But it happens much less frequently than you might assume. That's because these firms, their successes touted throughout the business press, are well-known and attractive to investors—and their stock prices are almost always already high. While you might want to buy their products, you'll generally want to avoid their stocks. Because they start out expensive, growth stocks' returns tend to lag behind those of value stocks, which are on the other end of the spectrum.

Unloved, unknown, or temporarily embarrassed, the riskier value stocks should be an investor's friend, as they outperform the broad market averages over the long term by as much as 3%. Of course, these are averages and trends. There are some growth stocks that start out expensive and just keep going up. And no one wants to get caught in the "value trap" in which they buy a depressed stock—after all, it is cheap for a reason—and then have it go bankrupt. These frightening emotional totems are what produce the value-stock premium, which is created anew each day as investors flinch at the thought of owning a value stock or smile at the thought of owning a growth stock, and adjust their prices accordingly. When the growth stock slips, it is mercilessly hammered down. Investors have long since given up on the value stock, so when the company finally turns around, the stock is brought up smartly due to the upside surprise. That is when the value fund sells it. And the cycle starts again.

5. The S&P 500 Index Is the Stock Market

MYTH: "I shouldn't try to time the market, pick stocks, or even pick a fund manager. I'm just going to load up the equity portion of my portfolio in a low-cost S&P 500 index fund and be done with it."

REALITY: Actually, this approach gets closer to long-term investment sanity than many myths. But the S&P 500 is only a part of the world's stock market—and not the most important piece at that. For example, it is among the most heavily skewed of the major indices, with just the top 22 stocks comprising a third of the overall weight or movement of the index and the bottom 150 stocks in the index comprising just 5% of the index weight. So tying your fortunes to the S&P 500 essentially ties you to the fortunes of a tiny fraction of America's firms. The S&P 500 is a convenient way to track some megacap firms, but to get real diversification into less-correlated asset classes—such as small stocks, international stocks, and value-tilted stocks—you will need to go beyond the S&P 500.

6. Foreign Assets Are Un-American and Unnecessary

MYTH: "Why should I bother with foreign stocks? After all, U.S. firms are bigger, safer, and better understood than all those other companies out there. And besides, American companies are so global in their operations that good times overseas will surely be reflected in my U.S. company stocks."

REALITY: While most people are drawn to invest more heavily in their local markets, there is little economic rationale for it any more. American stocks and bonds do represent about 40% of the world's financial assets, but now that investing overseas has become safe, inexpensive, and convenient, it is time for Americans to look further afield. The goal is to find low-correlation asset classes with liquid markets, quality securities, and reasonable transaction costs. While emerging markets and the chances for shenanigans still put those securities at the furthest limit of acceptable risk, well-documented scandals in major American companies don't measure up to a gold standard of corporate probity, either. In any case, the global marketplace is fast growing up and foreign companies offer great potential for returns at reasonable prices.

The idea that strong overseas operations for American firms will capture that growth in their stocks is not supported by reality. Global American stocks tend to rise and fall with other American companies; their international operations do not provide meaningful diversification. An investor gets far better diversification, both through nondollar currencies and the actual foreign companies themselves, by owning pools of foreign stocks.

Many people are initially concerned that if they spend dollars, they need to hold dollar assets. Early retirees spending just 4% of their portfolio values each year don't need to concern themselves with this. In this day of near-perfect liquidity, raising needed dollars by selling a foreign stock requires a simple click on a computer screen, exactly like any other asset. The same logic applies to having sufficient liquidity to feel safe in an emergency. Holding large amounts of underperforming cash "for liquidity" makes no sense when any traded asset can provide you liquid cash in a day.

D. Prize-Winning Portfolio Theory

After coming to terms with investing mythology and starting to shake your thinking from some common investing errors, there is one more important concept to grasp to fully appreciate how Rational Investing can help you meet long-term investing needs. Asset classes—logical groups of financial instruments—have been mentioned and you probably have some idea that choosing the right asset classes in the right proportions is important. It is.

In fact, this precise area has been the subject of major academic study in recent years, with a conclusion that can help the average investor in daily life. Known as Modern Portfolio Theory, Harry Markowitz and Merton Miller won a Nobel Prize for it in 1990. In a nutshell, Modern Portfolio Theory holds that the behavior—that is, returns and risk—of an overall portfolio can take on different characteristics from the behavior of any single component piece. As a hypothetical example, if one asset pays off only on rainy days and another pays off only on sunny days, these two risky assets together would produce a nice all-weather portfolio.

There is no magical alchemy in this; simply adding the different components will produce a blend with characteristics that are the sum of all the individual pieces. Like a chef making a soup, you add a bit of this and some chunks of that and get a deliciously pleasing dish that is different from the taste or texture of any single ingredient.

Portfolio Theory only becomes interesting when you are able to blend less-correlated asset classes; after all, adding chunks of beef to more chunks of beef won't enhance the soup. When this happens, you can begin seeing different risks canceling each other out, resulting in a blended portfolio with less volatility than each individual asset class has alone.

Then the high-tech part comes in, with reams of computer-based simulations of various combinations of assets over different time periods. These systems, known as Portfolio Optimizers, find a cluster of optimal blends for a portfolio or the best combinations of asset classes to achieve desired rates of risk and return—at least as seen through the rear view mirror of historical returns. Depending on where you want to be in the risk/return tradeoff, choose your proportions of asset classes and, to extend the metaphor, create a perfect soup.

But Portfolio Optimizers are not foolproof. They can point you in the right direction when choosing an optimal blend of asset classes, but they have foibles. First, optimizers can only tell you what the optimal mix was during past years. Left to themselves, they tend to spew out portfolios skewed to just one or two asset classes that performed the best over whatever period you are studying. It isn't much use to know that owning just the three asset classes—small U.S. stocks, gold, and Japanese equities—between 1970 and 1996 would have been your best portfolio; no one would have been willing to hold something so unbalanced as that. It is possible, however, to find acceptable compromises, reasonable blends of the major asset classes that have historically tended to work together to produce good returns with low volatility.

These optimal blends are sometimes referred to as portfolios on the "Efficient Frontier." At least historically, they produced the best combinations of risk and reward. The relationships between asset classes, their expected returns, and correlation with each other will vary year-to-year but tend to remain within stable ranges over time. While you can't expect to create *the* optimal portfolio going forward, you will have something reasonably good, and more importantly, something you can expect over time to deliver return and volatility roughly in line with its historical trends.

RESOURCES

FOR MORE HELP WITH PORTFOLIO OPTIMIZERS. A couple of Portfolio Optimizers, technically known as Mean Variance Optimizers, are available for individuals. After you input different combinations of assets or desired percentage ranges for different asset classes, these optimizers will find the portfolios that would have generated the best combinations of returns and volatility historically.

These Portfolio Optimizers include:

- Multi-period portfolio optimizer MvoPlus, sold by William Bernstein's firm, Efficient Solutions, Inc., along with a number of useful tools for historical returns analysis at www.effisols. com

- Hoadley PC Portfolio Optimizer at www.hoadley.net/options/ develtoolsoptimize.htm, and

- Wagner's Mean Variance Optimizer at www.mathfinance.wag-ner.com/PRODUCTS/MVOPT/MVOptimizer/mvoptimizer.html.

E. Rational Investing

With an appreciation for buy-and-hold low-fee investing, a sense of the common investment foibles, and some background on how asset classes can be combined to make a low-volatility and efficient portfolio, you are ready to be introduced to the basic principles of Rational Investing. Together, these rules function to form a coherent, effective, and easy-to-use investing method for individual investors—especially early retirees.

1. Own Diverse Asset Classes

Rational Investing begins by focusing on building a portfolio with the right blend of asset classes. A blend of stocks, bonds, and other noncorrelated asset classes will generate equivalent or superior returns with less risk than individual securities from just a few asset classes or even a simple blend of U.S. stock and bond index funds. The math and data show that this is true. The mix works because modest amounts of volatile but generally high-return assets will improve overall portfolio performance with little or no additional risk.

The fact that one asset class is zigging while another is zagging means the overall portfolio remains calm. Early retirees can take comfort in knowing that the successful large institutions all invest this way to ensure a safe endowment producing steady income. They don't spend their time picking stocks, bonds, or even funds. They pick asset classes that work well together in a blend and then find managers who can deliver that asset class's performance consistently and at a low price.

For most investors, the Rational Investing Portfolio consists of about 40% stocks, 40% bonds, and 20% other—which includes commodities, oil and gas, market neutral hedge funds, real estate, and private equity. These additional asset classes are less correlated with the main stock and bond asset classes, providing real benefits to the overall results. (See Section F for illustrations of the asset classes and percentage allocations in a Rational Investing Portfolio.)

THE SENSE AND NONSENSE BEHIND ANNUITIES

Annuities are a contract with an insurer that pays you a fixed amount each year until some specified period or until your death. Immediate annuities start paying right away and sometimes seem an attractive option for early retirees: Buy it today and collect a worry-free inflation-adjusted check every month until you die.

Unfortunately, even good low-fee annuities don't pay enough to be practical for most early retirees. And trusting that an insurance firm will be around to pay you every month for the next 75 years brings its own set of worries.

Zvi Body, a professor at Boston University, is a leading proponent of using annuities to fund long-term retirement costs. The approach has merit for those with very large savings relative to their spending needs who are able to lock in most or all of their income needs with an annuity and still have money left over to invest in appreciating assets. Those who must put their entire life savings into an annuity to fund daily living expenses risk having all their eggs in one basket—and perhaps worse, risk having the inflation-adjustments in the annuity fail to keep up with rising living standards over time.

One interesting approach to annuities is to keep them in the family. Essentially, a parent hands over a large initial payment to a grown child who then pays the parent a regular monthly or annual payment for life. Between the tax benefits and the appeal of keeping the money in the family, this approach may eventually become standard practice—though experts advise it makes the most sense when parents are physically well but quite elderly.

2. Demand Low Fees

Your portfolio's management fees, which you can find in the fund's prospectus or by entering the ticker at www.morningstar.com, should average below .5% per year, and some early retirees can get even lower. Fees higher than that simply eat up too much of your expected return each year.

In the past, leading fund management companies only offered this level of pricing to large institutional investors, but they now make these same prices available to small investors, too. You can now get international small stocks, emerging markets stocks, international bonds, commercial real estate, commodities, and many previously difficult-to-get asset classes at fees in the .2% to .5% per year range. The Rational Investing Portfolio has direct fees of .4%, with an assumed additional .1% to .2% for trading costs incurred by the mostly low-turnover index funds.

3. Use Tilts

A portfolio has a tilt when it holds more of an asset class than it customarily would warrant. For example, if the Total U.S. Stock Market Index contains just under 7% small stocks, then a portfolio that contained more than 7% small stocks—for instance, the Rational Investing Portfolio in which small stocks make up over 18% of the total value of the stock holdings—would be considered to be tilted toward small stocks.

The Rational Investing Portfolio tilts toward value stocks, international assets, and small stocks. The value tilt is justified by reliable academic studies showing that value stocks and value bonds—high yield bonds—outperform the overall market over time due to their higher risk. Holding these risky assets in funds, within an overall portfolio, means the rewards can be gained while keeping the risk manageable. International stocks and bonds as well as small stocks are also attractive asset classes to tilt toward since their low correlations with other asset classes means they can dampen overall portfolio risk while delivering good returns.

4. Keep Volatility Low

Volatility indicates the up and down swings in the value of your portfolio, typically measured by the standard deviation of how widely portfolio returns have been distributed around the average.

> **EXAMPLE:** The S&P 500 U.S. Stock Index is fairly volatile. Although its average return between 1988 and 2004 was 10.5% per year, those returns were distributed widely—with plenty of years with big gains and plenty of years with negative, sometimes large negative market performance. This wide distribution can be measured with a well-known statistical tool called standard deviation, which in the case of the S&P 500, is 15.6%. This means that, in any given year, the results of the S&P 500 can be expected to fall with 68% certainty within one standard deviation above or below the average return, or between –5.1% and 26.1%. If you move two standard deviations away from the average, between –20.7% and 41.7%, you can expect returns to fall within this wider range 95% of the time. Note that the Rational Investing Portfolio has a standard deviation roughly half of that of the S&P 500.

An early semi-retiree should not try to simply achieve the highest rate of return if that means an unacceptable level of volatility or risk. Early retirement will be made unbearably hard if you must watch a slow-motion train wreck in your portfolio—your entire retirement savings and lifestyle collapsing. Choose a mix of assets to maintain an acceptable level of return at the lowest risk, which generally means holding lower levels of equity than some other long-term investing models advocate.

5. Use Index Funds Whenever Possible

Indexes are designed to approximate the returns of different segments of the market. Often, but not always, an index overlaps neatly with an asset class you will want to hold in your portfolio. Usually, the index is comprised of most of the significant securities that make up that asset class held in proportion to their size. Indexes undergo periodic revisions, typically annually, with some securities being added, others falling out of the index, and the weights of those staying in the index being adjusted to reflect their relative changes in value over the previous year. All this detail is simply to impress on you that an index, while certainly a useful creation, is only an approximation of the actual returns for the asset class and tilt in which you are interested. Whenever the match is close, you are in luck. In those cases, your best choice for the portfolio will almost always be the low-fee, tax-efficient index fund or index ETF. (See Section B for a definition.)

But there's not always an index fund available that matches your needs. In some cases—for instance, for the foreign bond or GNMA asset classes—there may not even be an index, never mind an index fund, that tracks the asset class. You are then left with little choice but to find a low-fee actively managed fund to do the job. Likewise, a sub-index or tilt may not have an index or traditional index fund that properly tracks it—for example, international small stocks or international large value stocks.

To make matters more complex, a few actively managed funds, notably value funds, also have the annoying habit of consistently beating their equivalent index funds year after year. (Value indexes have a subtle but material flaw since they only adjust their component companies annually and value stocks' fortunes tend to rise and fall more quickly than that.) You may occasionally find other actively managed funds that, through some credible difference in trading strategy, develop a consistent deviation from their index or benchmark. For instance, the Vanguard High Yield fund consistently varies from the high yield index by holding only the better quality "junk" bonds. During good times, the fund underperforms the index; during bad times, its better quality bonds hold up better than those in the index. This may be a tradeoff you would feel comfortable making.

In other cases, such as the private equity, oil and gas, market-neutral hedge fund, and even commercial real estate asset classes, the fullest diversification and best returns may come, paradoxically, by moving outside the universe of indexes and funds entirely and making individual, illiquid investment—that is, investments in carefully researched private companies, partnerships or buildings which cannot be readily sold.

Later in the chapter, you will find a list of good choices of index and other funds for each asset class. (See Section F3c.) Choose from among these and compare them to other favorite or new funds as you set about implementing the Rational Investing Method for yourself.

TIP

NOT ALL INDEX FUNDS ARE CREATED EQUAL. After years of experience in reducing trading costs while still matching the underlying index, Vanguard has learned how to often produce marginally better returns than the index, even after its fees. And Dimensional Fund Advisors (DFA) offers a variety of funds called enhanced index funds that track asset classes and tilts rather than an index per se. These will give you, for instance, funds tracking the International Small or International Large Value asset classes, making them a good fit for investors following the Rational Investing Method.

6. Know Your Required Return

It is possible to create portfolios with almost no risk—for example, those composed of bank CDs or money market funds—but they will generally lack sufficient return. The early retiree's portfolio must remain substantially intact or grow against the triple assault of inflation (assume 3% per year), fees and trading costs (.5% or so each year) and a 4% to 5% annual withdrawal over short periods as well as over the long run. In other words, adding together these three demands on your portfolio, you know that you need at least a 7.5% expected annual return to keep the real value of your portfolio intact each year.

While an all-CD or all-bond portfolio may feel safe to you, it can't return 7.5% over the long run, though interest rates may change one day to make that possible again. In fact, an all-CD portfolio yielding 5.5% will safely and securely corrode the real value of your savings if you were to withdraw at anything higher than a 2.5% annual rate. The Rational Investing Portfolio has a 9.5% historical rate of return, giving you ample breathing room to accommodate volatile and unpredictable future returns and still have your portfolio remain intact against the eroding power of inflation, fees, and your annual withdrawal.

RESOURCES

THE RESEARCHERS BEHIND RATIONAL INVESTING. Rational Investing builds on the findings of a rogue's gallery of academic finance researchers, proven over decades of testing and retesting. See Appendix 2 for details on how to access these and other studies:

- "The Efficient Market Hypothesis," by Eugene Fama and Burton Malkiel, explains that although prices in the market may be too high or too low, they are mispriced randomly and there is no method to make use of this information to consistently beat the market

- "Modern Portfolio Theory," by Harry Markowitz and Merton Miller, proves how investing across less-correlated asset classes can produce a portfolio with lower risk for a given return, and

- "The 3-Factor Model," by Eugene Fama and Kenneth French, identifies and explains the premiums paid to holders of small and value stocks, with subsequent studies showing how these premiums persist through time and across multiple markets.

> ### SHIFTING INTO AUTOPILOT
>
> Perhaps the biggest benefit of Rational Investing is that it gives you a system of knowing what to buy and sell, and when.
>
> With your portfolio in place, you are only trading to rebalance the asset classes annually—or occasionally sooner if allocations have gotten seriously out of whack—and you should find that kind of buying and selling is easy and automated. Because you are buying and holding, except for modest rebalancing, your capital gains remain compounding in your portfolio tax-deferred, perhaps for your lifetime. By agreeing to match the market instead of attempting to beat it, you put yourself ahead of the game.
>
> And if you should feel the need to play stock guru, give yourself a little hot money—a few percent of your portfolio—to mess around with, possibly with a little bonus to yourself for outperforming the asset class. With a small amount you can have fun, safe in the knowledge that you won't damage the overall integrity of your portfolio.

F. Examples of Rational Investing Portfolios

The charts and tables on the following pages show you the details of three portfolios that broadly adhere to the Rational Investing goals and could be appropriate for early retirees. The third and most complex portfolio, the Rational Investing Portfolio, boasts the best performance with the lowest volatility, but requires somewhat more effort to implement.

1. The Soda Cracker: Single Mutual Fund

The person who is terrified of investing, or who wants the ultimate in simplicity, can potentially get by with just a single mutual fund. Vanguard, along with other major fund firms, offers several packaged blends of index funds, under their Lifestyle, Balanced, and Target Retirement Date series. A good choice might be Vanguard LifeStrategy Moderate or Conservative Growth (VSMGX or VSCGX), or an intriguing new balanced fund, DFA Global 60/40 Portfolio (DGSIX) from Dimensional Fund Advisors. These funds invest in a diverse mix of between 40% and 60% stocks, with the balance in bonds. Vanguard Conservative Growth LifeStrategy, for instance, VSCGX, holding 40% stocks, including some international stocks, has 20-year average returns of 8.84% and a standard deviation below 7%.

Most of these balanced funds have relatively short track records, however. If you gain confidence from long history, you might turn to the granddaddy of balanced funds, started just months before the crash of 1929 and continuing strong to this day: the Wellington Fund (VWEHX). The actively managed Wellington invests 65% in large cap U.S. stocks with a value tilt and 35% in high quality corporate bonds. Over its 76-year history, it has averaged an 8.33% rate of return, with volatility, as measured by its standard deviation over that period of 13.2%. If you go this route, you won't have international or small company exposure, unlike the balanced funds mentioned above. But you'll have a long track record on your side.

Either way, you'll have the simplest investing job imaginable. Have your dividends and fund distributions routed to your checking account—the funds all yield interest and dividends of about 3% a year—and sell some shares of the fund when you need more cash. You won't even need to rebalance your portfolio; you just own one fund. Expenses for the Wellington Fund are .31% per year, the balanced funds mentioned here have fees of between .25% and .4%.

2. The Sandwich: An Eight-Fund Portfolio

Despite the ease and simplicity of the one-fund approach outlined above, most people can't bring themselves to put all their eggs in one basket quite so confidently. With just eight funds and a money market account, you can achieve substantial diversification while meeting all of the Rational Investing goals. Your expected return, measured since 1988 at 8.4%, will undershoot that of the Rational Investing Portfolio. And your volatility, a standard deviation of 8.2%, will be somewhat higher, but you will be on firm ground going forward and have a "real portfolio" to tend and rebalance. Perhaps most importantly, you will be able to easily implement this portfolio within a single brokerage or mutual fund account.

The Sandwich Portfolio will get you coverage of all the major asset classes in percentages roughly similar to those in the Rational Investing Portfolio. Missing will be just four of the 16 asset classes: commodities, high yield, private equity, and market neutral hedge funds. All but one of the funds is a reliable Vanguard fund. The final one, American Century Foreign Bond (BEGBX), is a reasonable way to get quality, medium-term foreign bonds. Even if you don't have a Vanguard account, you should find all these funds or their equivalents through any brokerage account that allows you to buy funds through a mutual fund supermarket service.

Fees for the Simplified 8-Fund portfolio average .33% annually.

The Sandwich Portfolio: Eight Funds Plus Money Market

Percent of Portfolio	Fund Symbol	Fund Description
20%	VFINX	S&P 500 (or Value Index VIVAX or VWNFX)
8%	VTMSX	Vanguard Tax-Managed Small
6%	VGTSX	Vanguard Total International Index
10%	VINEX	Vanguard International Explorer
6%	VEIEX	Vanguard Emerging Markets Index
30%	VBIIX	VG Intermediate Bond Index
11%	BEGBX	American Century Foreign Bond
5%	VGSIX	Vanguard REIT Index
4%	VMMXX	Vanguard Prime Money Market
100%		

3. The Cornucopia or Rational Investing Portfolio

For those who want the full feast, the Rational Investing Portfolio is the way to go. Not only will you have better expected returns based on historical results (9.5%) but you will achieve them with low volatility (7.98%). Implementing this portfolio will put you in 16 different asset classes, but will likely require you to set up an account to purchase Dimensional Fund Advisors (DFA) funds. These funds, sold directly only to institutional investors but available to individuals through an advisor, offer the serious asset allocator unparalleled ability to match investments to desired asset classes and tilts. (See the explanation below.)

The following tables give more detail on the Rational Investing Portfolio and its asset classes and historic performance. (See Appendix 1 for a complete description of each of the asset classes.)

The percentage allocations are outlined in Subsection a, and the historical performance of the portfolio versus two standard benchmarks is given in Subsection b. A list of funds, by asset class, that you can use to implement the portfolio are listed in Subsection c.

a. Portfolio asset allocations

The table below lists the asset classes and their percentage allocations for the Rational Investing Portfolio. These percentages are the result of many inputs and choices and extensive computer modeling with DFA Advisor Tom Orecchio, of Greenbaum & Orecchio, Inc.

In the chart below, **ASSET CLASS** is the type or category of financial securities in which you hope to invest. (See Section B for a complete definition.) The **PORTFOLIO ASSET ALLOCATION** is the percentage of your total savings you invest in that asset class. The **HISTORICAL RETURN** shows the performance, in percentage terms, by which investments in that asset class have grown, including dividends and capital appreciation—that is, the increase in price over time. **STANDARD DEVIATION** (see Section E4) is a statistical measure of the volatility or variability in the annual returns of each asset class. Finally, for asset classes for which price history is available from earlier than 1988,

LONGEST HISTORICAL RETURNS shows this long-run performance. Notice that while many of these asset classes have high standard deviations, the portfolio overall does not, since price swings in these less-correlated asset classes tend to cancel each other out.

BUYING DFA FUNDS

While it is simple enough to buy Vanguard or other funds through a brokerage account, fund supermarket, or directly from the firms, it is not so easy for individuals to purchase DFA Funds. These funds are designed for institutional investors that are generally sophisticated asset allocators. As a result, DFA will not sell directly to individuals. Nonetheless, DFA funds are available to individuals if you purchase them through a DFA-approved financial advisor.

Reading this chapter and a good basic investing book such as *Four Pillars of Investing* by William Bernstein should give you the knowledge you need to be able to be taken on as a client by a DFA-certified advisor at a reasonable fee, as he or she will not need to spend serious time educating you on asset allocation. Shop around. And if you cannot find an advisor who will work on a fee-only basis or offer you reasonable fees, then skip DFA and stick with other fund options. Your advisor should be able to provide reasonable customization of Rational Investing for your situation.

You can find advisors at: www.dfaus.com/find_advisor.

Rational Investing Portfolio Asset Allocations, Historical Returns, Standard Deviation

Asset Classes	Portfolio Asset Allocation	Historical Return 1988-2004 **	Historical Standard Deviation**	Longest Historical Return++
U.S. Large Stocks - Value Tilt ++	12%	13%	15.65%	11.7%
U.S. Small Stocks - Value Tilt ++	8.5%	17%	18.73%	14.7%
International Large Stocks	5%	4.19%	16.25%	13%
International Small Stocks	10%	4.73%	17.97%	16%
Emerging Market Stocks	6.5%	9.61%	26.59%	14%
ST Corporate Bonds /Money Market	4%	7.25%	2.59%	3.7%
U.S. Government Bonds—Long	4%	9.44%	7.89%	5.4%
Medium-Term U.S. Bonds	10%	7.78%	4.44%	7.3%
Medium-Term International Bonds	12%	7.95%	7.50%	
GNMA Bonds	5%	7.91%	3.92%	8.88%
High Yield Bonds	4%	8.06%	7.96%	
Oil and Gas	3%	12.66%	15.25%	
Market Neutral Hedge Fund	2%	11.19%	4.59%	
Commodities	4%	7.85%	22.02%	12.24%
Commercial Real Estate	5%	11.95%	14.23%	16.5%
Venture Capital/Private Equity	5%	14.17%	18.48%	11.87%
	100%			

** *Source: Wilson International*

++ *Sources: DFA Matrix Book 2004, U.S. Equity Series 1928-present, Vanguard, Cambridge Associates Venture Index, Goldman Sachs Commodities Index*

b. Portfolio performance

The table shows annual performance since 1988 of the Rational Investing Portfolio versus the S&P 500 and a 60/40 blend of the S&P 500 and one-month U.S. Treasury Bills. By measuring the Rational Investing Portfolio against standard benchmarks such as these, investors can get a clear understanding of the benefit to be gained in terms of the kinder ride due to reduced volatility by going through the effort to get invested in the full portfolio. Note that the portfolio did not get swept up into the hype of the 1990s stock boom, but neither did it get crushed in the popping bubble. Very few years in the last 16 had negative returns—and even subtracting fees, those down years would have limited the worst years to just negative 1%. Although the S&P 500 had a higher return, someone holding 100% stock faces a gut-wrenching ride unsuitable for early retirees.

In addition to compound annual return (the rate by which the portfolio grew each year, on average) and standard deviation, two additional standard measures of portfolio performance are listed here, beta and alpha. Beta measures the riskiness of a portfolio compared to the overall market of large U.S. stocks. Alpha, considered the holy grail of asset managers, measures the percentage by which the portfolio outperformed the U.S. stock market on a risk-adjusted basis. By both of these measures, the Rational Investing Portfolio performs quite well.

Rational Investing Portfolio: Annual Performance

Year	Rational Investing Portfolio	S&P 500	60% S&P 500, 40% 1-month T Bill
1989	18.01	31.5	22.26
1990	-0.47	-3.2	1.2
1991	19.09	30.5	20.54
1992	5.05	7.7	6.02
1993	17.68	10	7.16
1994	2.57	1.3	2.34
1995	18.25	37.4	24.68
1996	12.79	23.1	15.94
1997	4.85	33.4	22.16
1998	2.07	28.6	19.12
1999	17	21	14.48
2000	2.65	−9.1	−3.1
2001	−0.2	−11.9	−5.62
2002	3.23	−22.1	−12.62
2003	28.44	28.7	17.62
2004	16.18	10.88	7.128
Compound Annual Growth Rate Return	9.5%	12.1%	9.14%
Average Standard Deviation	7.98%	15.7%	9.66%
Beta	.28%	1%	.6%
Alpha	6.10%	0%	3.0%

c. Fund choices

The following is by no means a complete list of all suitable funds for investing in the major asset classes, and you may well have some you own or prefer. However, the funds included here, mostly from DFA and Vanguard, would be strong contenders on any short list. For the less traditional asset classes, the funds listed here are a pretty good guide to the choices available. If you are particularly drawn to certain asset classes, such as real estate or private equity, you may choose to skip mutual funds and instead create a portfolio more heavily favoring direct investments.

Exchange Traded Funds or ETFs (see Section B), offer useful alternatives to mutual funds, and can generally be found for indexes and even sub-indexes. Sometimes, as in the case of Vanguard's VIPERs, ETFs will have even lower fees than the corresponding mutual fund and some tax benefits. If you do use ETFs, though, be aware that you will face both the annual management fees as well as any brokerage commissions incurred to buy and sell them initially and each time you rebalance.

Asset Classes and Funds for the Rational Investing Portfolio

Asset Class	Funds (* Denotes index fund)	Notes
EQUITIES		
U.S. Large 12%	VG S&P 500 Index (VFINX)	Growth
	VG HealthCare Fund (VGHCX)	70% U.S., 30% Foreign
	VG Windsor II Value (VWNFX)	Active Value Fund
	VG Selected Value (VASVX)	50% Large, 50% Small
	DFA High BtM (DFBMX)*	Enhanced Value Index
	VG Value Index Fund (VIVAX)*	Value Index
U.S. Small 8.5%	VG Tax-Managed Small (VTMSX)*	Blend of Value and Growth
	VG Small Value Index (VISVX)*	Value
	DFA U.S. Small (DFSCX)*	U.S. Micro Cap; smallest 4%
	DFA U.S. Small Value (DFSVX)*	Value among smallest 8%
International Large 5%	VG Pacific Index (VPACX)*	Mostly Japan and Australia
	VG Europe Index (VEURX)*	Europe Index
	VG Tax-Managed Int'l (VTMGX)	Blend of Value and Growth
	DFA International Large (DFALX))	Blend, Active Mgmt., low fee
	DFA International Value (DFIVX))	Value, strong compared to DFALX
International Small 10%	VG International Explorer (VINEX)	Growth
	DFA International Small (DFISX)	Blend
	DFA International Small Value (DISVX)	Value
Emerging Market 6.5%	VG Emerging Market Index* (VEIEX)	Index
	Emerging Markets Small (DEMSX)	Small Blend
	Emerging Markets Value (DFEVX)	Value
	DFA Emerging Markets Large (DFEMX)	Large Blend

Asset Classes and Funds for the Rational Investing Portfolio, cont.

Asset Class	Funds (* Denotes index fund)	Notes
BONDS		
Short Term/Money Market 4%	VG Short-Term Corporate (VFSTX)	Some credit and interest risk
	VG Prime Money (VMMXX)	Money Market
	VG State Tax-Exempt Money Market	If available for your state
Treasuries 4%	U.S. Treasury I-Bonds	Up to $30,000 per year
	VG TIPS Fund (VIPSX)	Hold in IRA
	U.S. Treasuries	Buy through Treasury Direct
U.S. Medium-Term 10%	VG Intermediate Bond Index (VBIIX)*	Corporate
	VG Convertible Securities (VCVSX)	Currently Closed
	CDs	Pentagon Federal, Bank rate
International 12%	Fidelity New Markets (FNMIX)	Emerging Markets Debt
	DFA Global 2-Year Bond (DFGFX)	Hedged for U.S.D. investors
	Pimco Foreign Bond (PFUIX)	5-Year Unhedged
	Pimco Foreign Bond (PFORX)	5-Year Hedged
	T. Rowe Price Int'l Bond (RPIBX)*	Tracks MS International Bond Index
	American Century Int'l Bond (BEGBX) *	Tracks Index, partially hedged
	Pimco Emerging Markets Bond (PEBIX)	Lower fee than FNMIX
High Yield 4%	VG High Yield Corporate (VWEHX)	Higher quality than index
GNMA 5%	VG GNMA Fund (VFIIX)	

Asset Classes and Funds for the Rational Investing Portfolio cont.

Asset Class	Funds (* Denotes index fund)	Notes
OTHER		
Oil & Gas 3%	VG Energy Fund (VGENX)	Broad energy equities
	FBR Natural Gas Index (GASFX)*	For natural gas
	Private investments in oil & gas partnerships	
Market Neutral 2%	Oppenheimer-Tremont Hedge Fund Index *	
	Rydex Sphinx	Details in Appendix 1
	Other Hedge Fund Investments	Beware high fees in all cases
	Master Limited Partnerships	See Appendix 1 for examples
Commodities 4%	Oppenheimer Real Assets (QRAAX)*	1.4% fee, overweight Oil
	Pimco Commodities Fund (PCRIX)*	Preferred
	Physical holdings of Gold	Unique timberland REIT
	Plum Creek Timber REIT (PCL)	
Real Estate 5%	VG REIT Index (VGSIX) *	
	International REITs such as (EGLRX)	
	Private investments in rental property	
Private Equity 5%	Direct illiquid investments in companies and new ventures	See Appendix 1 for details and examples
	Limited partnership shares in private equity pools/funds	
	Ownership or silent partner in franchise	
	Investments in illiquid public companies	
	Business Development Corporations	

RESOURCES

FOR MORE ON INDEXING AND ASSET ALLOCATION. The defining source of information on long-term buy-and-hold low-fee indexing is by Vanguard's founder, John C. Bogle, *Common Sense on Mutual Funds* (Wiley). Bogle also has a website loaded with numerous speeches and articles at www.vanguard.com/bogle_site/bogle_home.html.

A couple of books by William J. Bernstein are particularly useful at explaining asset allocation, the crucial contribution to Rational Investing. The first book is newer and more accessible:

- *The Four Pillars of Investing, Lessons for Building a Winning Portfolio* (McGraw-Hill), and
- *The Intelligent Asset Allocator* (McGraw-Hill).

Larry E. Swedroe has also written well on the benefits of low-fee index investing, though with less focus on the power of asset allocation. Titles include:

- *The Only Guide to a Winning Investment Strategy You'll Ever Need: The Way Smart Money Invests Today* (St. Martin's Press), and
- *What Wall Street Doesn't Want You to Know: How You Can Build Real Wealth Investing in Index Funds* (Truman Talley Books).

Another good online source of information is the Library section of DFA's website. It contains a particularly good article by David Booth, CEO and Chief Investment Officer of DFA, on their approach, which supports and enables the Rational Investing Portfolio to reach nuanced exposure to key international and value asset classes and tilts. You can find it at http://library.dfaus.com/articles/index_enhanced_funds.

You might also enjoy reading Scott Burns's columns online from the *Dallas Morning News*, www.dallasnews.com. Burns is a diehard indexer and asset allocator and makes it all clear to his loyal readers.

A good book covering the finance/investing aspects of early retirement with detailed discussion of portfolios similar to the Rational Investing Portfolio is: *Retire Early, Sleep Well*, by Steven R. Davis (Grote Publishing),

Finally, Frank Armstrong gives a good, easy-to-grasp explanation of the benefits of adding more asset classes to a portfolio in his book: *The Informed Investor* (Amacom).

JUST DO IT

You may be convinced that something like the Rational Investing Portfolio is right for you, but find that actually buying and selling to bring your portfolio into alignment with these asset allocations can be gut-wrenching. My advice is, in the words of Nike, Just Do It.

However, if you have large unrealized capital gains in a taxable account, back-end loads on some of your existing funds, or simply an emotional aversion to change, then take it slowly. You might want to move just half of the allocation in on Day 1, then move the balance in six or 12 months later or even over a period of several years.

In particular, if a new asset class has been moving up dramatically for some time, it is hard to want to buy into it feeling you may be at the top. A true indexer would say it doesn't matter, but for most investors, these are understandable, valid concerns. Take it in stages. The point is that you get there eventually at a speed at which you feel comfortable.

G. Rebalancing Your Portfolio

Rebalancing your portfolio is a crucial component of keeping a Rational Investing Portfolio on autopilot. By selling some of your winners each year to scoop up more shares of the losers, you bring your portfolio back to its target allocation while ensuring that you buy low and sell high.

Using this simple method helps you overcome the natural but self-defeating human urge to keep riding a winning investment while dumping a losing one or trading too frequently. Studies have shown that rebalancing once a year is about the right frequency. Rebalancing more frequently is usually counterproductive, and while letting assets run two or even three years between rebalancing appears to increase returns, it probably means taking on more risk than most early retirees would want.

1. How Rebalancing Works

Assume you hold a simple portfolio of four funds and put 2% in a money market that you spend down over the course of the year. Each fund then grows or falls in value during the year.

Here is the basic method for rebalancing. (See Section G2 for an illustration.)

Start with the new portfolio balance, which you compute from your year-end brokerage statements or perhaps have online if all your various financial holdings are held in a central report such as that provided by Vanguard.

EXAMPLE: Your portfolio has grown from $1,000,000 to $1,055,000.

Next, use the target percentage holdings for each asset class to calculate the dollar holdings you need.

EXAMPLE: If you need 40% of your assets in U.S. Bonds, then 40% of $1,055,000 will be $422,000. This is the amount of U.S. Bonds you should hold for the coming year.

Finally, buy or sell each asset class in sufficient quantity to bring it to its new target amount.

EXAMPLE: If your U.S. Bonds holdings were today worth only $350,000, then you would need to purchase $72,000 additional U.S. Bonds to bring its allocation up to the correct level: $350,000 + $72,000 = $422,000.

2. A Look at a Rebalanced Portfolio

Below is a chart showing the steps and final figures for the rebalancing in a simplified example of five asset classes represented by five funds (Column 1) held in proportion to their target allocation (Column 2).

In January 2005, the fund was balanced with holdings matching target allocations (Column 3), but over the course of 2005, some asset classes increased in value while others declined (Column 4). Overall, the portfolio rose in value from $1 million to $1,055,000, necessitating the calculation of new target holding amounts (Column 5). The difference between actual holdings at the

Rebalancing Calculations

1	2	3	4	5	6
Asset	Target Allocation %	January 2005 Value of Holdings	January 2006 Value of Holdings	Target Holdings % of 2006 Portfolio Value	Holdings Over (+) or Under (−)
U.S. Stock Fund	33%	330,000	400,000	348,150	51,850
U.S. Bond Fund	40%	400,000	350,000	422,000	−72,000
Foreign Stock Fund	15%	150,000	225,000	158,250	66,750
REIT Fund	10%	100,000	80,000	105,500	−25,500
Money Market	2%	20,000	0	21,100	−21,100
TOTAL	100%	1,000,000	1,055,000	1,055,000	0

beginning of 2006 and the new target holding (Column 5 minus Column 4) gives the amount by which each asset class is overallocated or underallocated, the amount needed to sell or purchase to bring the portfolio back into balance.

Note that in this example, not all the asset classes will have declined; some will have gone up, too. For example, the U.S. Stock Fund holdings, which should make up 33% of the overall portfolio, should now be 33% of $1,055,000 or $348,150 for the coming year. Since the value of the U.S. Stock Fund on January 1, 2006 has actually grown to $400,000, the holding is overallocated by $400,000 – $348,150, or $51,850.

By selling $51,850 worth of the U.S. Stock Fund, money is available not only to restock the money market fund, but also to buy either REIT Funds or U.S. Bond Funds, both of which are underallocated. The buying and selling in these four funds and the money market will net out to zero—meaning you will have raised just enough selling winners to purchase the additional amounts you need in the funds that have declined.

Note that putting about 2% in the money market fund at the beginning of each year, when added to the 2% to 2.5% that most portfolios produce in interest and dividends over the course of the year, together neatly fund annual spending needs at a 4% to 4.5% safe withdrawal level. ●

Take 4% Forever

Withdrawing money safely from your portfolio each year is the engine that makes early retirement viable for those without pensions. This chapter leads you through the two steps required to get that engine going.

First, choose a safe *rate* at which to withdraw—the percentage you can take each year from your portfolio. Second, withdraw in keeping with the safe *method*—making annual adjustments, depending on need and portfolio performance, that increase your odds of financial survival over the long run. When combined with Rational Investing recommendations (see Chapter 3, Section E), the Safe Withdrawal

> *Don't kill the goose laying the golden eggs.*
> —AESOP'S COLLECTED FABLES, CA. 550 BC

Rate and Safe Withdrawal Method explained here should offer an optimal blend of current income and long-run financial viability, whatever the future brings.

A. The Safe Withdrawal Rate

The idea of saving enough capital to live off the interest has long tickled the human imagination, well before Aesop wrote the tale of "The Goose Who Laid the Golden Eggs" about 2,500 years ago. At heart, Safe Withdrawal Rates are your golden eggs; stick to a safe level and your portfolio will stay whole and keep producing through thick and thin.

Getting this withdrawal number right should be the goal of any retiree. Take too much and you could deplete your portfolio long before your death. Take too little and you could be denying yourself many things along the way and leaving far more than you intended to your survivors.

The Safe Withdrawal Rate is the percentage, around 4%, that you can safely draw out of a diversified portfolio each year to use as living expenses. But despite its statistically rigorous foundations, it will always be an estimate because you can never know the two most crucial components with certainty: how your portfolio will fare in the years ahead and how long you will live. However, by making realistic assumptions: that you will achieve average returns, markets will continue to perform as they have historically, and that you will live somewhat longer than average—you can come up with a reasonable and safe rate.

Traditional retirees—for example, those 75 years old and collecting Social Security—can think about spending at a faster rate. Depending on luck, health care, and genes, they may have little need for living expenses past age 105.

However, an early-retiree, at least until he or she also reaches 75 or so, cannot think about spending down a portfolio too quickly; the math simply doesn't work. The excessive annual withdrawals when combined with a few bad years in the market can rapidly, even irreversibly, corrode a portfolio's value and leave you broke or severely diminished. If you need to withdraw from your portfolio for more than 20 or 30 years, you will need to keep to more conservative levels.

The recommendation here—a 4% Safe Withdrawal Rate, taken according to a Safe Withdrawal Method—is tested against historical data to deliver a portfolio that maintains its inflation-adjusted value over the long haul. Keeping the inflation-adjusted value of your principal intact is the goal. It means every year leaves you in the same relative position as the year before; since you are not eating into your principal, you can continue this way, in theory, forever. Those who need to have their portfolios support them through several decades into a potentially long old age, with few pension benefits or inheritances on the horizon, will generally need this level of safety. And since the Safe Withdrawal Rate would have ensured successful portfolio survival in nearly any past market period, there is a good chance you'll do even better than the minimum if financial markets perform even moderately well in the future.

Yet even if you happen to retire into a bleak period for financial markets, there is some wiggle room in the 4% Rule, though not a lot. While a 3.5% annual withdrawal rate should leave your portfolio essentially unassailable for life, a 4.5% annual withdrawal, with specific precautionary modifications, has historically done well about 90% of the time in the long run, though it will often fall short over ten and 20-year timeframes. Models illustrate slightly different results based on different assumptions—for instance, how you adjust spending each year for inflation and whether you are comfortable depleting the portfolio by the end of 30 years rather than attempting to keep the inflation-adjusted value of your capital intact.

Cases can be made and studies found that show how higher withdrawal rates can be achieved, with a bit of fancy footwork and less certainty, over long periods. You can probably even take up to 5% a year if the markets are kind during the early years of your retirement or if you only withdraw that amount in years you really need it.

But by the time you pump your withdrawal rate up over 5%, the models all start to become remarkably consistent. Rather than having a 90% chance of maintaining real portfolio value, the rate quickly drops to 75%. And by the time the withdrawal rate hits 6%, it becomes a coin toss as to whether your Golden Years will be spent in a less than golden condition.

BENDING THE RULES

If you are truly determined to leap into early semi-retirement, even without the financial resources recommended here, then do it. In the worst case, you can cut your spending down considerably. Or after a few years of sabbatical and a chance to refocus, you can go back to full-time work.

Overall, the benefits may outweigh any inconveniences. As long as you know the right way to plan for early semi-retirement, you can decide whether and how much you want to bend the rules.

For example, if you know you have a finite number of years ahead of you, or that an adequate pension or inheritance is waiting around the corner, or if you simply need to spend more, then you can eat into your capital, take more risks, and hope for the best. As each year unfolds, you'll be able to gauge whether you are comfortably holding ground or uncomfortably depleting your resources. And you'll be able to make any changes you feel you need to along the way.

B. The Safe Withdrawal Method

Markets can and do enter protracted times of depressed results, such as the years from 1965 to 1982 when real returns from U.S. stock prices were negative across the entire period. Anyone unlucky enough to retire in 1965 faced years of tough sledding. Those who took out more than their Safe Withdrawal Rates each year generally ran their portfolios down to zero in less than 25 years.

Even if you are not unlucky enough to begin your early retirement in the next equivalent of 1965, the actual order of good years and bad years during your retirement can make a big difference to your financial results. If the early years are fat, you'll build up plenty of reserves that will compound and give you ample breathing room in the years ahead. But if the initial years of your retirement are lean ones, you may spend a decade or more just getting back to square one: the amount you started with on the first day of your retirement.

In either case, the right Safe Withdrawal Method will increase your odds of success and may just make the difference between staying happily early semi-retired, then moving on to a traditional retirement—or having to return to full-time work when you reach your 60s or 70s.

1. The Old Method

The first generation of Safe Withdrawal Rate research was simple and a surprising number of research studies still use it. But they are of little value to early retirees, designed as they were for traditional retirees with 20 or at most 30 years left to live, perhaps already ill or disabled and collecting a pension.

The old method was as follows: On the first day of your retirement, determine a single percentage of your portfolio and use it to set a dollar amount for spending in your first year of retirement, then adjust it each year for inflation.

> **EXAMPLE:** You decide on a 4% Safe Withdrawal Rate for your $500,000 portfolio, taking $20,000 for living expenses during the first year. Each year, you adjust the withdrawal up for inflation. If the inflation rate were 5% in the first year, you would give yourself $20,000 + 5%, or $21,000 to spend the second year. If inflation dropped to 3% the following year, you would adjust up the $21,000 by 3%, to $21,630 the third year, and so on.

In this way, you could ostensibly enjoy the same standard of living throughout your retirement. The models typically used plain vanilla portfolio allocations and a "safe" withdrawal rate was one that historically would not have left retirees broke after 20 or 30 years.

Unfortunately, this method runs a high risk of depleting a portfolio during a period of below-average returns and above-average inflation. Such a period occurred in the 1970s and it could happen again. Early retirees won't derive any comfort from taking an inflation-adjusted annual withdrawal while their portfolios are being decimated.

THE NEW GENERATION OF RESEARCH

State of the art Safe Withdrawal research has moved on from these early studies, providing more realistic and adaptable methods that match the way retirees really want to invest and spend over the long run.

The new studies are evolving on three fronts in which they:

- seek to keep portfolio values intact, as opposed to running them down to zero over time and span 40 or even 50 years as opposed to the traditional 20-year or 30-year timeframes

- use not only historical data, but also "Monte Carlo" simulations—that is, those generating thousands of plausible scenarios to test, and

- create objective rules for varying the amount withdrawn each year in an effort to either improve portfolio survival or safely draw out more money. Examples include finding ways to raise withdrawals following years of strong market performance or spending slightly more during the early years of retirement.

Along the way, retirees and their planners have developed a set of best practices for portfolio asset allocation and rebalancing that are gradually being incorporated into new Safe Withdrawal studies. Fortunately, these techniques show improvements in portfolio safety over the long run or small increases in the Safe Withdrawal Rate. (See Appendix 2 for a summary of a number of research studies.)

2. The New Method

Clearly, early retirees need a better Safe Withdrawal Method than those aimed at traditional retirees.

Specifically, early retirees need a method that:

- models a broadly diversified, low-volatility portfolio
- maintains the portfolio's inflation-adjusted value over time, and
- allows reasonable adjustments to annual spending—more in good years, less in bad years.

Since no study modeled these early retiree needs satisfactorily, I have worked with a leading researcher in the field to create a suitable one. (See Section D for full descriptions of the research and results.) The method is simple yet powerful—and requires just a few commonsense steps to implement.

a. Use a diversified portfolio

Start with a diversified, low-volatility portfolio, similar to the Rational Investing portfolio. (See Chapter 3, Section E.) The portfolio should be overweight in value, small, and international assets—and ideally will include other less-correlated asset classes such as commodities, energy, and real estate to further dampen volatility.

b. Withdraw up to 4% each year

Each year, calculate 4% of the portfolio's value; you can go to 4.5% with slightly diminished safety. That is the amount you can safely withdraw or spend that year. Spend only as much of this amount as you need, leaving any extra in the portfolio. In bad years, you can give yourself a break by using The 95% Rule, discussed below.

c. In tough times, use The 95% Rule

Market conditions zig and zag, and your portfolio's value will go up and down each year. Following a bad year, you won't want to have to lower your annual spending in lockstep. It could be a difficult adjustment for anyone to lower spending by 20%, for instance, from one year to the next. Yet you should make some sort of accommodation to the reality of your falling portfolio or risk overwithdrawing during a string of bad years.

To address this issue, look to The 95% Rule, which states you can withdraw at least 95% of the amount you took the previous year, even though that may exceed your normal Safe Withdrawal Rate. Taking 95% of last year's withdrawal allows you to keep your spending relatively stable, even through a string of bad years. You'll tighten your belt somewhat, but you won't turn your world upside down. Maybe you can cut back on vacations and some other extras or do a bit more part-time work for more income. The adjustments should be manageable and your portfolio will still have a high probability of recovering its full value when markets return to better days.

d. Rebalance the portfolio annually

Rebalancing the portfolio is the buying and selling you do for each asset class to bring its weight in your portfolio back to the target. (See Chapter 3, Section G for details.)

e. Keep up with inflation

Success is defined as keeping the portfolio value intact, in real inflation-adjusted terms, over time. In other words, if you started early retirement with a million dollar portfolio in 2000, annual inflation adjustments would have required that it be worth about $1,140,000 by the end of 2005 just to have maintained the original buying power or real value. With an average inflation rate of 3%, your $1 million portfolio will need to grow to $2,090,000 in 25 years just to keep pace with inflation.

WHERE THE OLD WAYS WENT WRONG

The old models typically set an annual withdrawal amount in the first year of retirement, then adjusted that amount up for inflation during every year of retirement thereafter, regardless of portfolio performance. But early retirees consistently reported that, in bad times, they found it painful to give themselves the full inflation-adjusted raises that the old models prescribe. And following good times, they wanted some sort of reward in the form of elevated spending that the old models didn't allow.

What is more, those who go through the effort to implement the Rational Investing Portfolio for its good returns and low volatility find it frustrating to have to adhere to a Safe Withdrawal Rate diminished by the more-volatile and lower-performing portfolios typically used in the old models. These portfolios usually consisted of a simple blend of the S&P 500 with Long-Term U.S. Treasuries, or sometimes even just 100% S&P 500.

Finally, by defining success as keeping up with inflation over the long run, the Rational Investing Method gives early retirees much stronger assurance that the portfolio will support annual withdrawals across what may turn out to be decades of market ups and downs.

C. Data and Results

Most early retirees admit to feeling some initial fear or uncertainty about dipping into their savings and living off an annual withdrawal. And for many, seeing more details of the supporting studies and methods behind the Safe Withdrawal Rate will help assuage those uncomfortable feelings. This section includes that documentation—allowing you to build the foundation to understand why this method works and is safe over both near and long terms, through up and down markets.

FAST FORWARD

FOR THOSE NOT INTERESTED IN THE FACTS BEHIND THE FIGURES. If you're not concerned about learning more about the studies and methods supporting the Safe Withdrawal Method—or want to save that reading for later—skip ahead to Section D, which explains the nitty-gritty of putting the Safe Withdrawal Method into practice.

Because of the lack of long-term international market data, the studies in this section use portfolios that contain the closest possible approximation of the Rational Investing portfolio, including value and small-tilts, using only U.S. securities, as indicated below.

Composition of the Rational Investing Portfolio Proxy (50% Stocks, 50% Bonds)

S&P 500	11%
U.S. Large Value	9%
U.S. Small Value	9%
U.S. Small	10%
U.S. Micro Cap	11%
Intermediate Government Bonds	18%
Cash	2%
Long-Term Corporate Bonds	30%

1. Testing a Specific 30-Year Period

To understand the benefits of the Safe Withdrawal Method, start by comparing it to a traditional withdrawal method. For this, it is useful to look at a study published by William Bernstein in his book, *The Intelligent Asset Allocator.* To show the risks of the old withdrawal methods, Bernstein used traditional portfolios with varying percentages of stocks and bonds while the initial withdrawal amount was boosted annually to keep up with inflation. The results for a particularly bad period, 1965 to 1994, are dramatic.

From 1965 to 1994, traditional inflation-adjusted withdrawals at 5% of the initial portfolio value completely depleted the portfolio within 25 years—whether it consisted of all stocks, all bonds, or any combination of the two.

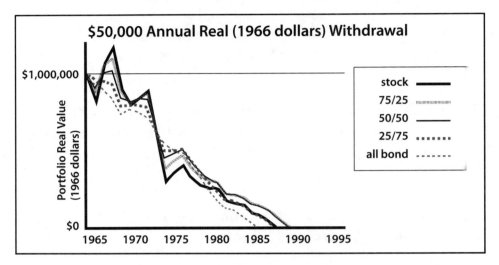

At a 4% initial withdrawal, the portfolios with at least 50% stocks survived, but only at a much depleted final value. The 50% stocks/50% bonds portfolio, for instance, was worth less than half of its starting value in 30 years.

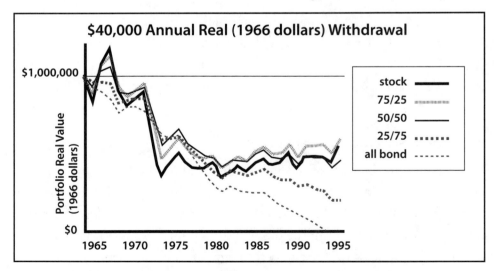

From The Intelligent Asset Allocator, *by William J. Bernstein (McGraw-Hill) © 2001 reproduced with permission of the McGraw Hill Companies.*

On the other hand, the Rational Investing Portfolio and the Safe Withdrawal Method with a 4% withdrawal rate survived these same years quite well, ending with a final value of $1.41 million in inflation-adjusted dollars, well above the $1 million starting value 30 years before.

An early retiree following this method would not have received automatic inflation adjustments to annual withdrawals and during the 1970s that would have meant some belt-tightening. However, this is the type of manageable adjustment that early semi-retirees generally are willing to make. In any case, The 95% Rule, allowing the withdrawal of at least 95% of the previous year's withdrawal and modeled in these results, would have softened the impact of falling stock and bond values. (See Section B2c for more on The 95% Rule.) During six of the years in the 1965-1994 period, an individual following this rule would have found it kicked in, and produced withdrawals higher than the normal 4%, sometimes going over 5%.

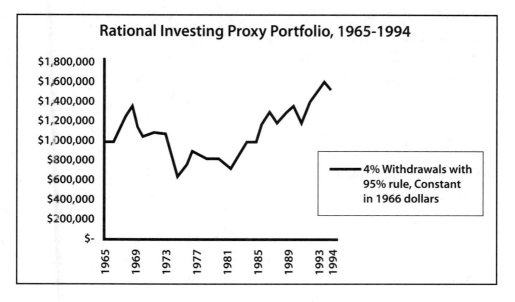

PLANNING TO LIVE TO AGE 105

No models, especially those based on historical data, can truly look out much more than 40 years into the future. If you plan to live 60 or more years, you may feel that the 40-year studies are insufficient.

Yet there is good news: The Safe Withdrawal Method keeps a portfolio's inflation-adjusted value intact over time. That means that 40 years from now, your portfolio in constant dollars should be at least as big as it is today. Getting that portfolio to last an additional 20 or 25 years should then be easy, even spending down its principal value if need be in your final years.

In principle, this portfolio should survive in perpetuity and be handed to your survivors—unless you develop a taste for very fast cars or space travel when you hit age 100.

It may be reassuring to note that foundations, which usually explicitly seek to exist in perpetuity, keep their annual portfolio withdrawals used to fund grants and disbursements to this same 4% to 5% range. They also invest along the same lines as the Rational Investing portfolio.

2. Testing Against Historical Data

Keith Marbach, of Zunna.com, has developed software for the new generation of Safe Withdrawal Rate researchers attempting to model conditions that more closely reflect the way retirees and early-retirees actually want to manage their long-term portfolios and withdrawals. Marbach and I developed enhancements to his previously published work to statistically test the Safe Withdrawal Method for Early Retirees. Our detailed look at a single 30-year period produced the results in the previous section. But it is essential to examine all possible historical periods to determine whether a Safe Withdrawal Method has merit.

To do that, we turned to a prized resource published by Dimensional Fund Advisors (*DFA Matrix Book 2005*) containing 78 years of returns from U.S.

stocks and bonds, including small and value stocks. We also used the corresponding Medium Term U.S. Treasury Bond series from Ibbotson Associates. The research methodology uses rolling historical observations—that is, it takes a first 30-year series, for instance, from 1927-1956; a second series from 1928-1957; and so forth for as many complete ten-year, 20-year, 30-year, or 40-year timeframes as history will allow. The portfolio value was recalculated to reflect each year's inflation, market results, and withdrawals.

This test of the Safe Withdrawal Method:

- used a portfolio similar to the Rational Investing portfolio with small and value tilts
- used different withdrawal rates in two separate studies: a basic study in which the Safe Withdrawal Rate is withdrawn as a simple percentage each year and another using The 95% Rule to soften the impact of falling markets on retiree withdrawals that year
- defined success as keeping the value of the portfolio intact on an inflation-adjusted basis over the targeted ten-year, 20-year, 30-year, or 40-year period, and
- assumed annual rebalancing of the portfolio. (See Chapter 3, Section G.)

As a separate benchmark to evaluate the benefit gained over time from using the Rational Investing portfolio, with its small and value tilts, we tested the identical basic withdrawal method against a portfolio consisting of 50% S&P 500 and 50% Medium Term U.S. Treasury bonds.

The data supports three important conclusions discussed below.

a. Sustainable withdrawal rate

A Safe Withdrawal Rate between 4% and 4.5% is sustainable from portfolios following the Safe Withdrawal Method.

To understand how the data support this point, look at the column below labeled 4%. The first number indicates that during 82.6% of the ten-year periods in market history, portfolios subjected to the annual 4% withdrawal ended with real values as least as big as when they started. Likewise, during every single 40-

year period (100%) indicated at the bottom of the column, portfolios ended up at least as big as their starting values in inflation-adjusted terms.

Success in Preserving Real Portfolio Value Over Ten, 20, 30, or 40 Years at Selected Annual Withdrawal Rates, Using The 95% Rule, Rational Investing Proxy Portfolio, 1927-2004

Timeframe	Rate					
	2%	2.5%	3%	3.5%	4%	4.5%
10 years	89.9%	87%	85.5%	82.6%	82.6%	79.7%
20 years	100%	98.3%	96.6%	89.8%	81.4%	75.3%
30 years	100%	100%	100%	100%	95.9%	91.8%
40 years	100%	100%	100%	100%	100%	97.4%

Timeframe	Rate					
	5%	5.5%	6%	6.5%	7%	7.5%
10 years	76.8%	68.1%	62.3%	53.6%	43.5%	36.2%
20 years	69.5%	55.9%	44.1%	33.9%	27.1%	20.3%
30 years	71.4%	42.9%	30.6%	14.3%	8.2%	4.1%
40 years	79.5%	59%	12.8%	5.1%	0%	0%

Source: Calculations Performed by Zunna.com using WATS Simulator

At the 4.5% withdrawal level, success rates are somewhat smaller across the board, reflecting the greater risk to portfolio survival from withdrawing more money each year. For the handful of 30-year and 40-year cases in which historical portfolio values fell short, further analysis showed that they did so by an average of just about 10%—meaning that the portfolio was still quite robust, but had fallen to about 90% of its original value, when adjusted for inflation. Clearly, this is a far cry from portfolio failure in the traditional studies in which failure is defined as running out of money entirely.

The figure below shows the same data in graphical form, dramatically showing how withdrawal rates above 4.5% rapidly decrease the chance that the portfolio will keep up its inflation-adjusted value over time. By the time an early retiree is withdrawing at 6.5% per year, the data show essentially no chance that the portfolio will keep its value over the long run.

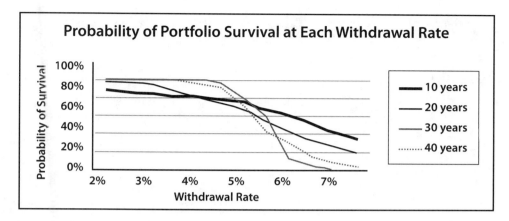

It seems reasonable to conclude that over longer periods, sticking to a maximum 4.3% rate of withdrawal and applying The 95% Rule during down years will give a very high probability of maintaining real portfolio value—in a way that is easy to live with and easy to stick to over the long run.

b. Minimal cost to The 95% Rule

Compare the columns in the chart below to see the impact of The 95% Rule. When an early retiree cushions the impact of falling markets by holding withdrawals to no less than 95% of the previous year's spending, there appear to be minimal negative repercussions.

The first column applies The 95% Rule, as above. The second column uses the standard method of holding withdrawals strictly to their applicable percentage each year. Success rates for The 95% Rule case are overall the same or slightly lower. At 4% withdrawals, for instance, there is about a 2% falloff in success rates at the 20-year level, from 83.1% to 81.4%, though none of the other time periods showed any falloff in success rates. For 4.5% withdrawal rates, the impact is more noticeable, with 2% to 3% falloffs in success rates at 20-year, 30-year, and 40-year levels.

For the target of 4.3% withdrawal level, assume that success rates would fall by a few percent in about half the cases going forward, a modest drop in security for the much-needed additional income during poor market conditions.

Likelihood of Maintaining Real Value at Different Withdrawal Rates With and Without The 95% Rule Withdrawals as Percent of Rational Investing Portfolio Each Year, Annual Rebalancing, 1927-2004

Rate	2%		2.5%		3%		3.5%	
Timeframe	95% Rule	Standard	95% Rule	Standard	95% Rule	Standard	95% Rule	Standard
10 years	89.9%	89.9%	87%	87%	85.5%	87%	82.6%	82.6%
20 years	100%	100%	98.3%	100%	96.6%	96.6%	89.8%	91.5%
30 years	100%	100%	100%	100%	100%	100%	100%	100%
40 years	100%	100%	100%	100%	100%	100%	100%	100%

Rate	4%		4.5%		5%		5.5%	
Timeframe	95% Rule	Standard	95% Rule	Standard	95% Rule	Standard	95% Rule	Standard
10 years	82.6%	82.6%	79.7%	79.7%	76.8%	76.8%	68.1%	71%
20 years	81.4%	83.1%	76.3%	79.7%	69.5%	71.2%	55.9%	62.7%
30 years	95.9%	95.9%	91.8%	93.9%	71.4%	81.6%	42.9%	55.1%
40 years	100%	100%	97.4%	100%	79.5%	79.5%	59%	64.1%

Rate	6%		6.5%		7%		7.5%	
Timeframe	95% Rule	Standard	95% Rule	Standard	95% Rule	Standard	95% Rule	Standard
10 years	62.3%	66.7%	53.6%	59.4%	43.5%	50.7%	36.2%	43.5%
20 years	44.1%	40.2%	33.9%	37.3%	27.1%	33.9%	20.3%	23.7%
30 years	30.6%	38.8%	14.3%	22.4%	8.2%	10.2%	4.1%	6.1%
40 years	12.8%	30.8%	5.1%	15.4%	0%	5.10%	0%	0%

Source: Calculations Performed by Zunna.com using WATS Simulator

c. Diversified portfolios survive best

A simple portfolio of stocks and bonds will not survive nearly as well as a diversified portfolio with small and value tilts.

To see the impact of the portfolio composition on success rates, compare the columns in the chart below. The first is the success rate data already seen above for the standard withdrawals from the Rational Investing Portfolio, (labeled RIP). The second column in each case models standard withdrawals from a generic portfolio blend of 50% S&P 500 and 50% medium-term U.S. treasuries.

Comparing these columns shows that success rates for withdrawals from the 4.5% column for the Rational Investing Portfolio reasonably match those from the 2.5% column for the generic 50% S&P 500/50% medium term treasuries portfolio. For instance, the 20-year and 40-year results at 4.5% withdrawals for the Rational Investing Portfolio are quite close to those in the 2.5% withdrawal level in the generic portfolio. Likewise, the 4% column for the Rational Investing Portfolio is roughly in line with the 2% column for the generic portfolio.

In other words, without changing anything else, investors can expect to increase their Safe Withdrawal Rate by as much as 2% a year simply by adopting something like the less-risky, diversified, value and small-tilted Rational Investing Portfolio.

Likelihood of Maintaining Real Value for Rational Investing Portfolio v. 50% S&P 500/50% Medium Term U.S. Treasuries, Withdrawals as Percent of Portfolio Each Year, No 95% Rule, Annual Rebalancing, 1927-2004

Rate	2%		2.5%		3%		3.5%	
Timeframe	RIP	50%/50%	RIP	50%/50%	RIP	50%/50%	RIP	50%/50%
10 years	89.9%	76.12%	87%	76.12%	87%	74.63%	82.6%	67.16%
20 years	100%	87.72%	100%	80.7%	96.6%	71.93%	91.5%	64.91%
30 years	100%	100%	100%	100%	100%	97.87%	100%	80.85%
40 years	100%	100%	100%	100%	100%	91.89%	100%	78.38%

Rate	4%		4.5%		5%		5.5%	
Timeframe	RIP	50%/50%	RIP	50%/50%	RIP	50%/50%	RIP	50%/50%
10 years	82.6%	62.69%	79.7%	59.7%	76.8%	52.24%	71%	40.3%
20 years	83.1%	61.4%	79.7%	45.61%	71.2%	38.6%	62.7%	28.07%
30 years	95.9%	55.32%	93.9%	34.04%	81.6%	19.15%	55.1%	6.38%
40 years	100%	64.86%	100%	45.95%	79.5%	10.81%	64.1%	0%

Rate	6%		6.5%		7%		7.5%	
Timeframe	RIP	50%/50%	RIP	50%/50%	RIP	50%/50%	RIP	50%/50%
10 years	66.7%	35.82%	59.4%	34.33%	50.7%	26.87%	43.5%	23.88%
20 years	49.2%	17.50%	37.3%	12.28%	33.9%	10.53%	23.7%	7.02%
30 years	38.8%	0%	22.4%	0%	10.2%	0%	6.1%	0%
40 years	30.8%	0%	15.4%	0%	5.1%	0%	0%	0%

Source: Calculations Performed by Zunna.com using WATS Simulator

DON'T BELIEVE IN ANY MODEL 100%

As Safe Withdrawal Rate studies all depend on predicting and preparing for an unknowable future, one respected researcher, William Bernstein, has written that attempting to achieve probabilistic success rates greater than 80% is probably not worth the effort. While readily admitting that conforming to a basic Safe Withdrawal Method is wise, he feels that too many early retirees put too much faith in getting to 100% secure withdrawal levels, reducing their consumption levels below where they could be—believing that this makes their finances 100% safe for life.

He notes that all manner of human and natural disasters have erupted on earth, unpredictably, through history. Dialing your Safe Withdrawal Rate down low enough to achieve perfect safety on the financial front hasn't ensured perfect safety overall. It just means that upsets to your plans will probably come from unanticipated personal or societal-level disasters, some of which might even have financial implications. While a super-low withdrawal rate clearly makes your financial life safer, you'll never achieve 100% safety. Better, he argues, to spend a bit more freely along the way and accept the fact that life will always carry unpredictable risks.

D. Using the Safe Withdrawal Method

Every month and year, you'll be making practical decisions to implement your safe withdrawals—taking cash that has accumulated, possibly selling securities to generate more cash, and rebalancing your portfolio. This section explains how.

Your 4% safe withdrawal will generally be funded by a combination of interest, dividends, capital gains distributions, and possibly the sale of appreciated assets.

Since some retirees are accustomed to living only from interest and dividend income, using capital gains or selling appreciated securities to raise additional cash may seem counterintuitive. But because the Rational Investing Portfolio is designed to generate solid long-term returns with low volatility, it does not generate a large amount of interest and dividends; it focuses instead on generating capital gains. Realizing a small amount of these gains at favorable long-term capital gains tax rates is not spending principal, but simply harvesting some portion of those gains while leaving the overall portfolio intact and growing.

As a practical matter, take the following steps to raise cash from your portfolio.

1. Use a Money Market Account

By requesting that the distributions from interest, dividends, and mutual fund capital gains be transferred to a money market account—as opposed to being reinvested in the fund they were distributed from—you can easily accumulate a source of ready cash for your safe withdrawals. This could amount to 2.5% or more a year, depending on the amount of capital gains distributions. These distributions are typically taxable, but as an early semi-retiree, the tax you pay is likely to be quite low.

2. Raise Additional Amounts During Rebalancing

If your needs for annual spending exceed the money automatically distributed out of your mutual funds, then you can raise a needed slug of additional cash each year when you rebalance your portfolio. Rebalancing is the annual tune-up you give your portfolio—selling some of the winners, using those funds to buy more of the down asset classes. (See Chapter 3, Section G for details of portfolio rebalancing.)

To raise cash during rebalancing, for instance, include the money market or cash component in your rebalancing plans with the needed amount or percent allocated to it. When the exercise is done, you will have the needed amount of cash in your money market account, and the portfolio will be balanced.

For instance, many early retirees opt to put 2% of the portfolio into a money market account during their annual rebalancing, which they spend during the year. They then count on the interests, dividends, and capital gains distributions trickling in throughout the year to fund the balance of their annual living expenses.

3. Sell Securities If Necessary

If you get stuck and need to raise additional cash during the year, sell the most appreciated equities first, if there are any. If not, sell fixed income assets, starting with the shortest maturities—probably short-term corporate bond or other short-maturity bond funds if you own them; otherwise, medium term bonds.

> **EXAMPLE:** Eva was $3,000 short in August, with not enough cash coming in from her dividends to pay for a bulge in expenses from her summer vacation. She looked through her holdings and found that the international small cap value funds were up over 30% that year, the asset class with the most price appreciation in her portfolio. Eva sold $3,000 worth of those funds for cash. At the end of the quarter, when some bond funds paid their dividends, she paid the $3,000 back to her portfolio, purchasing some additional REITs that happened to have been beaten down that year. ●

CHAPTER FIVE

Stop Worrying About Taxes

Given the complexity and ever-changing nature of the U.S. Tax Code, it's always risky to make blanket statements about taxes. But one safe assumption is that people moving from traditional wage-earning to early retirement will find themselves in an altered, more favorable tax landscape.

This chapter explains the tax benefits many early retirees can expect—along with tax strategies that can be beneficial to all. To bring the point home, you'll find tax return information from two families who spend

> *"Let the good times roll…"*
> —THE CARS

the same amount each year: one with essentially no savings living from annual salary income; the other early semi-retired living substantially off savings.

EXPERT

FOR TARGETED TAX PLANNING ADVICE. This chapter illustrates how an early semi-retiree's tax situation may be different from the more familiar tax situation of a salary earner. For specific advice on your tax preparation and financial decision-making, however, consult a retirement tax planning guide such as Ken Morris's *Wall Street Journal Guide to Planning Your Financial Future: The Easy to Read Guide to Planning for Retirement*, find online help at www.fairmark.com and www.smartmoney.com/tax, or speak with an experienced tax advisor.

> **ASSUAGING GUILT**
>
> Some people feel uncomfortable when they think of reducing their income taxes or paying none at all. It almost seems un-American—or just plain wrong.
>
> Rest assured that what you will learn in this chapter is completely legal and straightforward, a natural result of aligning your financial life with the terrain of the U.S. Tax Code.
>
> Early retirees can use their newfound free time and tax savings to contribute in other ways: by donating to charities—or, for those who feel very strongly, by making voluntary contributions to reduce the national debt.

A. Tax Benefits for Early Retirees

Get ready to smile. If you are about to become an early semi-retiree in America, your tax situation will likely be brighter than you imagined. The reason is simple: The highest tax rates are on salary income. And so it follows that since you already earned much of your money through working wages, you already paid most of your tax dues. Now, you will earn moderate amounts of dividends, interest, and capital gains—and perhaps a bit of self-employment income. Shelter this amalgam with various ordinary deductions and exemptions and you'll likely be left with a very manageable tax bill.

The bottom line is that most people who retire early can expect to pay combined annual state and federal taxes of between 0% and .3% of the value of their portfolios—or between 0% and 5% of their annual spending or budget as opposed to the 40% or so that high-earning salaried workers customarily pay.

After years of conditioning, discounting $1,000 earned down to about $600 in the hand, you may be in for a pleasant surprise when you look anew at your retirement budgeting. Realizing that $1,000 earned in early retirement is probably worth a weightier $950 in the hand means that those planning for early retirement are often a lot closer to their financial goals than they imagined.

> **TIP**
>
> **UNLEARNING OLD TAX-AVOIDANCE STRATEGIES.** Since you'll be in such a low tax bracket, some common tax-minimizing strategies may no longer help. For instance, it may no longer make sense to have a mortgage for its tax-deductible interest. You might also want to skip municipal bonds and take a higher yielding taxable bond instead. And after-tax contributions to a Roth IRA may be even more advantageous than pre-tax contributions to a regular IRA. The reason: You have such low taxable income that additional deductions give little or no added benefit.

B. Strategies for Lowering Taxes

This chapter describes the five main strategies early semi-retirees can use to significantly lower taxes—both immediately and over the long run.

By following these strategies, you are working to win the tax game on several fronts. First, you are simply earning less taxable income and deferring the taxation of the bulk of your portfolio gains, perhaps indefinitely. Next, if you need work income, you can earn it by being self-employed, which will offer you more ways to shield what you earn from taxation each year. And finally, by simply operating at lower dollar levels, you qualify for the lowest tax brackets and rates.

1. Receive Less Salary or Earned Income

Most early retirees, even those who continue to work part time, have left their high salary-earning days behind and rely instead on interest, dividends, and capital gains for much of their income. These types of passive income all come with a lower tax bite than does salary income.

Those earning salary, wages, or other income not only have state and federal income taxes to pay, which can be at combined marginal rates over 40%, but they also have growing Medicare, FICA, and Social Security taxes taken directly out of their paychecks. In 2005, that amounted to 7.65% on up to $90,000 of income or $6,885 per year, with no limit on the income subject to Medicare taxes, which are now running at 2.9%. Together, these taxes add up.

By comparison, dividends and capital gains are taxed at just 15% and possibly even at 5% if adjusted taxable income was below $59,400 for a couple, or $29,700 for an individual in 2005. Interest income is taxed at the same rates as earned income, but by keeping many of those interest-bearing investments in an IRA or in I-bonds, that tax can be deferred or eliminated. What interest income remains can generally be offset by credits, exemptions, and deductions. And what remains after that can still be taxed mostly or completely in the lowest 10% or 15% income tax brackets. (See Section B4 for more on these attractive brackets.)

WHAT TO PUT IN AN IRA

With the current 10% income tax rate and 5% capital gains tax rate, some of the traditional wisdom about what to put in an IRA is starting to look dated.

Traditionally, people put fixed income or high-dividend assets in IRAs to shelter them from higher tax rates. Although putting fixed income in the IRA still makes sense, if you are paying little or no income tax, you might consider an alternative strategy: Place your actively-managed mutual funds in the IRA, as these funds will tend to throw off a bit more capital gains distributions—possibly even some short-term capital gains—that could cause an unplanned tax bite.

Also, keep any Treasury Inflation-Protected Securities (TIPS) or TIPS funds in your IRA to avoid annual tax on the principal adjustment, which is a unique feature of these bonds.

2. Don't Pay Tax on All Portfolio Gains

Your portfolio should earn 8% or 9% a year on average, through a combination of interest, dividends, and capital appreciation in the funds you own. Because you only withdraw at a Safe Withdrawal Rate of about 4%, however, the rest stays in your portfolio, keeping you abreast of inflation and preserving your capital in the event of a protracted downturn. (See Chapter 4, Section A for a detailed discussion of Safe Withdrawal Rates.) As long as you don't sell these appreciating assets, you don't pay tax on them.

Of course, you do need income just to live, so you will realize some taxable gains. Start with the interest, dividends, and capital gains thrown off by your funds, which are taxed in the year you receive them. Along with any income you earn from part-time work, this may give you all the cash you need to meet your needs each year.

> **TIP**
>
> **CONSIDERING ETFS.** Note that Exchange Traded Funds, known as ETFs, do not throw off capital gains from investor redemptions, which can make them more tax-efficient during rising markets. They do, however, generate taxable interest and dividends.

If you need more cash, sell a few shares of winning investments during your annual rebalancing or as needed. (See Chapter 3, Section G for details on rebalancing.) This will also generate some taxable capital gains, but they won't be too high since much of the proceeds of your sale will simply be a return of principal, which is not taxable at all. Everything else stays right where it is, year after year, growing as unrealized capital gains and comprising the bulk of your annual portfolio growth. Eventually, if you stick to your plan and the economy does well, half or more of your portfolio may be in the form of these appreciated assets. Since you don't pay capital gains taxes until you sell, any taxes on these unrealized capital gains are continuously deferred, possibly through your entire lifetime.

Buy and hold investors, such as those following the Rational Investing Method (outlined in Chapter 3, Section E), have a big tax advantage over those who trade more frequently. Using the annual rebalancing method (described in Chapter 3, Section G), will ensure that only a relatively small amount of your assets are actually sold each year, which keeps taxable gains to a minimum.

Investors who don't follow an asset allocation method with systematic rebalancing tend to churn through their portfolios—changing course frequently, buying and selling as the mood strikes. As a result, they pay taxes on much of their gains each year. Sometimes they even pay capital gains taxes on investments in which they have lost money. Paying taxes frequently instead of deferring them means you have less capital working for you, less chance to let compounding add to long-run returns.

3. Cash in on Self-Employment

If you work for yourself after retiring early, you'll be able to deduct many of the expenses connected to your verifiable efforts to earn part-time income. Your self-employment can take many forms, from the simplest sole proprietorship requiring no special legal paperwork to formally structured corporations you establish and register with your state. Either way, deductions are numerous when compared to traditional salary earners.

For example, salary earners can't deduct the cost of driving to work, but if you are self-employed, you can deduct the cost of driving to see a client. Home office deductions can be problematic for a salary earner who commutes to a regular office, but you can deduct the expenses of your home office easily and legitimately. While you cannot take your spouse to lunch and deduct it, you can work on an investment idea with a friend over lunch and deduct that. As you slowly move toward working on things you are passionate about and earning income from them, you'll find more of your expenses are legitimate business deductions, which help shelter the business income you earn from income taxes.

TAX BREAKS FOR THE SELF-EMPLOYED

There are several deductions commonly available to the self-employed. They include:

HOME OFFICES—out-of-pocket expenses for equipment and supplies, but also a fair percentage of rent and utilities based on the square footage of your office; the office or portion of a room must be used solely for business purposes

USE OF CAR FOR BUSINESS—currently set at 40.5¢ per mile

BUSINESS TRAVEL—100% deductible for small businesses

MEALS AND ENTERTAINMENT—deductible at 50% if solely for a business purpose

HEALTH INSURANCE—personal premiums up to the limit of your profits from self-employment, and

YOUR CHILDREN WHO WORK FOR YOU—if they do identifiable, documented work for pay. If the business is a sole proprietorship, there will be no self-employment tax, either. And your children's earned income may also be used to fund a Roth IRA. (See Section B5.)

RESOURCES

FOR MORE INFORMATION ON TAXING MATTERS. For a detailed discussion of how to find and take advantage of all appropriate tax deductions for your business, see *Deduct It! Lower Your Small Business Taxes,* and *Working for Yourself, Law & Taxes for Independent Contractors, Freelancers & Consultants*, by Stephen Fishman (Nolo). And if you own rental property, see *Every Landlord's Tax Deduction Guide*, also by Stephen Fishman (Nolo).

4. Consider Whether Low Tax Brackets Apply

The U.S. Tax Code has special tax brackets for those earning low incomes. Early semi-retirees often find they qualify for these low rates: 10% or 15% federal tax on earned or interest income and 5% for dividends or capital gains.

Most early semi-retirees will also have significant itemized deductions from local property taxes, charitable donations, health insurance, and expenses from part-time businesses along with the personal exemption for each family member.

Here's how tax breaks work for them: These deductions and exemptions, with some twists, can be set against the income from various sources to calculate taxable income. After these deductions, many early retirees can keep taxable income—that is, the amount listed in the tax tables on which tax must be paid—in the lowest 10% bracket. For 2005, this amount was $14,600 per year for married couples filing jointly; $7,300 for those filing singly.

Even if this is not possible, additional taxable income up to $59,400 per year for married couples or $29,700 for singles was taxed in 2005, for example, at the still-attractive 15% federal income tax rate, with the added benefit of qualifying any dividend or capital gains for the special low 5% tax rate. Normally, capital gains (the amount by which your investments have appreciated) and qualifying dividends (payments made to stockholders) are taxed at 15%. So the 5% rate represents a significant savings.

WARNING

(!) BE AWARE OF THE ALTERNATIVE MINIMUM TAX. Generally, Alternative Minimum Tax or AMT kicks in when a taxpayer has regular earned income sheltered by large amounts of deductions and exemptions—for instance, from high state and local taxes or lots of children. AMT does not apply against normal capital gains, interest, and dividend income. As a result, AMT will probably not be a problem for most early retirees. Nonetheless, no blanket statements are safe when it comes to taxes, so you'll need to check your specific situation with a tax expert to be sure.

A NEWLY ER-FRIENDLY PROVISION IN THE TAX CODE

In 2005, a feature was added to the federal tax code that may help early retirees. Instead of deducting the *income* taxes you pay to your state, you can opt instead to deduct the *sales* taxes you pay each year on all the items and services you purchase.

Since all retirees tend to have low state income tax bills but continue to consume things and pay sales tax, deducting sales tax is likely to result in a bigger deduction. If you pay for most items with a debit card or check, it is fairly simple to produce documentation backing up the amount you spent during the year and either calculate the sales tax you paid on it, or use the table provided by the IRS in Publication 600, *Optional Sales Tax Tables*, available at www.irs.gov/pub/irs-pdf/p600.pdf.

However, since your federal taxes are already low, there is a chance that this deduction will not actually lower your taxes much. Still it can't hurt—especially in a year when taxable income might have spiked due to a Roth conversion or large capital gains distributions.

5. Convert to a Roth

A Roth IRA is a special type of IRA to which you contribute with after-tax dollars—often a terrific tool for long-term savers. It is generally better to have money in a Roth than a regular IRA or SEP IRA. The big attraction of a Roth is that not only does your money compound tax-free as in any IRA, but you will never need to pay taxes on the distributions. Nor will you need to wrestle with required minimum distributions (RMDs) inherent in the traditional IRA or SEP IRA, which can push you into higher tax brackets as you age. Indeed, you can designate beneficiaries for your Roth, who will receive the funds outside of probate at your death and can then withdraw them tax-free over the course of their own lifetimes.

Although you can always contribute into any IRA each year in which you have earned income (up to $4,000 a year in 2005; $4,500 if you are over age 50), the big win comes when you convert large amounts of your traditional IRA or 401(k) to a Roth.

Despite their many long-run benefits, however, the process of converting these other tax-advantaged savings devices into a Roth requires some pain and finesse, since you must pay the accrued income tax on the IRA at once instead of when you would have normally withdrawn the funds. Early retirees have a built-in advantage: Because their annual incomes are low and they are in low tax brackets, they can convert regular IRA funds into Roth IRA funds at a reasonable cost, ideally by paying federal income taxes on the converted amount of 15% or less. Note that regular IRAs can only be converted to Roth IRAs by those who have less than $100,000 of taxable income in a given year—a problem for many salary earners, but generally quite feasible for early retirees.

Here is how to get your IRA money into your Roth in the most advantageous way. Around November, make an effort to determine your expected income and tax for the year. Assuming you are within the low federal tax brackets of 10% or 15%, determine how much additional income you could realize without exceeding the limit of that bracket. Then file the necessary forms with your financial institution to convert traditional IRA money into the Roth in sufficient amounts to sop up any unused portions of these lower brackets.

By paying a modest amount of tax now, you are moving funds into the truly tax-free Roth, allowing this money to start compounding tax-free earlier. This means you pay tax now on a smaller total than you will in the future—and unlike a regular IRA with forced distributions, you will never need to withdraw the funds unless that is your wish.

Continue to add to the Roth IRAs or regular IRAs for eventual conversion into the Roth in any year you have earned income—a requirement for contributing new funds to any IRA. All in all, the tax advantages and compounding power of the Roth, for those who can plan long-term and especially for those who don't intend to spend the money, can be quite attractive.

FUNDING YOUR CHILDREN'S RETIREMENT WITH ROTHS

Now that you understand the potential allure of a Roth IRA, imagine being able to fund them for your children, too.

Putting maximum contributions in each year—currently $4,000 and increasing to $5,000 by 2008—over the later years of their childhood can pay large benefits down the road.

Assume the contributions continue for ten years and the money compounds at 8.5% a year until the child is 60 years old. This will produce an IRA worth over $2 million—or an estimated $550,000 in today's dollars, well over ten times the amount contributed.

Your child can then withdraw this money free of taxes during retirement, or even pass it on to his or her children. If you expect to live a long time, this can be a nice legacy to give your children who might otherwise have to wait well into their own retirements to get any money from your estate after your death. Note that if you were to give the children the same amounts in a taxable account or a regular IRA, the eventual value would be only about half as much.

To fund a Roth IRA, the child must earn income. The arrangement will work best if the children earn money from outside sources, or if you have your own profitable sole proprietorship and can verify that your child is doing work for the company—perhaps running products to customers, cleaning the office, maintaining a website and computers, or performing clerical work and mailings; allowances and payments for normal household chores won't count. To make the most of the benefit, aim to have the child earn at least $4,000 a year. Those earnings will be shielded from income tax, due to the child's standard deduction. These earnings, essentially all after-tax earned income, can then be used for an annual contribution to a Roth IRA. Not only does this arrangement allow you to teach your children the values of hard work and deferred gratification, it can help you plant the seeds for their retirement. And if they feel the need for some spending money after all that work and forced saving, you can always give them a little extra allowance to make up for it.

C. Comparing Taxes: Salary Earners and Early Semi-Retirees

This section looks at the taxes for a traditional salary-earning couple and an early semi-retired couple. Imagine these two families live in the same neighborhood, with similar homes, cars, and most other annual expenses. Of course, they are not directly comparable despite their other similarities, since one has a portfolio worth nearly $1 million and a fully paid home; while the other has a mortgage and no savings.

Still, a comparison highlights how different income types are taxed in the U.S and the specific ways early retirees can benefit taxwise. In particular, you will quickly see how the early retirees pay far less in taxes even though both couples have the same income and spending each year. By the way, as incomes go up, the tax savings grow even greater for tax-wise early semi-retirees living substantially from portfolio earnings.

1. An Early Semi-Retired Couple

Bill and Mary, early semi-retired with two children under 17, live in their fully-paid home. These prodigious savers have a financial portfolio of around $930,000 and tap it for $42,000 per year, or 4.5%, at the upper limit of the range of Safe Withdrawal Rates.

WORK INCOME. Bill and Mary earn $16,000 of self-employment income, $11,000 of which is net income to them as it is offset by $5,000 of business expenses they can deduct—including the costs of business materials and supplies, travel, promotion, and home office expenses.

EXPENSES. In addition to regular monthly and annual expenses totaling $45,000 a year, the couple also sets aside an additional $8,000 a year for expenses that early retirees must account for but may not necessarily see or spend every year: fund management fees ($4,500), home painting ($1,000), and car depreciation expenses ($2,500). (See Chapter 2, Section C for a discussion of these expenses.) In other words, although they only need $45,000 of cash to meet their normal expenses each year, Bill and Mary have correctly calculated their annual budget at $53,000 to account for annual fund fees, plus a new car and home paint job every ten years or so.

DEDUCTIONS. In addition to $5,000 of work expenses offsetting work income, Bill and Mary are assumed to have the following average deductible expenses and exemptions:

Property taxes	$3,000
Charitable donations	$2,000
Health insurance	$8,000
Exemptions (4 people)	$12,000
SEP IRA contribution	$2,045 (the maximum they are allowed)

However, they find it more advantageous to take the standard deduction, which is $10,000 in 2005, instead of itemizing their property tax and charitable donations. Health insurance is deductible directly for self-employed, as is one half of their self employment tax, an additional $777. The family also qualifies for up to $2,000 of Child Tax Credit.

PORTFOLIO DISTRIBUTIONS. Bill and Mary's portfolio produces roughly $25,000 in taxable distributions (2.6%). Overall, their portfolio is assumed to yield 3.5% in interest and dividends, but much of it is earned in their tax-advantaged accounts and not taxed or immediately available for spending in early retirement. Although this yield is slightly high for 2005, it reflects the possibility of higher interest rates and taxes on portfolio yields in the next few years.

Interest	$15,000
Qualified dividends	$10,000

Since $25,000 of distributions and $11,000 of work income are not enough to meet their need for $45,000 a year in cash for spending, Bill and Mary supplement it with the sale of $9,000 worth of appreciated assets during their annual rebalancing. These assets are assumed to have doubled in price and thus contain $4,500 of capital gains.

INCOME EARNED—ALL TAXABLE SOURCES. Summing up the income side, Bill and Mary have the following taxable income:

Source	Amount	Tax Rates
Interest	$15,000	10%
Dividends	$10,000	5%
Capital gains	$ 4,500	5%
Work income	$11,000	10% + 15.3% self-employment tax
Total	**$40,500**	

Note, however, that due to all their deductions and exemptions, discussed in the Deductions section above, and up to $2,000 from the Child Tax Credit, Bill and Mary will not end up paying any federal tax except for their self-employment tax. All their annual income—and up to an additional $17,500 more in dividends or capital gains—will be entirely sheltered with effective tax rates of zero.

TAXES DUE. Bill and Mary's total tax bill was:

Federal income tax	$0
Social Security/Medicare	$1,554 (self-employment tax)
State tax (New York)	$1,098
TOTAL tax on income:	$2,652
Percent of annual spending:	5% (2,652/53,000)
Percent of portfolio	.28% (2,652/930,000)

Note that the income tax Bill and Mary are paying is all self-employment tax (Social Security and Medicare payments on sole proprietorships, calculated and returned with IRS Form 1040), and state income tax, with their home state of New York being among the highest. They pay no tax at all on their portfolio distributions and withdrawals, and could contribute more money into a regular IRA than into their SEP IRA, though there would be no additional tax benefit. They could also contribute additional income into their Roth IRAs.

2. A Working Couple

Ralph and Alice are tax-paying salary earners saving at the national average of about .3% a year, who have few taxable financial earnings from their savings. Their tax situation will reflect income entirely generated as salary. They have two children and earn and spend $53,000 each year. Ralph has health insurance through his employer and the couple has a mortgage.

WORK INCOME. Ralph and Alice earned an annual salary of $53,000, which includes Ralph's full-time earnings as an ambulance driver and Alice's flex-time job as a dental assistant.

EXPENSES. The couple has expenditures, including taxes, of $53,000. Their spending levels for monthly and annual expenditures are closely comparable to the early retirees, Bill and Mary. For instance, the income taxes Ralph and Alice pay are close to the portfolio management fees that Bill and Mary set aside, leaving them with the same money to spend each year.

DEDUCTIONS. Ralph's job comes with health insurance benefits for the whole family, but the couple also has a mortgage interest deduction of $8,000 per year, which again keeps the families' discretionary spending on a par. Their deductions are as follows:

Property taxes	$3,000
Charitable donations	$2,000
Mortgage interest	$8,000
Exemptions (four people)	$12,000

Ralph and Alice also qualify for $2,000 of Child Tax Credit.

PORTFOLIO DISTRIBUTIONS. Ralph and Alice, if they saved at the average U.S. rate, would have just $120 a year of savings, and therefore no material taxes on interest, dividends, or capital gains.

INCOME EARNED—ALL TAXABLE SOURCES. Ralph and Alice have the following taxable income:

Source	Amount	Tax Rate
Salary	$53,000	10% and 15%

TAXES DUE: Ralph and Alice owe the following taxes:

Federal income tax	$1,211
Social Security/Medicare	$4,055
State tax (New York)	$1,735
TOTAL tax on income:	$7,001
Percent of annual income:	13.2%

3. Comparing and Contrasting

Comparing the two tax situations shows that not only has the early semi-retiree couple avoided all federal income tax, but their Social Security and Medicare taxes, due to their small part-time income, are also much smaller.

All together, the salary earners Ralph and Alice pay about $4,349 per year more in income taxes. This tax savings, an additional 8.3% of gross income, represents the benefits available to semi-retirees.

Note also that had they a larger portfolio or bigger spending needs, early retirees Bill and Mary could have received up to $17,500 more dividend and capital gains distributions each year without paying any more tax. ●

CHAPTER SIX

Do Anything You Want, But Do Something

In early retirement, "work" can be defined as the things you enjoy doing that keep your brain fresh, activities in which people count on you, or in which you develop and exercise your unique skills. And of course, if you need extra income, work can provide the means to obtain it.

If you're considering retiring early but haven't made the leap yet, you may already know exactly what you'll be doing to fill those hours: a part-time job with a former employer or a long-dreamed-for calling as a missionary or parachuting instructor. You may plan to take classes or earn a new degree to recast yourself into a new avocation.

> *Do not do what you hate.*
>
> —JESUS, IN VERSE 6 OF THE SECRET GOSPEL OF THOMAS, FIRST DISCOVERED AT NAG HAMMADI, UPPER EGYPT, 1945

Or it may all be a haze for you now—a vague hope that there is something out there with your name on it.

This chapter focuses on concrete examples of how early retirees solve the Work Question while still maintaining a balance with plenty of time for leisure and exploration. It also focuses on the types of part-time paid work possibilities that suit early semi-retirees especially well.

A Why Work?

"Do anything you want, as long as you do something." The legendary billionaire, Warren Buffet, reportedly doled out these words of advice along with a reasonable but by no means excessive gift to his children when they were young adults. Buffet believes that a key to a long and happy life is to have work that connects you to others, challenges you on many levels, and makes a difference. He felt that giving his children large cushions of cash would have undermined their incentives to find meaningful work.

And the advice is good enough to survive as one of the basic rules for early retirees. Even if you are one of the lucky ones who does not actually need income from work, you still must heed the heart of this message. You'll need to find some way to stay engaged and challenged, paid or unpaid, or your early retirement will almost surely sour into something surprisingly awkward and unpleasant. Killing time, relaxing, and being self-indulgent are terrific in the right doses—and great ways to recuperate from years of stressful overwork. But they alone won't get you what you really seek: a long, happy, fulfilling life.

During the early months of early retirement, just keeping your cars inspected and registered, your sidewalks clear of snow, and the plumbing leaks fixed may feel like enough responsibility. But at some point, you'll want to stretch out to something more challenging. Of course, you won't want to create the same old hyper-ambitious overachievement on a lower payscale; you have chosen to retire early to make time and opportunities for a more comfortably paced schedule.

But to be complete, you'll need something to do that engages and challenges you. Chosen well, this work can support and even enhance the changes you are making in your life, as well as provide needed income. If you still need more convincing, heed the scientists who are now quite clear that keeping the brain engaged is one of the few known ways to fend off Alzheimer's disease, and mental health professionals who stress that depression lurks in wait for those who cut themselves off from meaningful interaction with others.

B. How Work Evolves in Early Semi-Retirement

Many early retirees start off by feeling that they could never downshift their lifestyles. While certainly a valid sentiment, it reflects thinking anchored in the past. If, over time, they are fortunate enough to find work activities they feel are genuinely better and more fun than what they have been doing it becomes much easier to make any necessary financial tradeoffs to stay engaged in them. For example, a formerly hard-charging professional, after discovering her inner artist, might realize she would prefer to move to a pleasant inexpensive rural retreat than to go back to work to pay the taxes on an expensive home in the suburbs.

Early retirees typically go through many stages—seeking to find the right blend of paid or unpaid work activities and striking a balance based on need, appetite for challenge, and opportunity.

1. More Money in Less Time

Most early semi-retirees initially seek work that produces the amount of money they need in the shortest possible time on the job. They have a strong desire for leisure after years of overwork and look at work in fairly utilitarian terms.

If you are in this stage, staying close to former employers or industry contacts where your network and skills are still strong will likely deliver the biggest payback and most opportunity for cutting back to a limited number of hours of work. Working just a day or two a week can feel very liberating and your early pension or safe withdrawal amount will still allow you to cover your expenses. You can spend the bulk of your free time exploring and relaxing, finding the joy in life again.

2. Cutting Ties to Past Work

During the next stage, the effects of the time spent relaxing and thinking start to appear, and many early retirees begin to drift away from their former work, finding it uninteresting or even toxic.

You may be at this stage if your work starts to seem out of step with your emerging self, which is becoming steeped in new possibilities. You may start to be drawn to new ways to make money, preferring something as pleasant as possible, often something that requires a challenging shift of gears. You may not mind working longer or earning less if you can truly enjoy what you do. In your still ample free time, you can dig more deeply into some personal interests—perhaps taking classes, earning certificates, or otherwise retooling yourself for a new field of work. You are starting to be guided in work choices by your intuition that speaks to core values and passions.

3. Being Paid for Doing What You Love

Those who become proficient in new areas of interest usually come to trust that there may be a way to earn some income through them, and gradually switch to seeking them.

If you are in this stage, you may notice that your relationship to money has begun to change. Perhaps your financial portfolio has grown while this process has been occurring, giving you a bit more breathing room. Yet even if you don't feel flush with cash, you may find your way to a new equilibrium in which income is still covering outlays, albeit reduced outlays. And you may begin to spend your days doing the activities that are not only meaningful to you, but in which you now have skills, contacts, credibility, and experience. From this base, you have truly begun to experience the promise of early semi-retirement.

With luck, over time, additional income-generating possibilities will arise in these emerging areas of interest. But income will have stopped being the defining driver in your thinking; now, you would rather do what you love and live within the income you can comfortably derive from it.

HEARING YOUR CALLING

Knowing what you might want to do as an avocation or second career often takes some doing.

Sometimes the things we would like are hidden in plain sight, since a part of us, conditioned by years of pragmatism, drapes a little "not going there" cloak over them.

In early retirement, you can afford to be impractical at last. For example, if you'd love to be a swimming instructor but hesitated about exploring the possibility in the past because the post pays too little, take a fresh, unbiased look and give it a try. You may later decide it isn't right, but you'll decide that from a position of knowledge, not reflex. And you'll then be free to try the next thing on your list of intended activities.

4. An Illustration of the Evolution

The figure below captures the interplay between practical considerations and dreams, allowing for the evolution that people and their financial lives often follow as they seek a balance between changing demands on time while finding a way toward an avocation, or true calling.

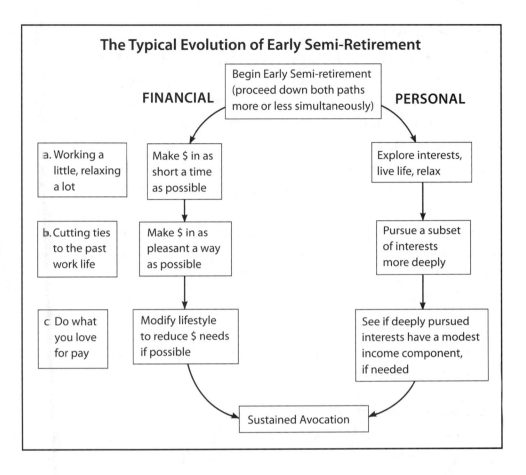

The Typical Evolution of Early Semi-Retirement

FINANCIAL — Begin Early Semi-retirement (proceed down both paths more or less simultaneously) — PERSONAL

a. Working a little, relaxing a lot

b. Cutting ties to the past work life

c. Do what you love for pay

Make $ in as short a time as possible

Make $ in as pleasant a way as possible

Modify lifestyle to reduce $ needs if possible

Explore interests, live life, relax

Pursue a subset of interests more deeply

See if deeply pursued interests have a modest income component, if needed

Sustained Avocation

C. Making the Shift

Maybe you've been able to finesse the financial part of early retirement—that is, with a pension or a safe withdrawal from your portfolio and a bit of work income, you can make the numbers come together. Or perhaps you have started early retirement and find that changed circumstances or your optimistic miscalculations now make it essential that you earn a bit to supplement each year. Or you might not need income at all, but have noticed the limits of going out to lunch and surfing the Internet for hours on end. Finding work that is satisfying and rewarding sounds great, but you aren't sure how to find it. Here's how to get started.

1. Have Patience

The process of finding satisfying work will almost surely take time, perhaps several years. In fact, you will likely continue throughout your lifetime collecting a kaleidoscope of interests, skills, commitments, income sources—wearing many hats through the years.

Keeping a sense of evolving and exploring will let you enjoy this quest much more than trying to nail everything down tight. Keep in mind that after longing to be a teacher, an artist, or a minister, you don't simply wake up one morning changed into one. And even though signing a paper will make you a landlord overnight, getting into the mindset of being an early retiree rehabbing homes, renting them out, or flipping them into the next deal is an evolution that requires slow and patient growth over years.

2. Decide How Much to Work

There are two broad approaches to finding satisfying work. Pick the one that feels right to you.

a. Limited work hours in your current career

In the first approach, typical among new early retirees who opt to stay near to their former profession and networks, you focus on the hours you would be comfortable working, the level of demands you could comfortably take on, the amount of flexibility in your schedule that you need to keep from feeling compromised by your work commitments. Think about building a blend of activities that provide the right amounts of work time, commitment, and expected income, while also offering variety and a chance to explore new opportunities.

> **EXAMPLE:** Erika was a lawyer in a large law firm for 22 years. Today, a few years into early semi-retirement, she teaches a college class as an adjunct professor, sits on a board of directors, and does a bit of consulting work with some old clients. Erika aims to keep her total weekly work time under 15 hours and likes the pace and freedom that comes with a blend of several smaller commitments as opposed to a single job.

EXAMPLE: Hugh retired early from a large private equity firm and soon after started a small partnership to invest in commercial real estate. He appreciates the chance to do deals with old colleagues—but especially appreciates being able to set and limit his own schedule. As a father of two young children he has decided he just won't go back to a 65-hour workweek, but will devote more time instead to the full range of family activities, from coaching and church to camping trips and crafts project during the years that his kids are growing up.

b. Finding new interests and roles

The second approach to finding satisfying work, best suited to those ready for bigger changes, is to let yourself be guided by one overarching question: What do I really care about doing, even if it doesn't involve financial rewards?

That gets you focused on new fields, new professions, perhaps new credentials or training, and a chance to create newfound passion and energy. This may naturally come as a second stage in the evolution of your work during early retirement. (See Section B2.) Or you may be ready to skip straight to it upon first leaving full-time work. (See Section D for more on converting an interest into a new career direction.)

EXAMPLE: Jim left a large Wall Street firm a few years ago with the goal of never working again. He quickly immersed himself in several nonprofit and volunteer pursuits and started a small fee-only financial planning practice. In time, however, he felt a desire for a more focused endeavor—and a prolonged dip in the stock market made him realize he would also be more comfortable with additional income. Jim became clear about his true work passion, which was to be involved in private secondary school education. As a first step, he has taken a part-time position working in the fundraising department of his alma mater and hopes to develop the necessary skills there to grow further, possibly becoming a headmaster there one day. Meanwhile, he is working in an exhilarating environment, raising funds for a cause he cares about, with people he enjoys and admires.

BEING 19 AGAIN

As you seek to discover what you want to do now that you don't have to work full time for a living, it might be helpful to picture yourself as a new undergraduate college student: You arrive on campus without a clue as to what you would like to be and spend the next four years—or maybe longer—exploring and discovering.

Bring that same sense of possibility to your life again. It will take some time to settle into the right thing, but as long as you are open and questing, you'll be well clear of the daytime TV or the online brokerage day-trading screens.

You may not end up sticking with any of your early ideas, but they will open your eyes to many ways you can earn the income you might need to supplement pension and investment earnings while feeling challenged and energized.

3. Take a Sabbatical

When first beginning early retirement, budget for and try to make a clean break: at least three months of unstructured and uncommitted time off leavened with a trip to Italy or a long-postponed raft trip down the Colorado River. You may even want to give yourself a whole year away from any work-like activities if you are leaving your old job feeling burned out and frazzled.

That time will allow you to reboot and start to clearly understand your true needs and interests and goals. Set a low bar: Nothing significant is going to happen, so you won't have to worry that things are quiet. Give yourself that initial delicious sabbatical—the feeling of playing hooky—that you have looked forward to for so long.

You don't have to travel far from home to get a respite, either. Have lunch with people you've wanted to see, read the books you've been meaning to read, rearrange the closet or workshop, fix the house, buy that boat. Get to know yourself again.

4. Start Back Slowly

You may worry that spending time away from the job will cause you to forget how to work. But rest assured that it is like riding a bicycle: Having been wired up to work your whole life, you won't forget how.

I spent my first six months of early retirement in a psychological state of detox. Picking up the phone made me cringe inside and I heaved a little internal sigh of relief if I had no new email messages. But eventually the feeling of dread passed and I was back on a normal footing. Several months of regular exercise, a slow pace, and healthy eating did the trick; it just took some time.

When you reach your own normal footing, you can start to think about work again. Perhaps you've been making plans to switch careers and you can get that back in motion.

> **RESOURCES**
>
> **FOR MORE HELP WITH NEW WORK OPTIONS.** If you are looking to start completely fresh in a new direction, there are plenty of workshops and fine books on starting a particular new business or advice on working in an established field.
>
> You may also want to consider consulting a career counselor who can put you through a battery of tests that might lend insight into your underlying aptitude or match with various lines of work.
>
> See *What Color is Your Parachute*, by Richard Nelson Bolles (Ten Speed Press), for additional tips on how to open your mind to new work possibilities.

D. Common Work Options for Early Retirees

Here are some of the most common approaches early semi-retirees take to finding paid work.

1. The Filler Job

This is the job you take on with the goal of making a modest amount of steady money in a comfortable, usually casual environment. Look for something part time connected to an area of interest, a favorite community activity, a hobby or service to which you feel drawn. Whether taking the slot as the weekend dockmaster at a nearby marina, starting golfers at the local golf course, or working in an independent bookstore, these are jobs that are meant to make you feel good and immersed in a world you love while picking up some extra cash.

Not to say there will never be any tension or problems to solve there; every workplace can have those. But the job can fill in the gap in your budget with plenty of flexibility and enjoyment—and allow you to go home without thinking about work.

> **EXAMPLE:** Petra works part time as the administrator at a community nature center. Her children attended environmental courses and camps at the center over the years, and when the opening became available when Petra was seeking some additional income, she was hired. The board appreciates having a mature "insider" in the position—and Petra finds the flexible, family-friendly atmosphere, in which she can work 20 hours a week with 12 weeks off each year, a good fit. She enjoys the low-stress work environment, surrounded by naturalists, animals, and young people.

> **EXAMPLE:** Phil landed a part-time job as a greeter at PNC Park, home of his favorite team, the Pittsburgh Pirates. He is free to watch the ball games, earns $12 an hour which mounts up to help cover his expenses, and gets to meet and assist fans attending the games. Best of all, he never feels guilty about watching a ball game now: He's at work.

2. The Avocation

An avocation can be defined as the work you might do even if you didn't get paid for it. As a rule, avocations don't pay much, which is why you might have pushed dreams of doing them aside in the past in favor of a better-paying career. Examples might include minister, martial arts instructor, model, pastry chef, or possibly something requiring a bit more of a financial investment, such as running a dive shop or antiques store.

> **EXAMPLE:** Don trained initially for life in the ministry but never felt comfortable there, embarking instead on a traditional banking and human resources career and working in management and outplacement counseling roles. After nearly 20 years, though, Don was feeling the limits of his corporate life, and while recovering from bypass surgery in his late 50s, decided to go back to the ministry. He now works full time as an executive pastor, putting his business skills to use organizing operations in a church with 16 full-time staff, and taking his turn preaching, performing weddings and all manner of other pastoral duties. "I have never been happier," Don enthuses, "but my circuitous route back to the ministry was the only way it could have ever worked for me."

Be aware, however, that some people who finally begin doing the job of their dreams find it is not all they had imagined from afar. Learning that a dream is actually a bad fit is generally a helpful step to uncovering what you are going to do with the rest of your life, so don't fight it or feel remorse. Move on to other things that draw you. At least with a basic safe withdrawal or pension underwriting the bulk of your annual expenses, you can afford to change work options without facing financial hardship.

> **EXAMPLE:** Jon left a ten-year investment banking career to begin his long-held passion of teaching high school math. But he found that aside from a handful of exceptions, most of the students seemed simply determined to shoot themselves in the foot and learn nothing, despite the teachers' heartfelt efforts to help. Frustrated and saddened, Jon switched to a new public experimental school the second year, but found the problems even more severe. Midway through that year, he pulled out and began writing a book about his teaching experiences.

> **TIP**
>
> ! **ONLY FOOLS RUSH IN.** Rather than lose time, money, and heart by trying out an avocation as a job and finding it to be a bad fit, do some sleuthwork first. Find business owners or workers who seem to be doing the job of your dreams—and ask if they'd be willing to give you five minutes of candid conversation on the benefits and pitfalls of their posts. Most people will be flattered to be asked. And you will get a clearer idea of the realities of your dream—and possibly find a new direction to take it.

3. Your Former Job, But Less of It

In this approach, you downshift from your old job to a lighter, flexible schedule working for the same company or doing the same type of work you did previously with another employer or work arrangement.

Because of the likely lack of benefits or full-time salary, you may even be paid more per hour. Use your network and word-of-mouth contacts to find these arrangements. If your skills are transferable, you might find that an employee leasing, contract worker, or professional temping service can place you flexibly and profitably. Examples where this has worked are in medicine, programming, engineering, design, writing, and editing, though many other possibilities exist.

Obviously, there can be psychological changes in working with your former co-workers from your new vantage point. If you were a boss before, you may need to get over the feeling that you're not in charge anymore. But if you had a specialist role, you might find your status increases if you are brought in for only the most challenging jobs.

EXAMPLE: Gerry worked as an anesthesiologist with a private practice when malpractice worries and the pace of surgical work got to him. He longed to spend more time on his boat, but also wanted to keep professionally active. He now works as a temporary staff anesthesiologist at rural hospitals, choosing his workdays around his sailing schedule, keeping his bank account full and his professional skills sharp.

BEFORE MAKING THE TRANSITION . . .

Well before starting early semi-retirement, it is worth thinking about how you might make a work transition.

If you know what you want to do, begin to lay the groundwork. For example, if you are staying in the same general line of work, check whether any noncompete or nondisclosure agreement you may have signed is likely to keep you from particular employment avenues, and if so, for how long. See if you can negotiate or obtain the right to send a single email message to the relevant database of your employer's clients telling them how to contact you.

With this preparation, it is quite possible that your own employer or another industry player will agree to hire you on a part-time basis.

If you know you are going to switch gears to a new profession or avocation, you can lay groundwork for that, too. Whether through networking and attending conferences or taking on unpaid internships or projects, you'll begin building momentum and confidence about your decision to change work domains. Kicking around in a new area for a few years allows you to build contacts, understand your personal fit and aptitude, and think through where and how to make some income in this area.

Once you stop working full time in your old career, you'll have the time to progress in the new one. But the more time you have to make the transition, discovering if your heart is really in it and confirming the fit, the better.

4. Consulting or Freelancing

Much as you might choose a job working fewer hours in your former field, you might also use your expertise and contacts to work as a freelancer or consultant in small, project-based doses, either for your former employer or for one or more new ones.

Freelancers generally focus on practicing specific readily-defined skills, such as design, editorial, or specific computer-based tasks, whereas consultants are hired more for expertise, relationships, or an ability to plan for The Big Picture. Either way, organizations typically choose to hire such workers rather than regular employees when they need such specialized skills for a finite project.

If you decide to work as a freelancer or consultant, expect to earn more per hour than a salaried worker doing the same type of work. But you will still likely earn far less annually since you will be working only a limited number of days. Ideally, the arrangement will allow you to secure small, controlled commitments that leave time free to do the other things you want to do.

But there are also some risks to working this way. For example, you may spend quite a bit of unpaid hours just trying to drum up business. Also, because you will only be working occasionally, your skills might become outdated, reducing your value to clients and losing you potential projects.

Still, many early semi-retirees find the consulting role a comfortable one, as it gives them a legitimate role in the workworld without the fixed time commitments of their former full-time jobs. They can attend conferences, go to lunch with co-workers, and generally keep busy with little or no pressure—all the while steering themselves to people and projects of genuine interest.

> **EXAMPLE:** After taking an attractive exit package from a large investment firm, David entered early retirement with no particular plan for the future. Old industry contacts began calling to see if he would tackle specific projects—for instance, sorting through the financial paper trail to identify the extent of a trading fraud at a bank. Later, David was drawn to work raising money from investors to help get a new hedge fund off the ground. Those projects required intense bursts of activity, though the pay was so good that David was able to earn enough to cover his entire living expenses during a few good years.

EXAMPLE: Frances retired at age 60 after a career in pathology, most recently running her county's forensics laboratory. In early retirement, she plans to help other counties in the state upgrade their laboratories with new equipment. That will involve writing the paperwork for funding and analyzing vendors' bids for equipment and installation services. She is also looking into becoming an expert witness for court cases involving pathology questions.

RESOURCES

FOR MORE ON SELF-EMPLOYMENT. Unless you plan to make money in early retirement solely as an employee, you'll probably be self-employed and should consider forming a company to gain maximum tax and liability advantages.

For information on which form of business to use—sole proprietorship, limited liability company (LLC), or another type of corporation, see *LLC or Corporation?, How to Choose the Right Form for Your Business*, by Anthony Mancuso (Nolo).

5. Dealer, Agent, or Broker

For the early semi-retiree who has sales or business development skills, working as a dealer, agent, or broker can be the perfect match. Some call this the "Eat what you kill" approach to business. If you put together a deal, you get paid; otherwise, nothing. Examples include working as a boutique investment banker, business broker, real estate agent, or in commission-only business development.

You use the relationship networks gained on your former job to find people who need investors, clients, business relationships, or contacts that will bring buyer and seller together. Typically, you enter a formal agreement with one side, generally the seller, who pays you only if a deal comes together. By living with no guarantee of income, you can offer clients more flexibility than full timers doing the same thing.

You might also become affiliated with an established firm to give you the backup resources and credibility to win clients. If you do affiliate in this way, however, be careful not to start back down the slippery slope toward a traditional career mindset and work hours. It may take some real effort to explain to work colleagues and some understanding on their part to avoid conflict. Finding partners who are sympathetic to your early semi-retirement, perhaps because they long to do it themselves one day, may help. You might also outline a relationship in which you are independent but bring deals to the bigger firm for a cut of the fee while the staff there handles other key parts of the work. Don't expect much work to flow the other way, however. A firm is unlikely to toss an independent part timer much business or cut you in on in-house deals, since it might not trust that you would pull the same weight as a full-time person during a crunch.

Because you are an early semi-retiree, with the bulk of your spending needs covered by pensions or safe withdrawals from savings, you can likely withstand a lumpy or dry income stream far more readily than the worker living paycheck to paycheck. For example, you may find you can win clients by not requiring them to pay a regular monthly retainer, bearing more of the risk that a deal does not come to a successful conclusion, but winning business with more flexible terms. Use your expertise to sniff out and focus on clients who are most likely to be rewarding. Play your cards right and you may still get a retainer fee regardless of the outcome, possibly enough to cover your annual needs for work income. The commissions or stock options or other outsized rewards from a successful deal are then gravy.

> **EXAMPLE:** Cathy left the company she founded during a management shakeup and now helps other firms in that industry raise venture capital or be acquired by larger buyers. When a deal comes together, she can make $100,000 or more, but may go a few years without a deal at all. As an early semi-retiree who needs less than $20,000 of work income each year, Cathy doesn't mind a few dry years. One successful deal every five years would cover her needs, though her earnings have been much better than that. Cathy enjoys the thrill of the hunt when helping clients and still has plenty of free time to pursue outside interests.

6. Angel Investing

Angel investors make direct investments in small private companies, often working closely with the company's management to help with introductions or other advice to make the company more successful. This can open the door to occasional income-generating opportunities as an advisor or board member to the private firm, with others managing daily operations.

One potential pitfall is that chronically understaffed entrepreneurial companies can devour free time, so be careful to not overcommit or you'll find yourself right back in a rat race of a different stripe. Also, while angel investing can be very rewarding emotionally, the financial risks are higher than many naïve angels think. Small, prosaic cash-generating businesses are probably your best bet: dry cleaners, gas stations with small convenience marts, fencing installers, moving companies, or other small service providers that might never get institutional venture capital or go public but can pay investors a regular tax-efficient dividend.

Traditionally, however, most angels focus on small entrepreneurial technology companies, hoping for much bigger investment gains. Regrettably, these small tech product companies are statistically likely to return a goose egg for initial angel investors, even if the company survives, due to the dilution and onerous terms from follow-on institutional venture investors. Then again, they could be big winners; it's a high-risk gamble.

Try to invest in experienced or impressive management teams, and get the technology vetted by a trusted and knowledgeable technical resource. Invest with other angels and do not put in any more money than you can afford to lose.

> **TIP**
>
> (!) **BEWARE OF COMMON STOCK.** As an angel, require some sort of coupon-paying preferred stock, senior to the founders, for your investment. Also, if the company is public or profitable, it can probably pay you a stipend for your participation on the board or a regular retainer for advising the company in addition to any dividends or eventual returns on your initial investment.

Retail shops and consulting companies sometimes also seek angel investments. In general, steer clear of these types of companies. The successful
ones tend to throw off just enough cash to pay salaries to employees, but not
enough extra to compensate investors for the risks.

One promising possibility, if you can find it, is a nontechnical service
company looking to expand rapidly. If you have prior experience and contacts
in that field, you might be a big help to the founders. This inside knowledge
can be your backstage pass to be able to invest in the company even at its less
risky later-stages, right alongside larger venture capital funds.

RESOURCES

 FOR MORE ON ANGEL INVESTING. There are several matching
networks and local networking groups to link angel investors with
entrepreneurs seeking funding.

The oldest and best-known of these networks is the Technology
Capital Network, now run at MIT and renamed The Capital Network.
You can find out more from its website at www.thecapitalnetwork
.org.

- You can also find a directory of other local networks at www
.angeldeals.com/angelnetworks.
Angel investors now have a trade association that has useful
information for prospective investors at www.angelcapitalas-
sociation.org.

- Finally, local business incubators set up to help startup firms and
the lawyers and accountants who work with small growth firms
can also provide leads to good angel investing opportunities.

TALES FROM THE CRYPT: THE DAY TRADER

Some might consider day trading to be a form of early semi-retirement, but a look at the reality of it disavows this myth. Unless you were a Wall Street insider, money manager, analyst, or trader in your career, you are probably on thin ice going into day trading as a sideline to make cash. And even then, be wary of overestimating your knowledge: Professional fund managers, on average, match the market and fall short by the amounts of their fees.

Usually the cycle starts when a professionally successful but unemployed person gives up looking for work and decides to stay home and manage the portfolio for a living. On the surface, this makes sense to friends and family: Savings managed properly can pay almost a salary-sized benefit compared to portfolios that are ignored by those who are overworked. But one day, the faithful steward takes a draught of the dreaded potion, sells a stock he—this is usually a Guy Thing—bought that morning for $1,000 profit, and the beast is born.

Day trading becomes a worklike obsession filling the days from early morning onward. The newly minted trader has little personal growth, exercise, family time, or chance to explore new hobbies and projects. He becomes a locked-down, pasty, twitchy drone putting the family's financial future at risk. This isn't early retirement and it isn't work; it's some sort of addiction.

If you have the potential to take this bad turn as a day trader, see Chapter 3, Section E for ways to invest sensibly for the long-term in a modest amount of time, keeping you from obsessive churning of your portfolio, and panic selling. Your brain and your schedule will be free to gain all the benefits of real early semi-retirement. And if you just love to pick stocks, you'll also find in that chapter a way to do it without putting your health or your home at risk.

7. Real Estate

Investing in real estate is one of the archetypal early semi-retirement work activities. It can be a way both to build up the real estate asset class for your portfolio as well as to earn income.

And if you are handy and enjoy doing needed repair work yourself, you have a big advantage in making your investments work out well financially, since you will save the cost of paying outside contractors and repair services.

Rehabbing—going deeper than cosmetics to make structural repairs and changes or additions—is a more significant commitment. However, if you know your housing market and have the skills to do the work yourself, this can be a solid moneymaker, akin to buying a beaten down stock and holding it as the company's fortunes and value are restored. Uninformed rehabbing with expensive outside contractors, however, can turn a decent investment into a money pit.

The classic model is to buy properties carefully with mortgages—seeking to make the investments generate cash or at least not consume cash, then improve and refinance them at their higher value. Ideally, refinance with a non-recourse loan—that is, one that leaves the building and its rents, not personal assets, as the only collateral. Since you have pulled out your initial capital through the refinancing, you are free to start the cycle again. Your property will then be paying off its mortgage. And over a long period, you will own the building outright, adding real frisson to your portfolio and earnings over the longer term. Capital gains might also occur over that period, making the investment that much better.

EXAMPLE: Ted, early retired four years ago and recently married to Cati, spent an intensive three months fixing up Cati's former home to resell. While the house, in a fairly rough neighborhood, could have sold for $150,000 in its original condition, Ted's three-month blitz and $40,000 of construction costs helped the house sell, from first visit to final closing, in just seven weeks for $240,000.

Ted and Cati felt that pocketing $50,000 for three months' work was a good tradeoff. Improvements were extensive—including a new roof, new siding, and extensive landscaping, along with a nearly complete gutting of the home's interior, renovated kitchen and bathrooms, new major appliances, carpets, flooring, and a complete paint job, inside and out. One of Cati's cousins was a contractor and did most of the bigger work, but Ted provided plenty of long hours, too. Together with the cash from Ted's former home, sold at a profit the year before the marriage, the couple has nicely supplemented their savings and ensured a financially secure early retirement with a Safe Withdrawal Rate now hovering around 2%. (See Chapter 4, Section A for more on the optimum Safe Withdrawal Rates.)

RESOURCES

An early semi-retiree and Washington DC resident, Mike Dulworth, writing with Teresa Goodwin, has outlined the main points for both the financial and project management facets of successful rehabbing in a recent book, *Renovate to Riches: Buy, Improve, and Flip Houses to Create Wealth* (John Wiley and Sons).

TIPS FROM THOSE WHO LEARNED THE HARD WAY

A number of successful early semi-retired rehabber/landlords offer some tips that might help save you time, money, and angst.

FIND FIXER-UPPERS IN GOOD NEIGHBORHOODS. Once you improve the property, you will be able to attract good tenants, which will make your life much easier. The value of the property will also be preserved, since the neighborhood will not deteriorate during the time you can expect to own the property. Those who knowledgeably get into the "fix and flip" mode, selling the property immediately, may be able to ignore this advice about neighborhoods.

DON'T BE AFRAID OF MAINTENANCE EXPENSES. Maintenance is an essential expense in owning and keeping up any real estate, so just budget for it. Develop a roster of trusted service people you can call in on short notice.

CONSIDER THE LONG HAUL. Rental property owners reap tax benefits over the long run. Chief among these is the ability to deduct depreciation as an expense each year, which reduces income taxes long before any loss is realized through the sale of the property.

KNOW THE MARKET. Good properties at higher rents generally come with fewer headaches, but might be less attractive investments in terms of the percentage return. But if you know your market, you can do well in other segments such as student housing, which will need more maintenance than normal residential properties.

GET A GOOD SECURITY DEPOSIT. Getting a month's rent or more as a security deposit mitigates and seems to keep at bay a multitude of tenant problems such as damages, skipped rent payments, and the like.

BE PREPARED TO DIG HARDER THAN EVER. Deals today are harder to find than they were ten or 20 years ago. Expect them to take more creativity, more work, more research, and possibly a different method of profiting than the plain vanilla cash-flow-positive deals of a few decades ago.

KEEP A SENSE OF REALISM. Don't expect all real estate investments to go up over time or to provide a hedge against inflation. For example, Peter bought a townhouse in suburban Dallas in 1980—a bubble there—that 25 years later was only just back to the market value at which he bought it.

8. Innkeeping

Many early semi-retirees find that owning and operating an inn or bed and breakfast is the perfect way to blend home and work.

If there is a season or attraction that draws visitors to your locale—whale watching, skiing, annual arts or music festivals—then you can even close the inn off-season and have large chunks of the year free to relax or do your own travel.

Most innkeepers and B&B owners, however, will quickly tell you that, while for the right person or couple it is ideal, innkeeping is a labor of love that requires a commitment and a lot of work. It is not generally financially remunerative until the place has at least five or six rooms and managing that size of an establishment often starts to feel like a full-time job.

RESOURCES

FOR MORE ON THE INS AND OUTS OF INNKEEPING. Two books about running an inn or B&B include:

- *Start and Run a Profitable Bed & Breakfast*, by Monica and Richard Taylor—a Canadian early semi-retired couple (Self-Counsel Press), and

- *So—You Want to Be an Innkeeper: The Definitive Guide to Operating a Successful Bed-And-Breakfast or Country Inn*, by Susan Brown, Pat Hardy, Jo Ann M. Bell, and Mary E. Davies (Chronicle Books).

9. Artist or Creative Worker

For many people, a good way to have a long and successful retirement is to start in the middle years uncovering and developing creative talents.

Not only does this enrich life and trigger many useful personal growth and stress-reducing benefits, but also it is work that can be done over many years. Picasso was still producing prolifically at age 90. And Grandma Moses took up painting at age 75 and produced some 1,600 works of art before she died at 101.

If you have the inclination and more than a modicum of talent for making pottery, painting, or writing, for example—you may be able to turn your creative passion into something that earns income, as well. Don't count on getting rich at this, but there is certainly some possibility of making income creating and selling artistic work. At the same time, you will be developing a talent and avocation that might just make the difference in your long-run mental health.

> **EXAMPLE:** Jean took up painting as an early semi-retiree ten years ago. Over the years, she has shown her work in community co-op galleries and art fairs, building up a local following. Today, she receives commissions several times each year from families for portraits of the children or other family members, painted in her signature abstract style, at prices in the thousands of dollars.

> **EXAMPLE:** Al started playing trombone in elementary school—adding guitar, piano, and various wind instruments along the way. At age 22, he relegated his music to hobby status and pursued a career in government service. With a solid pension and early retirement benefits now in hand, Al has begun gigging with local music groups and has started getting referrals and calls to perform at parties, weddings, restaurants, and clubs. In a good week, with about ten hours of actual playing time, Al makes $1,000 and loves every minute of it.

> **EXAMPLE:** Wendy, an early-retired attorney who uncovered her talent at jewelry design just after closing her practice, now creates necklaces, bracelets, scarves, and other accessories and sells them at local arts fairs or trunk shows, netting several thousand dollars a year. Wendy finds the challenge of presenting and selling her creations directly to the people who will be wearing them to be invigorating—a different but no less exciting aspect of the process than creating the works themselves.

10. Hobby Turned Business

On any given weekend, somewhere near you, retirees and early semi-retirees are setting up tables and selling their antiques, crafts, and collectibles. They are happy with the camaraderie, the chance of a sale, and generally by being surrounded by people and the things they love.

There are even more opportunities to make a buck with other hobbies—from scuba divers cleaning boat bottoms for a dollar a foot, foodies opening catering businesses, car enthusiasts trafficking in vintage car parts, to power paraglider enthusiasts customizing and marketing propeller-packs for the newcomers to the hobby.

If the thing you make or sell can be shipped, you can join the legions of people worldwide who have become eBay entrepreneurs, selling or reselling things they have made or acquired to a worldwide audience.

EXAMPLE: Beth and Emmy are close friends who both have an eye for design and unique products. Recently, they began frequenting the wholesale gift shops and buying unique home décor items for resale at community craft fairs and fundraisers. Every month they have at least one event and sometimes two or three. Typically, they sell products at prices between $25 and $75 dollars, bought at about 1/3 to 1/2 that price. They generally pay the show organizers 15% of their gross sales and gross about $3,000 at a successful show, giving them each about $500 profit. With about 20 shows a year, they have a lot of fun seeing old friends and making new ones—and each earns about $10,000 a year.

EXAMPLE: Doug buys and refurbishes old pinball machines, jukeboxes, and arcade video games he buys at auctions. With his practiced eye, Doug knows which machines can be repaired with parts salvaged from other units and which are terminal—and makes his bids accordingly. He sells the gaming machines through ads in the local papers, flyers on local bulletin boards, and an occasional booth at flea markets. Doug tries to make $300 to $500 on each one, after investing one or two hours of work, and moves about 30 machines a year. The one drawback is his garage has never had a car in it and is unlikely to as long as he lives there.

One caveat is to be careful that you do in fact run your hobby as a business and don't end up just putting it on steroids, acquiring masses of gear with the hope that you'll sell it. For one thing, your business expenses may not be fully deductible if you can't show you've made an honest effort to turn a profit. Be aware too, that while some people find the commercial element actually enhances their enjoyment of a hobby, others find that all the buying and selling starts to ruin the fun they originally found in it.

11. Teaching

Those who like to teach but aren't interested in plunging into a full-time teaching job or obtaining a current teaching credential—which typically requires at least a year of school plus many hours of supervised practice teaching—might try tutoring or teaching in an alternative setting.

Tutoring is no longer simply remedial. High schoolers who do A-minus work are increasingly turning to tutors to help them get that straight A. Math and science are especially popular, and in an average suburban area, pay about $85 per hour with plenty of flexibility in hours and scheduling.

You can find students through word of mouth referrals from guidance counselors at the schools, as well as through targeted mailings to parents of school-aged children in your area. School fundraisers also give you exposure to your target market: Offer five free tutoring sessions as a silent auction item and interested parents will soon have your contact information.

> **EXAMPLE:** While looking to be hired as a full-time high school math teacher, Larry, early retired from IBM after 25 years, was tutoring and substitute teaching math for ten hours a week. Larry taught kids at all levels and ages, made his own schedule, and took off on a cheap flight whenever he had a week free. His last trip before starting full-time as a teacher took him to a country music contest in West Virginia, where he heard the world's best fiddlers.

There are also other venues available for those who yearn to teach—from classes at community centers, prisons, and retirement centers, to kids' after-school programs. Junior colleges and university extension programs typically hire instructors without the usual teaching credentials if they have experience in a relevant profession. Adjunct professors at larger schools make around $5,000 for teaching a semester-long course versus about $3,000 at a smaller school or junior college.

Teaching avocational interests such as yoga, martial arts, or knitting may also present opportunities for early-retirees with those skills or interests.

E. Unpaid Work Alternatives

As an early retiree, you will want to do all sorts of things with your newfound time that are engaging, productive, and challenging. Many of these fulfilling activities may be unpaid, even though the activities themselves are often in-distinguishable from paid work.

If you are stuck not knowing what to do, start to uncover opportunities by asking yourself what you want to learn about. Then creatively think of where you can place yourself to learn those skills or develop that expertise. By making a commitment based on the experience you can gain, rather than based on a salary or title, you can be richly rewarded beyond money—and may build the skills that give you credible experience for moving to paid work in a related avocation.

1. Volunteering

Volunteering is the most obvious avenue for unpaid worklike activities. The possibilities are nearly endless. In any school, community group, nonprofit agency, church, or social service organization, opportunities for service and personal growth abound. Participating in something fun and interesting while at the same time helping to solve a need in the community can help complete a rewarding cycle.

Of course, you can volunteer by simply logging a few hours on a task set up by someone else. But for many people, the most rewarding projects are those that offer more independence or creativity in shaping something new. What seems to work best for most new volunteers is to pick something they care about, own a piece of it—and give it the time and mental energy needed to become competent at it. Most volunteer organizations are chronically short of people to take responsibility for projects and will gladly let you take on as much work as you like, providing you deliver the goods.

Early retirees who come straight from the world of business to work at nonprofits sometimes have trouble slowing down and adjusting to the pace and standards of a volunteer-heavy organization. If you find yourself frequently frustrated by what you perceive as inefficiency or amateurism in a volunteer organization, you have a few choices, assuming you want to stay involved with it. First, you may simply need a little more time out of the fast lane before you've slowed down enough to get the rhythm and expectations in the organization. Or you may find there is indeed a leadership vacuum you can fill, bringing greater levels of effectiveness to the organization in which you are interested. In that case, work over time helping to build up other talented people around you and transfer responsibility to them. If you are too indispensable to the organization, you'll face your own burnout as more and more responsibility falls on your shoulders and you have no one to share the load.

RESOURCES

 FINDING VOLUNTEER OPPORTUNITIES. You might match your skills and interests with local needs for volunteers at www.volunteermatch.org.

DIFFERENT WAYS OF GIVING BACK

Many, though not all, early retirees feel a profound sense of gratitude that life has dealt them the financial resources and circumstances to allow them the option of early retirement. They feel a desire to capitalize on their good fortune—and this often takes the form of volunteering or giving back. Service becomes a sort of privilege they are able to enjoy—the time, state of mind, and resources with which to help others.

But plenty of people are uncomfortable with traditional forms of giving back, feeling them insincere or burdened with an unwelcome sense of obligation. The good news here is that if you are simply pursuing what you love to do and being a decent human being, then you are probably going to be able to do more for society than 99% of the poor souls out there who are heaving themselves into work they hate and trying over time to fulfill somebody else's view of who they should be.

You may be skeptical, but look at how this might be true.

Let's say you are an engineer in early semi-retirement, spending your days tooling around in your shop and fiddling with stuff you find interesting. While it may sound selfish, your puttering might lead five or 20 years from now to some sort of interesting invention that people desperately need. Suddenly those years in the shop wouldn't seem to be a mere selfish luxury.

On the other hand, you might never do anything more than quietly fool around in your shop for the rest of your life. But even in that case, you are probably exuding a calm contentedness that is inspirational to those around you. As a result, young people in your neighborhood—even if you don't know them, they know who you are—may grow up being able to point to at least one adult who is genuinely content. That can have a major impact on the lives of those young people for decades to come. Even just being a good friend and readily available to your older parents or extended family is a way to give back.

2. Other Unpaid Opportunities

Apart from traditional volunteer work, there are some other useful roles and activities that offer the opportunity to learn or contribute, yet which pay little or nothing.

Among these, consider:

- becoming an active member of a board of directors
- organizing a discussion group or nonprofit association of people around a topic of interest
- getting involved in local politics, city or municipal advisory boards, school boards, neighborhood associations, or planning review committees
- setting up a garage workshop and inventing something useful
- writing thoughtful letters to public figures, editorial pages, or online message boards
- raising money for a charity, health care, or educational foundation
- mentoring kids
- organizing public seminars of useful information you would like to share
- investing a month in a monastery praying for world peace, and
- pursuing focused higher education courses, either online or in a traditional college setting.

(See Section F for additional examples of unpaid work options along with a large number of leisure activities in which early retirees commonly engage.)

AIM HIGH

You are going to be retired for a very long time. Chart a course for audacious challenges that you secretly believe have your name written on them. Then take frequent, small, steps toward those goals, finding the fun along the way.

Think big. If you have decades to make goals happen, you won't want to choose something that you could completely master in a matter of a few months. Work on something in stages over a long period of time—some activity that will keep your brain fresh and your heart light.

For example, Dana, a top grad 25 years ago, had been a stay-at-home mom while her kids were young. When they got to middle school, Dana felt the urge to open a new chapter in her life. She began participating in public discourse on foreign policy and began tentative steps on a cautionary book about the directions of U.S. empire building. At the same time, she became involved in grassroots political activism educating people in her local community about these and other national issues.

Dana and her early-retired husband love Washington DC and she envisions moving there in ten years or so when their children are grown. Her goal 20 or 30 years from now is to be one of the people whose opinions are sought in Washington, who is quoted in TV or news stories, writing white papers, and giving speeches. Dana knows it will take decades to achieve and that her current steps are decidedly modest, but she feels confident that she is now on a mission that will occupy her for many years to come.

F. Advantages for the Early Semi-Retired Worker

Many contemplating slowing down, even a little, become terrified that they will lose their edges and never be any use to an employer again. That fear of "losing it" may in fact have been a propelling force in your final years of work, causing you to push yourself ever harder with mobile email, late night wireless laptop sessions in bed, or weekend conference calls. You'd love to relax, but fear that if you ever did, you'd never get back in the game.

While you may never wish to get back into the same Overwork Mode, be confident that should you choose to, you can be effective and valuable to others on your own terms. By approaching work differently, as something you care about and enjoy doing, you will be able in the words of the Zen saying to Work Less, Get More Done.

1. Better Focus

By being relaxed, with more free time, you'll be able to bring fully focused attention to work when everyone else seems to be so overloaded they can barely return a phone call.

2. More Time for Connecting to Others

When it comes to people and relationships, you can afford to take the long view. Eventually these contacts may bring in business, but in the meantime, you will likely enjoy just getting to know people and seeing how you can help them, what you can learn from them. And you'll know exactly who to call when an opportunity for a new project or collaboration arises.

3. No Commuting

Unless you love to drive, arrange to work out of your home or at least an office close to home. You'll save time, money, and aggravation as you flexibly and easily meld your work with your other interests and activities during the day.

4. Cherry-Picking Assignments

You are free to choose work projects that you can approach with the same spirit that you address each day: What would you like to explore and learn about? Will you be working with people of integrity? Work that passes this sniff test is more likely to be successful, as you bring your full enthusiasm and mental energy to it.

G. Finding New Activities

If you secretly fear that you'll never have enough things to do in early retirement, this section is for you. It includes lots of descriptions of activities and pursuits in which early retirees are currently engaged that can give you inspiration and ideas. Whether you are an investment banker who is now free to pursue her dream of painting or a dad who can now devote large chunks of the day to your kids, early retirement gives you the time and the opportunity. And if you're stuck, perhaps the activities here can help spark your own ideas.

1. Travel

Travel is a staple activity of early retirees who now have plenty of free time. But you will need to be creative. Simply taking the travel options presented to regular working people is unlikely to fit your budget. Many early retirees find plenty of ways to travel for extended periods on a shoestring. From using a tent or trailer and staying in parks to home swaps and work for room and board, or simply going native and renting homes the way the locals might, options abound for logging all the travel you could want at prices that are a small fraction of the normal hotel and resort rates. (See Chapter 2, Section F2b for suggestions about traveling on a budget.)

Beyond travel, many early retirees take up residence abroad, restore homes, and adopt another culture, either full time or for part of each year. While prices of European real estate have climbed in recent years, home prices or long-term rentals in pleasant rural locations can still feel like bargains. Use travel as a chance to learn a new language, meet new people, pursue a hobby such as hiking, bird watching, or photography—or just to find beautiful places to stimulate the senses and imagination.

Some examples culled from the lives of early retirees who have wanderlust:

- Plan and go on a long trip or adventure.
- Qualify for and join the local racing club by racing 500 miles offshore in a sailboat.
- Buy a house in the European countryside and restore it.
- Explore low-cost, "Plan B" retirement living destinations overseas or in rural parts of America.
- Rent a canal boat and putter through Europe at four knots.

RETREAT!

When the going gets tough, the tough get going—out of town. Many people find that a week or even a few days in a retreat center at critical times of great change can help restore calm and perspective. The simple living, free from distractions, seems to loosen up old habits and conditioning. Answers to questions that have been perplexing you seem to mysteriously appear, often a few days after you've returned home.

If you have a spiritual tradition with which you are comfortable, look for something within that framework which meets your needs. If you have no spiritual traditions, now might be a good time to begin that exploration. There are plenty of retreat options, from spas or ashrams to Buddhist temples and Trappist monasteries. A fine guidebook is *Sanctuaries*, by Jack and Marcia Kelly (Belltower Publishers), which gives details on several hundred such locations in the United States.

This could also be a great time to learn to meditate, do yoga, pray, or live in silence for a few days—or get a series of massages or physical therapy while eating healthy food.

For a mini-retreat, don't forget that some inspirational music in the car or through the headphones on a plane or train can turn travel time into relaxation time.

2. Recreate

It may come as a surprise to find that many early retirees neglect their hobbies and recreation almost as much as they did when they worked full time. You may be one of them, getting so caught up in the ebb and flow of investing, Web surfing, community activities, or managing daily life that you neglect your opportunities to really delve into the things you find fun. Although it is a mistake to think of early retirement as some sort of middle-aged summer camp, filled with nonstop organized activities, it is appropriate to plan to immerse yourself in the many things you enjoy and never seemed to have time for during your years of full-time work.

Make it a scheduled priority to dig into your recreational activities; don't leave them as something you get to when there is nothing else more pressing going on. You'll be surprised where these interests can lead you—and the satisfaction you can gain from them.

Some recreational activities suggested by experienced early retirees:

- Be part of a community theater production or play.
- Restore a vintage car.
- Take up hot air ballooning.
- Join a samba band or a church choir.
- Get an old 4 x 5 frame camera and build a darkroom to develop and print photos.
- Build a deck and put a hot tub in it; invite friends over frequently.
- Get a dog.
- Do a lot of fishing, hunting, golf, watching sports live or on TV.

3. Get Healthy

You retired early to live a long fulfilling life: Make sure you are healthy enough to enjoy it. Use some of your ample free time to finally get fit. Find a class or join a gym if that helps motivate you or find a piece of exercise equipment you like, a friend to walk with, a team of adults who scramble around doing something vigorous on Saturday mornings.

Just find something and do it until your body's natural desire for healthy living takes over. At that point, you may discover yourself actually wanting to order salads and fresh vegetables when you go out to eat and the things you graze for in the kitchen may less often come from the baked goods shelf at the supermarket and more often from a farmer's market.

Some healthy suggestions from early retirees:
- Ride a bike or take regular walks.
- Hike the Appalachian Trail or the Milford Track in New Zealand.
- Get unhooked from coffee.
- Study homeopathic medicine.
- Learn how to give great massages.
- Learn yoga and practice it regularly.
- Start a regular tennis game with some doubles partners.
- Join an adult softball team.

4. Learn

Formal courses, either in a classroom or via online learning abound these days—and increasingly offer learning options focused on retirees and lifelong learners. While learning for its own sake is always fun, most people find targeting a concrete area of interest gives a focus to their learning and helps sustain commitment. Learn about DC electronics in the context of wanting to make repairs to the electrical system on your boat, or to invest in a promising new technology. Learn about 18th century European art as part of an overall effort to immerse yourself in that period in history, so much so that you could consider writing a novel set in the period or act as a consultant to movies being made about the period.

Don't forget that learning comes in all forms, with traditional "sage on the stage" classroom learning often being among the least effective. Learn by doing, immersing yourself in situations and projects with others where learning happens of necessity along the way as you muddle through. You'll not only have fun and have something to show for it at the end, but you're likely to have retained more relevant information to build on the next time around.

Some suggestions tried and passed on by early retirees:

- Go to Italy and learn the language while taking cooking classes.
- Develop a good layperson's understanding of genetic engineering or biotechnology.
- Go to a seminary and become a deacon or lay minister
- Research your ancestry or genealogy and visit places your family lived.
- Read classics from East and West.
- Learn how to refinish furniture or take an interior design course and redesign your home décor.
- Learn to play the bagpipes or piano.
- Be an intern in a gourmet restaurant's kitchen.
- Become a wine expert.

RESOURCES

FOR MORE ON LEARNING OPPORTUNITIES. Directories of online courses and degree programs abound, many of them poor, but two good ones are: www.elearners.com and www.worldwidelearn.com. Fathom, a grand lifelong learning collaboration between several great universities and cultural institutions, failed as a business, but the archives of its high-quality seminars are still available at www .fathom.com. ●

CHAPTER SEVEN

Don't Blow It

Early retirement often starts with an initial giddy period, a delicious feeling of playing hooky or skinny-dipping. You can't quite believe your good fortune at leaving behind the demands of full-time work and may pinch yourself some Monday morning at 10:30 to be sure that you are indeed relaxing in your sunny kitchen with the newspaper, scratching the cat instead of worrying about logging billable hours.

But this euphoric period inevitably ends—within a few months or a year or two. The list of repairs around the house gets down to the dregs, the CDs are all categorized, the bills filed, the computers upgraded and cleaned of spyware, the yard is looking trim. You stare out

> *Free at last, free at last! Thank God Almighty, we are free at last!*
>
> –MARTIN LUTHER KING, QUOTING A TRADITIONAL BLACK AMERICAN SPIRITUAL IN "I HAVE A DREAM" A SPEECH DELIVERED AUGUST 28, 1963, WASHINGTON, DC

the window and look into the abyss of an endless future with nothing to do. Fears, doubts, and stomach churning become your companions and if you're not careful, you become as stressed sitting at home as you ever were on the worst days at work.

Rule #7, Don't Blow It, is a warning and an appeal that having made the heroic efforts to get this far, you should not squander your days in mental anguish or physical torpor.

This chapter lays out the various pitfalls early retirees routinely face and offers prescriptions that have helped others put these issues behind them and move on. These problems are all entirely manageable. You just need to know about them, plan for them, and take strategic countermeasures when they arise.

A. Challenges of Early Retirement

Compared with the complexities and stresses of full-time employment, especially in a job you find unfulfilling, it's hard to imagine huge challenges in being retired. But the challenges are there, and as anyone who has experienced them will tell you, they rarely go away if ignored.

While not everyone faces all of the pitfalls described here, a surprising number of people do experience the whole list—at least to some degree. In many cases, no real prescription or cure is needed beyond time, acceptance, and patience. Then again, if you don't learn to cope with these demons, your early retirement will suffer a setback—and you may even be pulled back to working full time just to restore your personal equilibrium.

1. Guilt

Perhaps surprisingly, the first "gotcha" for many people is guilt. It can be harder than you imagine to sit in the yard and relax on a weekday afternoon when every other able-bodied person seems to be working. You begin to questions what you have done that's so wonderful that you deserve not to work—and guilt sets in.

Trained early on by parents, teachers, and bosses continuously leaning over to judge productivity or chastise idle moments, many people internalize those values and feel that someone must be watching and disapproving of perceived idleness. Those feelings may even be reinforced by a parent or in-law who thinks you're becoming soft and lazy.

Approach this demon of guilt with a multi-pronged attack. One method—a sort of self-subterfuge—that works for many early retirees is not to schedule too many highly indulgent activities during the core of a normal workday. Take out the boat for a sail or have that motorcycle ride at the beginning or end of the day. During the middle of the weekday, in addition to any actual income-generating part-time work, do worklike tasks such as email and deskwork, going to lunch with people, making phone calls, reading to keep up with your interests, studying and managing portfolio-related matters, or spending time on nonprofit activities. Because this is pretty much what your typical workday consisted of anyway, you will reassure yourself or anyone else who is concerned that early retirement is not turning you into a sloth.

Also be aware that there are plenty of people who never experience even the slightest twinges of guilt about their unstructured days filled with pleasant activities and their wealth of free time during early retirement. They tend to be internally-referenced people—often engineering and artistic types—who are highly absorbed in their interests and ideas. If you are feeling guilty, they can help point to a lasting solution: As soon as you, too, discover new interests or work options that passionately engage you, your feelings of guilt will probably fade away. But while you are in transition, the scheduling ruse can help.

Another approach is to remind yourself that you "deserve" early retirement because you paid your dues and you are now enjoying the fruits of your efforts. This approach doesn't work for everyone, but it can help some. Remind yourself, for instance, of how you sacrificed and lived below your means for a number of years or how you worked an extra job to be able to save more money. You chose to retire early and earned the right to do it; others have chosen to keep working. Don't let their values influence how you feel about yourself.

2. Boredom

Psychologists, especially those who work with teens, have plenty to say about boredom. Their general assessment is that boredom results when a person is pushing something away, trying to avoid a reality that seems less appealing than some other imagined activity. But boredom can also arise for those who simply don't feel challenged enough to fully use their talents.

Those forced to work with little choice about how to spend their days may be forgiven for feeling bored. As an early retiree, however, you have virtually complete freedom to choose how to spend your days and create your life. If boredom arises, you are fully empowered to squelch it.

Remarkably, boredom is usually a fear of those considering early retirement rather than an affliction of those who have actually retired. Once you are early retired and setting about finding new and varied challenges, boredom rarely arises. Should things get quiet, early retirees who've mastered the boredom issue simply wait a while knowing that a new project inevitably appears and feel grateful that they have the time and energy to engage it.

But not everyone handles boredom so gracefully. The world of work tends to turn many people into "doers"—addicted to the endless juggling of projects and priorities with a few quick doses of adrenaline-laced vacation thrown in. If you are one of these people, your sense of identity may have become tangled up with being busy; if you aren't busy, you fear you risk becoming expendable. When stuck in this mode, boredom is the penalty box, the result of not having planned ahead to keep sufficient activities and projects lined up. You can't imagine why anyone would ever want so much unstructured time; it seems terrifying.

Successful early retirees have learned that mere busyness should not be confused with having a life and that being quiet or underobligated is not a cause for alarm. When working on the right priorities—as opposed to making every green light or answering every email message—even slow, imperfect progress is fine.

I'M NOT WORKING, BUT I STILL HAVE NO TIME

A few years into early retirement, most people find boredom is low on their list of worries. Instead, they get to the end of the week and wonder where the time went.

Obviously, this isn't a problem for you if you are working on projects you feel are rewarding and valuable. But if your days are simply slipping away, full of errands and busywork and not much more, you'll need to reassess.

This book offers concrete suggestions to help you get your life more in tune with what you feel is important, (See Chapter 6, Section D for copious suggestions on activities.) In the short term, take a stern look at how your time is spent and make sure a significant amount is devoted to meaningful endeavors. Like an overgrown garden, it may be time to prune—dropping some activities and saying No to others. Some early retirees look at their time as unlimited and therefore not very valuable. A wiser approach is to look at your time the same way you might look at your budget, making sure nothing is wasted.

Reread the section describing the Rocks in the Jar exercise. (Chapter 1, Section D2d.) Reassess to make sure you allot time in your life first for the really important things and then let all the less important stuff find a way to fit into your week around the edges. Some early retirees have been known to ignore the important things entirely and start obsessing over little concerns—making scheduling a lunch or going to the dry cleaners into an event to be planned and fussed over ad nauseam.

Another way to look at boredom is to note that people get easily bored when they themselves have become boring. In that case, the solution is simple: Keep daring to learn new things, being of service, investing time and effort into things in which you believe. Be open to fresh ideas and the people who embody them. Not only will you not be boring, you won't be bored, either.

3. Panic

Typically tied to boredom, panic tends to rear up when there is little hope for the future or little imagination about the many positive things that could be in the offing.

For instance, you may begin to panic as the markets and your portfolio are mired in a downturn or your part-time business seems to be headed for the rocks. To fight the growing constriction in your throat and chest, you cast about wildly for something to do to make it better.

It's better to attack panic with two principal approaches: physiology and reason. First, breathe deeply and move purposefully; plenty of panic attacks are resolved by a brisk walk or a good workout.

Second, don't be afraid to examine the details of your concerns—laying out the worst things that could happen in detail and brainstorming responses to address them. If you worry about a boring day turning into a lifetime of boredom, try to dig into exactly how you are feeling and what the worst outcome from this might be. On examination, most people will understand that the problems are transitory, that a quiet day does not in fact translate to an entire life without meaning or joy.

But take practical, concrete steps now. Generate a series of responses and solutions. This might consist of joining a health club, calling a local environmental group that interests you, or signing up for a class at the local community college. Or your preferred approach might be going for a jog, then sitting down to meditate or curl up with a good book while realizing what a treasure each hour of your time is—and recommitting to finding useful ways to spend it. (See Section A5 for specific help on addressing financial worries.)

SPECIAL HELP FOR TYPE AS

Few people achieve early retirement by sitting around and waiting for life to happen to them. Chances are you were able to retire early because you are conscientious, energetic, and thrive on accomplishments.

Now, you may suddenly feel you have nothing to do. To cope, many Type As start applying their well-hewn skills to whatever is at hand, no matter how small or inconsequential. Trying to manage the kids and their sports "careers," bulldozing the poor souls on the church committee, or ruining the fun of a hobby by trying to make it a mini-career are all typical Type A responses. A better approach it to slow down and give it a rest.

A Type A friend who went through it the hard way offers the advice he wished he had been given: Don't make any major decision or financial commitment for a year after leaving full-time work.

Taking that small step can be a huge help in facing down the powerful urge to instantly throw yourself into the next big thing—which, precisely because of your haste and desperation, is likely to be a move you'll come to regret. Instead, during your first year, treat yourself gently and kindly. Notice your feelings, but don't pay much attention to them or invest them with huge importance. Hopefully your chicken with its head cut off feelings will subside on their own and you will discover or rediscover a palette of interests to approach calmly and thoughtfully.

4. Bruised Ego

Sometimes known as an Identity Crisis, this cluster of status losses often hits hard-charging early retirees hardest. To earn and save enough money to retire early, many pushed hard to become respected masters of their career domains—and without domains to master, they feel they have little purpose.

If you are used to perceiving yourself and being perceived as a super-achiever, it may be especially hard to accept that once you leave the workplace, nobody is going to miss you that much. If you wanted another full-time job, the headhunters would probably be interested. But once you've retired, don't expect your former employer and co-workers to be hovering around solicitously hoping for a few scraps of your wisdom. Instead, in less time than it takes to readjust your lounge chair, a new generation of workers will adopt new ways to do things, new loyalties, and you'll be old news.

If you want to stay a lion in your field, you might need to stay at work. However, if you are content to be involved but no longer the big cheese or if you're ready to move onto being an enthusiastic beginner in a new field, then the transition to early retirement should bring few negative jolts to your self-esteem.

Still, there are a few ego barbs waiting for virtually all early retirees—and it is best to steel yourself to withstand them. First, you are unlikely to have as much disposable income as your neighbors and former work colleagues. They are spending most of what they earn each year while you are living off your portfolio earnings and a bit of work income. Clearly, they'll be able to spring for that new sports car a lot more easily than you can. They'll probably be able to stay in a nicer resort on vacation, too, or fly business class while you sit in the back of the plane. About the only thing you can do about this, besides being happy for them, is to remind yourself that they still need to work full time while you have the luxury of spending your time more or less as you please.

Also, be aware that as an early retiree, neighbors and others in your community might mistakenly view you as an unemployed or even unemployable type struggling through a fruitless job search. Fearing this stigma, some early retirees actually avoid community events during the normal workday just to stay out of sight. Again, once you've discovered new passions and interests, your concerns about what other people may think of your lifestyle will likely fade away.

RESOURCES

 SOURCES FOR SOLACE AND SYMPATHY. No one understands quite how you're feeling like another early retiree. The message boards are filled with other early retirees who can buck you up when you're down and give you reassurance and perspective.

Some cyberpossibilities:

- www.early-retirement.org
- www.retireearlyhomepage.com
- http://raddr-pages.com/forums, and
- www.nofeeboards.com.

DARE TO BE ORDINARY

One approach to quashing ego worries is to "Dare to Be Ordinary."

Notice how often you associate personal success and self-worth with being connected to the best, the brightest, and the famous—and how often you name-drop. If you worked for a prominent corporation, associated with famous friends, belonged to exclusive clubs, or even drove a luxury car, you might be at risk of defining yourself with these outer trappings.

None of these things is bad in itself, but taken together, it's easy to become addicted to life in the Famous Label Zone and have trouble living any other way. Early retirees need to learn how to hang out and just be, rather than struggle in this invisible and often expensive dimension of prestige. Your way will be filled with quieter, more personal challenges and triumphs, but they probably won't be things likely to impress the casual observer. Challenge yourself to just be ordinary, without losing your sense of self-worth.

First, pay attention to how your mind operates. When do you feel insecure? Why do you feel you get a boost by owning or associating with some external source of prestige, particularly something purchased? Noticing this, do you feel a tad bit embarrassed or childish?

When you are ready for the next step, begin to challenge your emotional dependence on external sources. For instance, if you have a famous friend or associate or a noteworthy accomplishment, commit to not mention that person or accomplishment for a month. If you went to a prestigious college, don't let the school's name cross your lips.

Next, tackle insecurity on the financial front. For instance, use a serviceable but unstylish product in public—an old backpack or pair of shoes. When people ask what you do for a living, practice telling them that you don't work. When people ask where you are going for vacation, practice telling them that it is not someplace chic or expensive. And as you grow in confidence, practice confiding in casual conversation that you would gladly buy a new computer, go on a cruise, or shop at a certain store, but that you are on a strict budget and can't afford to do so. If all these become easy and natural, then you are well past the grip of the consumer status culture.

Ultimately, you may have the financial resources to buy the computer or go on the cruise. But in some fundamental way, you have come to see that you are not your vacation destinations, or your car, or people's understanding of your annual spending power—an important step to building emotional comfort with the tradeoffs inherent in early retirement.

The point of Daring to Be Ordinary is certainly not to change your life into something drab and pedestrian, but rather to break the grip of pride and ego, helping your motivations be rooted more often in a place of integrity. An early retiree can certainly aspire to soar, living an interesting life filled with fun and accomplishment.

5. Financial Worries

For many people, feeling financially secure is the ultimate challenge of early retirement. At least when you were working, you could marshal your paycheck to fight against the tide of unpaid bills or sustained portfolio losses.

Now should some major unbudgeted expense rear up or your investments suffer a drop, you may feel vulnerable. Even a little daily stock market volatility can be wrenching for those people whose moods rise and fall with the day's Dow Jones averages.

The first step in assuaging your money worries is to reread Chapters 3 and 4 and look into some of the books and resources cited there on asset allocation and Safe Withdrawal Rates. If you have implemented something like the Rational Investing Portfolio (outlined in Section E of Chapter 3), you have likely done all that is humanly possible to create a long-term portfolio with which to navigate the shoals of short-term economic fluctuations.

Then take a deep breath and promise you won't overreact to daily or even quarterly rises and falls in the value of your assets. One effective technique for this is to play "What If." For example, if the market went down 5% this week, what would you do? If you are hewing to the long-run investing methods, you realize that you would do absolutely nothing except perhaps a bit of rebalancing at the end of the year. This can take the obsessive urgency out of following the ups and downs of the markets and your changing portfolio balance.

If you do arrive at what you recognize as a psychological breaking point and seriously consider returning to full-time work, first play out in your mind how you would feel if you abandoned your dream of early semi-retirement only to find that within a year, investments spring back to their former levels. If your answer is that you would feel foolish or disappointed, then you should probably continue to stay the course with regular bouts of deep breathing.

Another approach that may help keep things in perspective is to remind yourself of all the great things going on in your life as a result of early retirement. Chances are your free time is far more precious to you than a small amount of additional annual spending, which can help you become resolved to a bit more belt-tightening to keep yourself in the equivalent financial condition.

If you still remain too worried about finances, a good interim step may be to get ready to return to full-time work should you later need to do so. For example, keep your work contacts honed and perhaps take a course or two to keep your skills refreshed.

Another mental strategy that can help get you through market downturns is to begin putting some flesh on an Early Semi-Retirement Plan B that you could execute in the future if you really needed to do so. For example, you might check out some inexpensive places to live such as the Dominican Republic, New Zealand, or some affordable part of the United States. Visualize a scenario in which you move to cut expenses if things really unraveled and where you could live on a 1% or 2% annual withdrawal, even from your diminished portfolio, if you needed to while you waited for Social Security to arrive and help cover your expenses. Or think about staying in your same locale but moving to a smaller home as a way to make all the numbers work again.

Finally, you might contemplate how a budding interest could, over a period of years, grow into a money-earning avocation, giving you more future income or capital.

By tying all these plans together to neutralize the hypothetical persistence of a negative financial trend into the long run, you can train yourself to be calm in the short term—and restore the peace of mind that you sought by early semi-retiring in the first place.

TIP

DON'T SELL STOCKS IN A PANIC. No matter what you do, don't start selling equities to load back up on allegedly safe CDs or bonds. The Rational Investing Portfolio (described in Chapter 3, Sections E and F), is both conservative and quite likely to deliver gains over the long run. But one sure way to undermine the portfolio's performance would be to make a panicky decision to sell stocks at their lows, putting the money into low-yielding fixed income investments with no chance of long-run appreciation.

B. Special Advice for Couples

"How do you put up with him around the house?" My wife has heard this one more often than any other source of wonder or confusion over early retirement. The answer she always gives is that she barely sees me any more during the day as each of us go about our various activities. Fortunately, our house is designed so that, even if we are both home, we can both disappear into our studies for much of the day. We have lunch and go to exercise class together every few days, but otherwise are not under one another's feet.

But for many spouses or partners—especially those who are used to staying at home—having a primary breadwinner give up full-time work for early retirement can cause problems.

1. Don't Interfere With the Other Person's Routine

If you are a new early retiree, here is an important piece of advice: Don't even consider monitoring or improving your spouse's or partner's daily routines.

Don't ask what your spouse or partner does or where he or she goes, much less make comments about how an hour seems like a long time to go to the store for milk. Nobody needs a full-time cop or nag in the house. Your stay-at-home spouse or partner is probably quite content with his or her life. Be happy he or she is relaxed and happy and try to get up to that level yourself.

2. Develop Your Interests

Make sure you are developing your own interests and don't depend on your spouse or partner to provide you with entertainment or constant companionship.

If you find yourself padding around like a lonely puppy looking for a few scraps of attention, you can be sure you're bugging your spouse or partner even more than you're boring yourself. Plan and do things together—perhaps share some sort of new activity such as working at the same nonprofit or trying a new sport or exercise class together, but take responsibility for your own activities and social plans.

WARNING

PLAN TIME TOGETHER—AND APART. One of the best things about early semi-retirement is that it allows couples the freedom to spend more time together. But don't overdo the joint activities: Keep plenty of separate interests so that overexposure doesn't deplete the magic in your relationship.

3. Honor Your Own Time

If you are newly retired and starting to feel like your spouse's or partner's on-call personal concierge, here are a few suggestions.

First, understand that it takes two to play this game. If you secretly yearn to have someone tell you what to do or to feel useful, then you are likely playing along with the other person's practice of delegating lots of new household chores your way. Be especially wary of overcommitting to projects that are not leading you toward your goals. The way to break the cycle is to find other things you like to do more, ways to be useful other than as a home repair expert or pediatric chauffeur.

Second, simply learn how to say No. Think of creating a little bubble of space around your time so that other people's obligations don't invade and interrupt you. Even if you don't have other activities and projects yet, remind yourself that having free time to think, meditate, exercise, or do research is one of the key reasons you chose to retire early. Reassure yourself that you have meaningful projects to work on; you may not know what they are yet, but uncovering them takes time, too. All these thoughts can make it easier to keep other people's priorities from swamping your own in their nascent stages. ●

CHAPTER EIGHT

Make Your Life Matter

Reclaiming your life through early retirement is a great first step, but the benefit doesn't stop there. When you are doing what you love, you'll find it easy to help out others in a pinch. You'll have more time in early retirement to say yes, or to take on a new project—and you'll have the chance to grow, reflect, and share. This is precious stuff in any day and age—and particularly valuable in today's attention-deprived world.

It may never be possible for more than a small minority of people to retire early. It might not even be a great thing if large numbers of people did it: Think of the potential shortage of lawyers and the long lines at checkout counters in the middle of the day. Kidding aside, if more people could find their way to early retirement, immersed in the things they care deeply about rather than just doing anything that pays the bills, progress might be possible on many fronts.

> *Now that we've found love, what are we going to do with it?*
> —THE O'JAYS (KENNETH GAMBLE AND LEON HUFF)

For instance, tired social and political problems could start to buckle under compelling fresh solutions as early retirees throw themselves into local politics and grassroots activism. And if enough early retirees spent more time with their children and other young people, a whole generation could grow up kinder, wiser, and a little happier than their parents or grandparents. If numbers of people who seldom had time to roll up their sleeves in local volunteer activities brought fresh perspective and energy to important community institutions, they could help bind the fabric of the public sphere at a time when community seems to be in decline across the country. Churches could grow stronger if long-time and new members had the time and passion to begin their spiritual questing in earnest. And as men began to leave full-time career pursuits in numbers similar to women's, their health and longevity could even begin to come in line with those women enjoy. People with more time to stop and talk—or even better, stop and listen, could help make life a little better for everyone.

Pacifist icon Mahatma Gandhi said, "Be the change you want to see in the world." As an early retiree you are uniquely blessed with the time, resources, and energy to take a stand and make a difference. If something is important to you, you can do something about it.

EARLY RETIREMENT WORKS

While there are no large, academically rigorous studies assessing the impact of early retirement on the population, some smaller polls of early retirees on the www.early-retirement.org website were done for this book.

The results showed that:

- 62% of early retirees feel their marriages are stronger now that they have early retired, while only 10% found them worse, and
- 65% feel their overall fitness and health is better, while just 12% feel it is worse—notable since these early retirees are older now than during their working days.

Most impressive of all, but perhaps least surprising, fully 95% feel their stress levels are lower after early retirement.

Taking to heart Rule #8, Make Your Life Matter, can help you at any stage of early retirement to see your efforts as part of a bigger solution and can give you a bit more perspective and courage to plow past difficulties that arise along the way. While others can be there to help, the journey forward is yours. It's up to you to decide what you will make of your life.

In parting here are a few more useful tools to help. Think of them as a sort of survival kit, a simple set of practical guidelines that can keep you moving through all kinds of terrain that lies ahead. With all the time you free up through early retirement, you have every opportunity to consciously and deliberately try to make your life better. The steps discussed here can help

A. Simple Steps for a Life Well-Lived

No matter how clear you are about your goals, how sound your financial condition, and how well-planned your early retirement, there will still be periods in which you feel stuck. Whether due to actual depression or just a period of vague confusion, you may yearn for tangible, day-to-day steps you can take to keep your life on track. While these steps can benefit anyone who practices them, they may be especially useful to early retirees who often find themselves in a questing mode, open to constructive reorganization in their lives.

Follow these guidelines in any way you like, from simply reading and thinking about them to taking baby steps in a few of them to embarking wholeheartedly into one or more as a defining feature of who you are. Over time, consider how you might attend to each of the topics covered here: body, mind, relationships, activities, attitude, fun, and home. Though you might spend ten or 20 years simply noting that one of these areas needs honing in your life and doing nothing more about it, this gestation period is important and need not be rushed. With luck, one day you'll be ready to change it in a natural and effective way.

The Indians called this path "yoga"—meaning to yoke together mind and body—an overarching and systematic approach to living that reaches far beyond the exercise classes most people now associate with the word. Many other cultures, too, assembling the wisdom of thousands of years of human experience, have arrived at the same general methods for transforming your life from the inside out.

1. Healthy Body

Regularly do some sort of stretching, walking, or other more vigorous activity in an unpolluted environment. Eat sensibly. Breathe deeply.

2. Healthy Mind

Engage in some sort of calming, reflective activities. Be honest with yourself and with others. Find and follow a spiritual path, whatever that means for you. Be prepared to stand against the tide of common opinion.

3. Healthy Relationships

Make time to participate in activities with family, friends, neighbors, or other people in your extended community. Cultivate empathy and kindness, helping and sharing with others where you can. Open up your heart to love and be loved.

4. Meaningful Activities

Have regular activities—not necessarily paid—that you deeply enjoy. At various points, these activities should engage you into the wider world so that your efforts touch and help others in some way.

5. Healthy Attitude

Feel gratitude for all you have been given and an inquisitive openness about what life may bring. Try to forgive others and move past things that annoy you. Make a genuine effort in the things you undertake.

6. Fun

Do things just for the sheer joy of it, as long as they don't hurt others. Create something beautiful. Immerse yourself in music.

7. Home

Create physical surroundings that help you stay centered and comfortable, preferably in a healthful environment that you find both invigorating and calming.

> ## YOU ARE NOT ALONE
>
> As you make profound life changes, it helps to have support from others. Whether in your spouse or partner, old friends or new, seek kindred spirits and those who support the small steps you are making.
>
> Be aware that old friends may be confused or even threatened by your changes in direction, but real friends will understand. For example, when I first started eating less meat years ago, I was easily coerced into leaving the salad bar and joining the gang for a burger. Now the people I tend to hang out with seem to be more in synch and loyal friends understand me even if they still like steak.
>
> New friends, met in the new activities in which you spend your time, may surprise you with their depth and support. When you start living your values, you support and inspire those who share them.

B. Taking Your Pulse

Periodically monitor your progress, formally as well as casually, and see how you are stacking up against the goals you have set. Are you making a difference, standing for something you deeply value? Or are your days once again becoming cluttered with obligations that are no longer important to you? Can you work out a way to shift some of these off to others to make time for the things that are aligned with your priorities?

Likewise, if you are making good progress aligning your actions with your deepest values and fulfilling those hopes you had during the long years of stress and overwork, take some time to celebrate that.

You won't want to spend too much time reveling in self-congratulation, though. From your new vantage point, you've probably found a half-dozen or more new things you can't wait to tackle. No problem. You've got your whole life ahead of you!

Peace

Bob Clyatt

bob@workless-livemore.com ●

The Asset Classes in the Rational Investing Portfolio

This appendix includes a brief description of each of the 16 assets classes that comprise the Rational Investing Portfolio outlined in Chapter 3, Sections E and F. The portfolio is made up of roughly 40% stocks, 40% bonds, and 20% other asset classes to provide broad diversification, good return, and modest volatility.

Stocks

Large U.S. Stocks, Value Tilt

Large U.S. Stocks make up a big proportion of the world's stock markets and should be well-represented in your portfolio. By favoring value stocks, you put historical returns on your side, as these shares have tended to outperform the average large stock over time.

This was first shown by Eugene Fama of the University of Chicago and DFA and Kenneth French, now at Dartmouth, in their widely cited Three-Factor Model documenting the persistence of premiums for owning high book-to-market or value stocks. Over the years, this disquieting theory that provides a sound theoretical rationale for bad companies' stocks outperforming good companies' stocks has withstood sustained assault, and with minor modifications, still stands.

Use it to add value stocks to equity holdings, gaining a slight performance edge and reducing overall risk or volatility.

Small U.S Stocks, Value Tilt

The small company premium has also been documented by Fama and French as part of their 3-Factor Model. Small companies can still be quite large by most people's standards: They are the smallest 20% of the NYSE firms, sometimes referred to as the CRSP Deciles #9 and #10, as well as smaller publicly traded firms. Even smaller private companies are covered in the Venture Capital/Private Equity segment of the "Other" portion of the Rational Investing Portfolio.

Small companies seem less attractive, less well-known, and more subject to financial fluctuations from external market and competitive conditions. This generally keeps their prices lower for a given dollar of earnings, but as these companies grow or move into favor, they can produce an outsized return for investors.

Whether a small company's shareholder is generously or merely adequately compensated for the additional risk taken on, Rational Investors like the fact that small—and especially small value—stock returns are less correlated with the overall market, reducing volatility in the overall portfolio.

International Stocks: Large, Small, and Emerging Market

Some 60% of the world's equity assets are non-U.S. stocks. The Rational Investing portfolio allocates roughly 45% of equity holdings in International Stocks (21.5% of the overall portfolio) which is aggressive by most Americans' standards but is still less than a true market weighting.

Owning International Stocks gives a portfolio exposure to a different set of risks and thus continues to give diversification benefits.

New studies confirm the traditional wisdom: Over the long run, International Stocks do indeed provide reduced volatility in returns. International Small Company Stocks and Emerging Market Stocks tend to be particularly volatile and less correlated with U.S. stocks, with periods of great performance offset by periods of abysmal performance. Over time, though, the growth in these economies provides not only risk reduction, but strong returns.

Bonds

Short-Term Bonds/Cash

This is the typical money market fund in which cash is swept or left while awaiting investing, spending, or rebalancing. An alternative that might have slightly higher yield would be Vanguard's Short-Term Investment grade Corporate Bond fund.

Treasuries

For this asset class, buy Treasury Bonds or inflation-adjusted I-Bonds directly through Treasury Direct at www.treasurydirect.gov, buy a U.S. Treasury bond mutual fund, or buy Treasury Inflation-Protected Securities (TIPS).

For a short while in the late 1990s, TIPS offered a 4% real rate of return that could have given investors a chance to effectively lock in their Safe Withdrawal Rate at no risk. (See Chapter 4, Section A for more on the Safe Withdrawal Rate.) And in retrospect, this could have argued for a massive allocation to TIPS. However, for all the planning and obsession over the 4% Safe Withdrawal Rate, it is designed to keep investors approximately 90% safe. So in the majority of real-world scenarios, a portfolio will do even better than simply keeping up with inflation and allowing the safe withdrawal amount.

Thus, a long-term TIPS-only strategy, while producing 20 or 30 years of carefree time in which you need not think about your portfolio and guarding against the small risk of underperforming, guarantees no real growth either.

Today the point is moot, since TIPS yields are under 2%—far below what most would consider a reasonable Safe Withdrawal Rate. However, if real interest rates rise in the future, the debate will resurface.

One final negative about TIPS: They are taxed on the inflation-appreciation component in their redemption value each year. Thus, if you hold TIPS outside a Roth IRA, you will owe taxes on the inflation-adjustment either annually (for taxable accounts) or whenever you withdraw (from a traditional IRA).

Medium-Term U.S. Bonds

Financial researchers Eugene Fama and David Plecha have shown that the slightly higher yield from Long Maturity Bonds is not fair compensation for their much higher volatility and risk when interest rates change. Also, Medium-Term Bonds are less correlated with equities than longer term bonds.

By sticking with a blend of 2-Year and 5-Year Average Maturity Bonds you can capture the bulk of the yield while still ensuring reasonable protection from rising interest rates. Some investors prefer 3-Year to 6-Year CDs instead of bonds in this portion of their portfolio.

International Bonds

Like International Stocks, 2-Year and 5-Year International Bonds give assets held in currencies other than the dollar, which adds to diversification. DFA hedges currency risk in its bond funds, which costs money and takes away this currency diversification benefit. But both PIMCO and American Century offer International Bond funds that are not hedged.

In general, bonds serve to dampen volatility from equity returns, but don't add much to long-term returns.

High Yield Bonds

This category of fixed income investment bears special mention for two reasons. First, it comes with high annual interest payments. And second, returns tend to be countercyclical, less correlated with other bonds. During periods of rising interest rates, the high yield market generally does not fall as quickly as other bonds of similar maturity. Likewise, it will not prosper during periods of falling interest rates, but is rather tied to the perceived fortunes of the stock market.

Its uniqueness makes it attractive—and fortunately, Vanguard has a good low-cost fund: High Yield Corporate (VWEHX). This fund will move differently from other high yield funds in that it invests in only the highest quality high yield bonds, and thus underperforms the high yield index in the good years. But it has nowhere near the credit risk and defaults in the tough years—and there are tough years in the high yield bond segment. Hold high yield in tax advantaged accounts if possible to reduce taxable income.

GNMA Bonds

GNMA Bonds are issued by the Government National Mortgage Association, an agency of the U.S. government, and as such are considered to have creditworthiness comparable to U.S. Treasuries. These bonds are less risky than Fannie Mae or Freddy Mac bonds.

Investors' funds have been lent directly to GNMA, which pays a coupon and returns principal and are not affected by individual mortgagees repaying their loans or prepaying their mortgages. GNMA yields tend to be about .5% higher than comparable Treasury Bonds.

Other

Oil and Gas

Energy markets, driven by the prices for oil and gas, are not highly correlated with other asset classes and as such have a place in your portfolio. Ideally, you might be able to directly own partnership shares in an oil or gas producer, lock yourself in for ten or 20 years and reap a steady, high return. Certainly many investors have been able to follow this script. Unfortunately, others have ended up with dry holes or fast-talking operators who made investor money disappear into thin air. Investigate carefully before buying.

If you don't have access to this type of investment, there are alternatives. In particular, the FBR Gas Index (GASFX) is a mutual fund that gives you pure exposure to the natural gas market which is under-represented in the commodities indices relative to its importance in the economy—and the Vanguard Energy Fund (VGENX) can give you focused exposure, albeit via stocks, to the oil and related energy markets.

Market Neutral Hedge Funds

The hedge fund industry has taken off in recent years among institutional and individual investors alike. Hedge funds tend to attract great fund managers due in no small part to the lure of up to 20% of the profits they make from managing them. The "Market Neutral" moniker is a catchall for a number of different hedge fund strategies that use esoteric methods to seek profits uncorrelated to stock and bond markets. Several investment strategies are generally grouped under this heading—including index arbitrage, convertible-warrant hedging, merger arbitrage, interest rate arbitrage, Long-Short strategies, and others.

Rather than invest directly in a single hedge fund, you may want to invest in one of the new variety of funds of hedge funds. If you are an accredited investor and can stomach the 1.95% fees on top of the fees the hedge funds themselves charge, then you can invest in the Rydex SPHINX fund of hedge funds that tracks the S&P Hedge Fund Index. Alternately, the Oppenheimer-Tremont unit of CSFB has now lowered to a $50,000 minimum on its Market-Neutral fund of funds. With a 1.96% fee and 5% profit-sharing bonus and a 2.5% load, it is still a bit of a toss-up whether this will be good for investors—and there is little history to go on.

You might also consider investing in Master Limited Partnerships for this part of your portfolio. Often they own pipelines, but are generally not correlated with the oil and gas markets themselves. Possible new funds include Energy Income & Growth (FEN), Fiduciary/Claymore (FMO), Kayne Anderson (KYN), and Tortoise Energy (TYG).

In general, don't invest in hedge funds that simply offer a manager who is talented at picking stocks and bonds. At these fees, you should get something more esoteric than that.

Commodities

It is reasonable to ask whether commodities belong in your portfolio. Traditionally considered too risky for retirees, asset allocators have given them much attention lately due to their occasional high returns and consistently low correlation to equity and bond markets. But until recently, investors who wanted commodities exposure had to either buy stocks in natural resources firms (which would then tend to correlate more closely with stock markets), or invest in futures (complex, high risk, and by nature short-term and high-maintenance).

Both Pimco and Oppenheimer began offering a unique vehicle a few years ago that directly purchases commodities contracts and Treasury Bonds in the correct proportions to track an index of commodities: the DJ/AIG Commodity Index, or the Goldman Sachs Commodity Index. Although the retail versions of these funds carry loads and high fees, there are ways, through Vanguard and other fund supermarkets, to get into the low-fee, no-load institutional versions of these funds. (See Chapter 3, Section F3.) That brings your fees down within range to consider, though the Oppenheimer fund's fee, QRAAX, is still 1.5% per year; the Pimco fund's fee, PCRIX, is half that.

A timberland REIT, Plum Creek Timber (PCL), may also offer a way to invest in this high-performing and relatively uncorrelated-to-equities asset class. Timberland is difficult to invest in any other way short of buying into timberland limited partnerships—nearly as difficult and expensive for individuals as buying actual land and arranging to have it managed and harvested.

You may also wish to hold physical stocks of gold coins for the ultimate time-tested safety asset. Precious metals funds are also available with unusual, and for some investors, attractive counter cyclicality and risk reward profiles. Over the long run, these tend to be poor investments, though they do react well as short-term hedges that can be psychologically comforting during market turmoil.

Commercial Real Estate

Direct investment in real estate has been a cornerstone in many early retiree and other wealthy investors' portfolios. If you don't want to make the effort to become a landlord directly, you might try to learn—perhaps from an accountant or financial planner—about becoming part of a limited partnership that invests in commercial real estate such as mini-malls or medical services buildings.

These investments, highly illiquid, have tended to do well for investors through good and bad economic times, but they are hard to find. Until such an opportunity comes along, you can invest in REITs. These are usually best held in your tax-advantaged accounts, since they do tend to throw off relatively large amounts of taxable income. Vanguard's REIT index fund (VGSIX) is simple and inexpensive. International REITs are starting to form, such as Alpine International (EGLRX), that give further diversification into overseas real estate markets.

Beware of viewing the purchase of a second home as a "real estate investment," however. Unless you gain rental income from it on a par with other rental investments, this is an expense, not an asset. Merely hoping for a capital gain does not convert a second home into an investment.

Private Equity

Investing in small, private firms less correlated with the public stock markets helps add resiliency to your portfolio. A few Private Equity funds have recently gone public and you can now buy into them as easily as buying an ordinary share of any stock or fund, though they remain expensive and unproven investments.

If you are an accredited investor—defined as $1 million of net worth for a couple or $300,000 of annual income for a couple during the past two years—you can try to become a limited partner in a venture capital fund. Alternately, you can make independent angel investments or work with small firms to gain stock or options in their firms as partial payment for your services. A private investment in a small public company (PIPE) could give you the type of preferred stock that big investors tend to favor with more protections than the public common shareholders.

While you wait to be able to assemble these deals, you might choose to invest this allocation in the smallest cap NASDAQ stocks—including pink sheet or OTC NASDAQ stocks. Compared to the effort you will undertake to select and invest in a single private equity deal, the risk and illiquidity you face in a small OTC NASDAQ stock is minor. You may even be able to meet management or get to know the company if it is local, as you would expect to do in any private equity deal in which you invest. ●

Resources

The following resources are included for those seeking to dig more deeply into some of the financial and academic issues raised in the book. A number of useful online resources are here, as well as books and articles.

Early Retirement

The resources listed are written by and for early retirees. They include several key free message boards and early retirement blogs as well as the more noteworthy books not already mentioned in the chapters.

Online

The best message board for early retirees has traditionally been http://early-retirement.org/forums/index.php. Use it to read up on all the issues early retirees and those planning for early retirement face daily. A caring and knowledgeable community.

Other good early retirement message boards include:

- www.retireearlyhomepage.com
- http://raddr-pages.com/forums, and
- the FIRE (Financial Independence, Retire Early) board at www.nofeeboards.com.

Paul and Vicki Terhorst have a nice Web page to keep the early retirement community abreast of their adventures at www.geocities.com/TheTropics/Shores/5315.

Akaisha and Billy Kaderli, the delightful beacons of positivity profiled in the Introduction, also keep early retirees posted at www.geocities.com/ba264.

A 29-year-old Microsoft employee seeking to retire at age 40 with at least $1 million runs a blog at http://pfblog.com. It is well organized and full of personal finance and investing links, but long on advertising.

Print

Buford. *Halftime,* by Bob Buford (Zondervan). Buford started a series of books aimed at men seeking to create a second half of their lives committed to Christian values. The series now includes *Stuck in Halftime, Game Plan, Halftime Participant's Guide, Halftime Leader's Guide, Finishing Well: What People Who Really Live Do Differently,* and more.

Dominguez and Robin. *Your Money or Your Life,* by Joe Dominguez and Vicki Robin (Penguin), published in 1992, is a classic early retiree tome describing the late Joe Dominguez's experiences in a frugal early retirement, committing his time to community causes.

Edmunds. *How to Retire Early and Live Well,* by Gillette Edmunds (Adams Media), contains little data or quantitative analysis, but gives a great explanation of the need for an early retirement portfolio of diverse, noncorrelated asset classes. Contains good descriptions of the pain of living through a portfolio deterioration, as well as how to manage illiquid alternative investments such as real estate and private equity.

Personal Finance

General resources on personal finance topics are too numerous to catalogue, but the resources here are those most relevant to early semi-retirement. Other general personal finance sites of interest are also listed.

Online

Risk Grades offers a useful, free service for measuring portfolio risk at www.riskgrades.com.

A useful directory of links to personal finance resources can be found on the Web at www.geocities.com/finplan825.

A professionally written and edited blog with links to large numbers of other personal finance blogs and resources is at www.soundmoneytips.com/2005/04/the_personal_fi.html.

And finally, the truly frugal hangout on the Web at http://frugalforlife
.blogspot.com.

Print

The bibles of personal finance are by:

- **Morris.** *Wall Street Journal Guide to Understanding Personal Finance,* (4th edition) by Ken and Virginia Morris (Fireside), and
- **Quinn.** *Making the Most of Your Money,* by Jane Bryant Quinn (Simon & Schuster).
- **Stanley and Danko.** *The Millionaire Next Door,* by Thomas J. Stanley and William D. Danko (Longstreet Press), is the classic book on living frugally.

Rational Investing

Rational Investing has roots in the index investing world, informed by academic research in Modern Portfolio Theory and the 3-Factor Model. Resources here range from online newsletters for index investors to books and academic studies underlying various aspects of the Rational Investing approach.

Online

Two subscription sites from Index Investors, Inc., can be found at www
.IndexInvestor.com and www.retiredinvestor.com. The more expensive ($100 per year) www.retiredinvestor.com has model retirement portfolio creation and historical testing capabilities coupled to actual Vanguard and other funds that fulfill the strategies. The 5% Target Real Return portfolio is a good proxy for the Rational Investment Portfolio in this book. Several free resources are also available on these sites.

William Bernstein has an online complement to his books, *Four Pillars of Investing* and *The Intelligent Asset Allocator* at www.efficientfrontier.com.

Scott Burns, columnist in *The Dallas Morning Post*, offers tangible, sensible advice and an asset allocator's perspective. The site is free with registration. A good sample column is: www.dallasnews.com/sharedcontent/dws/bus/scott-burns/columns/2005/stories/032005dnbussburns.153f93882.html.

"Twelve Steps to Investment Peace," by Paul Farrell, is available online at *The Wall Street Journal*'s site. The website requires a subscription, though two-week trial subscriptions are available. Farrell's article describes a step-by-step approach to bringing yourself from wherever you are currently invested to something very similar to the Rational Investing Portfolio. You can find it at http://online.wsj.com/public/article/0,,SB111428448981715157,00.html?mod=sunday%5Fjournal%5Fprimary%5Fhs.

Ibbotson Associates has great research on asset allocation topics, usually aimed at institutional investors, but of use to early retirees, as well at www.ibbotson.com/content/kc_published_research.asp?catalog=Article&category=Knowledge%20Center%20Published%20Research#Asset%20Allocation.

Bill Schultheis offers online musings at www.Coffeehouseinvestor.com following up on conclusions from his book, *The Coffeehouse Investor* (Longstreet). Schultheis is a kindred spirit advocating a Rational Investing approach.

Here is a link to the components of the capital-weighted S&P 500 index, showing how concentrated it has become, with just 13 stocks now comprising a quarter of the index's value: www.indexarb.com/indexComponent-WtsSP500.html.

An example of the way large institutional investors such as Common Fund, which manages many college endowments, pursue sophisticated forms of Rational Investing is at www.commonfund.org/NR/rdonlyres/9B2AAC71-E458-46A5-8A5F-1D583D7469D5/0/How_efficient_is_your_frontier.pdf.

Print

Armstrong. *The Informed Investor*, by Frank Armstrong III (Amoco), a financial planner, gives a very readable discussion of the benefits of diversifying among key asset classes with Small, International, and Value Tilts.

Bogle. *Common Sense on Mutual Funds*, by John C. Bogle (John Wiley and Sons). This book and anything written by Bogle are the gold standard for advice on cost-efficient indexing and long term investing. As founder of the investment firm Vanguard, Bogle has arguably done more for the small investor than anyone in history and continues to rail against excessive fees and conflict of interest in the mutual fund industry.

Clements. Here are two good articles by Jonathan Clements, the *Wall Street Journal* personal finance journalist who advocates Rational Investing principles:

- "Getting Actively Passive: Index Funds Still Win—If You Go Beyond the S&P 500," *Wall Street Journal*, January 12, 2005, Page C1. (Written with Rex Sinquefield, CEO of Dimensional Fund Advisors), and
- "Real Simple: Using Just Three Funds to Build a Globally Diversified Portfolio." June 15, 2005. Page D1.

Davis. *Retire Early, Sleep Well*, by Steven R. Davis (Grote), gives a clear, engineer-friendly exposition of Rational Investing for Early Retirees using DFA funds.

Ibbotson Associates. *Stocks, Bonds, Bills and Inflation: 2005 Yearbook,* by Ibbotson Associates, is a useful source for historical data series, recently made better with the 2005 addition of Dimson, Marsh, and Staunton international data going back to 1900.

Swedroe. Larry E. Swedroe has written on the benefits of low-fee index investing. His titles include:

- *The Only Guide to a Winning Investment Strategy You'll Ever Need: The Way Smart Money Invests Today* (St. Martin's Press), and
- *What Wall Street Doesn't Want You to Know: How You Can Build Real Wealth Investing in Index Funds* (Truman Talley Books).

Academic Studies

Brinson. "The Determinants of Portfolio Performance" (1986) and "The Determinants of Portfolio Performance II, An Update" (1991), by Gary Brinson. For a detailed clarification of this oft-misunderstood study, see: "Does Asset Allocation Explain 40%, 90% or 100% of Performance?" by Roger Ibbotson and Gary Kaplan at www.ibbotson.com/download/research/Does_Asset_Allocation_Explain_Performance.pdf.

Chensvold. Support for the Value Premium is in Christian Chensvold's article at the IndexFunds.com site at www.indexfunds.com/archives/articles/chensvold_christian_20040101_dfavsvanguard.htm.

Dimensional Fund Advisors. Dimensional Fund Advisors' (DFA) Library section contains, among other useful papers, literature describing the 3-Factor Model, that is, the persistence of the Value, International, and Small Company Stock premiums through time at http://library.dfaus.com.

Hechinger. A Lipper and *Wall Street Journal* study explains and estimates the hidden trading costs incurred by mutual funds, cited in John Hechinger, "Deciphering Funds' Hidden Costs," Page D1, March 17, 2004.

Wermers. "Mutual Fund Performance: An Empirical Decomposition into Stock-Picking Talent, Style, Transactions Costs and Expenses" by Russ Wermers; *The Journal of Finance,* Vol. 55, No. 4, *Papers and Proceedings of the Sixtieth Annual Meeting of the American Finance Association*, Boston, Massachusetts, Jan. 7-9, 2000 (Aug., 2000).

Safe Withdrawal Rates

This section reviews the tools and resources that have attempted to quantify Safe Withdrawal Rates for retirees. Although the study most applicable for early retirees is likely to be the one introduced in Chapter 4, Section A, the studies here provide useful reference points.

Calculators and Analytic Tools

FIRECalc, the best of the bunch for early retirees, is available at www.fire-seeker.com.

Engineering-types may appreciate www.retirementoptimizer.com, a safe withdrawal modeling tool similar to FIRECalc, which is available for purchase online to be downloaded and run on a computer, though free trials are available. Contains useful features for modeling annuities.

A simple, online calculator for retirement finances can be found at www.i-orp.com/TaxCutForm.html.

A former Boeing planning executive has an extensive series of articles and some software and books for sale to help retirees plan withdrawals with a more nuanced appreciation of what to do if the plan goes awry at www.analyzenow.com.

Gummy, an intelligent, idiosyncratic retiree, offers several useful resources and papers on his site; be sure to explore. You can find a discussion of the Safe Withdrawal Rate at www.gummy-stuff.org/sensible_withdrawals.htm.

Academic Studies

Bengen: Bengen is a financial planner whose pioneering study concludes that a 4.1% inflation-adjusted safe withdrawal from a 50% stock, 50% bond mix holds up over 30 years. Limitations: Only two asset classes, and success is defined as having a nonzero portfolio balance by the end of 30 years, so more appropriate for traditional retirees than for early retirees. Favors a 75% stock allocation. You can find it at www.fpanet.org/journal/articles/2004_Issues/jfp0304-art8.cfm?renderforprint=1.

Bernstein. The following links to William Bernstein's site provide supporting data for applying a constant percentage withdrawal rate instead of an inflation-adjusted original withdrawal:

- www.efficientfrontier.com/ef/998/hell.htm
- www.efficientfrontier.com/ef/101/hell101.htm
- www.efficientfrontier.com/ef/901/hell3.htm, and
- www.efficientfrontier.com/ef/403/hell5.htm.

Cooley and Hubbard. This is the classic "Trinity Study," which is considered the cornerstone research project for all Safe Withdrawal Rate investigations. The authors validate a 3.75% safe (100% success) withdrawal. Limitations: Only a two-asset model and assumes the retiree dies within 30 years. Uses traditional inflation-adjusted withdrawal methodology. Some analyses in the paper also fail to adjust for inflation. Highlights: Stock mix includes 75/25 as well as 50/50. The original paper is available at: Cooley, P.L., C.M. Hubbard, and D.T. Walz, "Retirement Spending: Choosing a Sustainable Withdrawal Rate That Is Sustainable." *Journal of the American Association of Individual Investors*, 20, 1 (1998): 39–47.

A 2003 upgrade to the original paper improves the analysis by adding International Assets, though the data series used are relatively short and limited. A 4% inflation adjusted scenario running 25% S&P 500 25% EAFE, and 50% bonds moves up from 95% success to 96% success over the longest (30-year) periods. Correlations are shown in the paper at www.fpanet.org/ journal/articles/2003_Issues/jfp0103-art10.cfm.

Greaney. John Greaney offers a downloadable compendium of SWR studies and recommendations for a modest fee at www.retireearlyhomepage.com/re-ports1.htm.

The paper summarizes studies that tend to have 75% stock/25% bond portfolios, generally comprised of S&P 500 and TIPS, and adds one of its own, the Retire-Early Study. Using data going back to the 1870s for 50-year payout periods, Greaney finds optimal stock/bond allocation at around 80% stocks, with a resulting 3.35% safe withdrawal rate, inflation-adjusted annually. Studies results are primarily focused around establishing a 100% safe rate. The study affirms approximately 90% safety around the 4% withdrawal rate level.

Guyton. Jonathan T. Guyton develops and back-tests various additional withdrawal rules that would have helped permit higher withdrawal rates while maintaining portfolio safety over time. Specifically, he develops rules for limiting inflation-adjustments following "down" years and limiting any inflation adjustments to 6%.

Problems would arise with these rules, however, since there is no "catch-up" in future years—a down year or inflation cap permanently lowered the real value of withdrawals for the lifetime of the early retiree. Likewise, even when times are good, there is no way to increase the low spending levels. There are other concerns with the methodology, particularly the fact that no true historical analysis is done except for a single "Perfect Storm" period from 1973 on. However, even this is not a full 40-year period; the author assumes that if you've made it this far, you'll make it through until 2013.

The paper does make useful additions to the literature, however. It uses a diversified blend of stocks and bond funds in its models, including international stocks and bonds and REITs as opposed to the simple blend portfolios in almost every other Safe Withdrawal Rate study. And it seeks to model rules consistent with human psychological tendencies to produce a more dynamic/responsive annual withdrawal and in the process get a somewhat higher withdrawal rate. From the *Journal of Financial Planning*, October 2004. You can find it online at www.fpanet.org/journal/articles/2004_Issues/jfp1004-art6 .cfm?renderforprint=1.

Jarret and Stringfellow. Jaye C. Jarrett and Tom Stringfellow use a three asset-class model including small U.S. Large Stocks (25%), U.S. Small Stocks (25%), and Medium-Term Bonds (50%). They have a 100% safe inflation-adjusted withdrawal rate of 3.3% while leaving the principal intact in real terms over 30 years. The 75/25 split, with stocks split evenly between small and large caps, produces a better result, with 3.54% safe withdrawal rate over 30 years. Payout is increased annually for inflation. They use rolling averages of market data since 1927. The paper is available online at www.fpanet.org/journal/articles/2000_Issues/jfp0100-art11.cfm.

Kizer. A 2005 article by Jared Kizer, "Drawing Down and Looking Abroad," uses new long-term international data to credibly show, for the first time, the value of international diversification in increasing the likelihood of success in a portfolio subject to 4% or 5% annual inflation-adjusted withdrawals. The study uses international data series going back to 1900 from Dimson, Marsh and Staunton (DMS), recently made available from Ibbotson Associates. You can find it at www.journalofindexes.com/contents.php?id=535&np=1.

Marbach. Keith Marbach's original published study shows what happens when a retiree spends a fixed percentage of the portfolio each year while attempting to maintain the full spending power of the portfolio at the end of the 30-year time horizon. This scenario comes up with a 100% confident spending percentage, based on historical rolling average methods, of 4.16%. Since this method of spending a fixed percentage of the portfolio each year cannot ever deplete the portfolio to zero, it is possible to consider scenarios with lower probabilities of success—for example, the 90% scenario. Coincidentally, in the 10% of cases that fail to keep up with inflation, the portfolio value drops by an average of 10% in real terms and supports a 4.5% safe withdrawal rate. Many retirees could stomach a one in ten chance of losing 10% of their real purchasing power over 30 years if it allowed them to increase their annual spending from 4.1% to 4.4%.

Negatives are that the optimizer model selected a 100% all U.S. Large Cap Stock allocation for all these portfolios, which would be quite volatile. The Safe Withdrawal Method presented in Chapter 4, Section B makes needed refinements to this study to produce results tailored to the needs of early retirees.

You can find Marbach's study in the *Journal of Retirement Planning*, "A Choice of Risks when Spending in Retirement," Sept./Oct. 2002; and online at www.zunna.com/Research/ChoiceOfRisksInRetirement.pdf.

Work/Life Issues

The following are resources from organizations and academic studies validating concerns about overwork to practical books that can help you find your own work/life balance.

Online

Take Back Your Time is a grassroots political action organization working to educate people about issues of Overwork, and for legislation to mandate longer vacations for American workers. You can find it at www.timeday.org.

Center for the New American Dream is an organization with a mission to help Americans shift toward saner and sustainable lifestyles summed up as: Live Consciously, Buy Wisely, Make a Difference, with a website at www.newdream.org/make/index.php.

Print

Covey. A systematic way to align your values with your actions is presented in *The 7 Habits of Highly Effective People*, by Stephen R. Covey (Simon & Schuster).

Dlugozima, Scott, and Sharp. This book helps anyone figure out how to get a six-month sabbatical during the years before actually early semi-retiring: Six *Months Off: How to Plan, Negotiate, and Take the Break You Need Without Burning Bridges or Going Broke*, by Hope Dlugozima, James Scott, and David Sharp (Henry Holt).

Gomes. A longtime chaplain at Harvard describes a well-rounded and intellectually sound basis for moving beyond the values of popular culture in: *The Good Life, Truths That Last in Times of Need*, by Peter J. Gomes (Harper Collins).

Vienne. This lovely and inspiring little book can help you keep perspective when the going gets rough: *The Art of Imperfection, Simple Ways to Make Peace With Yourself*, by Veronique Vienne (Clarkson Potter).

Academic Studies

de Graaf. *Take Back Your Time: Fighting Overwork and Time Poverty in America*, edited by John de Graaf (Berrett-Koehler); 2003.

Hill. *History of the Work Ethic*, by Roger B. Hill, Department of Occupational Studies, University of Georgia, Athens, Ga.; 1996.

Rodgers. *The Work Ethic in Industrial America, 1850-1920*, by D.T. Rodgers (University of Chicago Press); 1978.

Schor. *The Overworked American, The Unexpected Decline in Leisure*, by Juliet Schor (Basic Books); 1992.

Index

A

W

Y

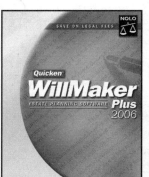

Remember:

Little publishers have big ears.
We really listen to you.

Take 2 Minutes & Give Us Your 2 cents

Your comments make a big difference in the development and revision of Nolo books and software. Please take a few minutes and register your Nolo product—and your comments—with us. Not only will your input make a difference, you'll receive special offers available only to registered owners of Nolo products on our newest books and software. Register now by:

PHONE	**FAX**	**EMAIL**	or **MAIL** us
1-800-728-3555	1-800-645-0895	cs@nolo.com	this registration card

fold here

Registration Card

NAME _____ DATE _____

ADDRESS _____

_____

CITY _____ STATE _____ ZIP _____

PHONE _____ EMAIL _____

WHERE DID YOU HEAR ABOUT THIS PRODUCT? _____

WHERE DID YOU PURCHASE THIS PRODUCT? _____

DID YOU CONSULT A LAWYER? (PLEASE CIRCLE ONE)   YES   NO   NOT APPLICABLE

DID YOU FIND THIS BOOK HELPFUL?   (VERY)   5   4   3   2   I   (NOT AT ALL)

COMMENTS _____

_____

_____

WAS IT EASY TO USE?   (VERY EASY)   5   4   3   2   I   (VERY DIFFICULT)

We occasionally make our mailing list available to carefully selected companies whose products may be of interest to you.
❑ If you do not wish to receive mailings from these companies, please check this box.
❑ You can quote me in future Nolo promotional materials.
   Daytime phone number _____.

RECL 1.0

Nolo
in the
NEWS

"Nolo helps lay people perform legal tasks without the aid—or fees—of lawyers."

—USA TODAY

Nolo books are ..."*written in plain language, free of legal mumbo jumbo, and spiced with witty personal observations."*

—ASSOCIATED PRESS

"...Nolo publications...guide people simply through the how, when, where and why of law."

—WASHINGTON POST

"Increasingly, people who are not lawyers are performing tasks usually regarded as legal work... And consumers, using books like Nolo's, do routine legal work themselves."

—NEW YORK TIMES

"...All of [Nolo's] books are easy-to-understand, are updated regularly, provide pull-out forms...and are often quite moving in their sense of compassion for the struggles of the lay reader."

—SAN FRANCISCO CHRONICLE

fold here

Place
stamp here

Nolo
950 Parker Street
Berkeley, CA 94710-9867

Attn: RECL 1.0